ONE HUNDRED YEARS OF SERVICE THROUGH COMMUNITY

A *Gould Farm Reader*

Edited by
Steven K. Smith
Terry Beitzel

Foreword by
Robert D. Patterson

University Press of America,® Inc.
Lanham · Boulder · New York · Toronto · Plymouth, UK

Library of Congress Control Number: 2014931242
ISBN: 978-0-7618-6226-0 (paperback : alk. paper)
eISBN: 978-0-7618-6348-9

For Nancy and Kent Smith

For all Gould Farmers

"The past is our definition. We may strive, with good reason, to escape it, or to escape what is bad in it, but we will escape it only by adding something better to it."

Wendell Berry
From "The Specialization of Poetry" (1974)

TABLE OF CONTENTS

FOREWORD

Gould Farm is a non-profit organization which helps people (whom the Farm refers to as "guests") with mental health problems through living at the Farm and participating in its therapeutic milieu, especially its work-oriented rehabilitation. Today the Farm still has many of its original characteristics, importantly its conception as an intentional community, but it is also now a licensed mental health facility and fully embraces using current best treatment practices.

It has a 100-year history. This book lets us learn about the Farm by reading what participants and observers said about it during those 100 years. It is a fascinating story. You will read text before 1925 (the year the Farm's charismatic founder died), but not a lot because he was emphatically much more into action than words. There are letters to and from famous people exchanged by the founder's wife who took over after his early death. There is a 1955 scholarly sociological study of the Farm. It used objective quantitative measuring instruments to study it sociologically and then had to struggle with why their instruments did not seem to capture important parts of what the researchers saw in the Farm.

There is part of an Oxford University thesis (1999) which analyzes the Farm from a social service and psychological perspective. Throughout, there are observations (including two book excerpts) by guests and their families.

You will see the connection between the Gould Farm and Harry Hopkins, who was a major architect of the New Deal in the Roosevelt administration. So there is plenty here for readers with many different interests—history, theology, psychiatry, psychology, anthropology, and sociology. It will help orient guests and their families and other people who become involved with the Farm.

As you follow the Farm's history through these writings you will feel the tension as you ask yourself: will this deeply religious charismatic founder be able to set in motion an organization which can be sustained for decades? Will his early death lead to the demise of the organization? Will the organization be able to adapt to external forces without watering down its initial high ethical goals?

I think an important insight about the Gould Farm comes from Infield (1955). He says that most self-organized intentional communities do not survive long, but Will Gould's wisdom to fuse an intentional community with a clear overarching goal to help rehabilitate people with mental illnesses was a unique combination that probably contributed to its ability to survive. These twin goals propelled the Farm to be attentive to both internal and external forces rather than succumb to excessive focus inward, which Infield says was a common failing of intentional communities.

Infield's observation also makes clear why there has always been a tension between the goal of having the Gould Farm be "one family" and the necessity to frequently accept new guests who are different in many ways from the staff and, therefore, always in danger of not being absorbed into the 'family.'

What impact can the Farm have beyond the benefit it provides to guests? This is addressed in documents starting in 1935. Stucker (2012) discusses several programs which modeled themselves to varying degrees on Gould Farm.

My association with Gould Farm since 1976—as psychiatrist for the Boston area program and for a shorter time the Monterrey program, as Associate, and as board member—has been the most rewarding experience of my professional life. I always experience that satisfaction when I go to the hardware store near my home and can talk to any of four former Gould Farm guests who have been employed there for several years.

Robert D. Patterson, M.D.
Lecturer on Psychiatry, Harvard Medical School, Boston MA
Attending Psychiatrist, McLean Hospital, Belmont, MA

PREFACE

Ten years ago, while working at Gould Farm, I began interviewing individuals who, like me, grew up on the Farm. This exercise later prompted the idea of a Gould Farm "Reader." Why not, I thought, not only record the recollections of teenagers through octogenarians, but also collect excerpts written about Gould Farm from books, letters, and dissertations, roughly spanning the Farm's history?

Such written material slowly began to supplement my interviews, which I placed in five "generations," from those who grew up on Gould Farm in the 1930s through those who lived there in the 1990s. What began to emerge were common understandings of shared values, communal idealism, social service, and remembrances of honorary aunts who died years ago. Created also were shared bonds between interviewer and interviewee, ranging from concern that certain traditions were changing to appreciation for having lived and shared our lives, in a community context, devoted to helping others.

I later wrote in 2004, after synthesizing transcripts of these interviews:

> (I)nterviewees identified "tradition" as a critical dynamic that has sustained Gould Farm as a therapeutic community. Tradition also meaningfully contributed to the Farm's distinct therapeutic functions, especially in the sharing of common meals. The Farm's communal experience fostered a unique awareness among its children toward those with mental illness and, by extension, to other disadvantaged populations. This awareness, along with a communal identity, shaped Gould Farm children long after they left Gould Farm.[1]

Viscerally understanding the value of communal dining, at least in my experience and observation, it was not until I read the following, written in 1955, that shared, communal meals really did help foster the Farm's therapeutic purpose, and its community:

> All (Gould Farm) activities are essentially optional, including work as well as attendance at regular Sunday morning service...The only regularity that, for obvious reasons, must be insisted upon is attendance at meals. These are all taken in common, with the exception of breakfast which some of those who live in the cottages may arrange to have at home. The seating of the guests is not left to chance, but is planned with some care, especially in cases that need such attention.[2]

This, I thought, would be the first selection for a Gould Farm Reader!

Though communal dining has changed since 1955, it has not disappeared. Yet how an institution's traditions change, why they disappear, how they are "created" then recognized as "tradition," were questions I would later consider, when choosing selections for the Reader. Aware of how certain "old ways" burden as much as liberate, their disappearance, sometimes at the whim of an individual, concerns me; change, uninformed by historical memory and historical sensitivity, may prove blind to institutional nuances and needs. Gould Farm has been fortunate to have elders who are historically sensitive, have preserved historical memory, yet to varying degrees, embraced change when change was due.

Rose "Roma" Foreman, was one of the last guardians of Gould Farm decorum. She scolded those who read newspapers at the dining tables. She switched off lights when not needed, watered plants from near-empty dining room glasses. For years Roma also assigned napkin rings to each community member (some of us held the same ring often for decades), not leaving their placement on the dining tables to "chance." While the rings' original use had long been discarded, they, to this day, identify one's place at the table. This sense of place made many, I believe, feel more at home than they might otherwise if seating was self-chosen. Yet she, and so many other elders, were more than guardians; they devoted their working years to the Farm while organizing activities, raising families, making the newcomer feel at home. Roma, who came to the Farm in 1930, was 99 when she died in 2009.

Gould Farm pioneers Faith Colt and Rose McKee, who arrived at the Farm in 1916 and 1920, respectively, also loom large in my memory. They, perhaps more so than Roma, were more open to change, being active in certain administrative positions that demanded their leadership when profound change occurred, especially Will and Agnes Gould's deaths, in 1925 and 1958, respectively. Rose and Faith both died in 1985; their children and grandchildren serve in leadership roles at Gould Farm.

Finally, I remember the beneficiaries of Gould Farm's purpose and what it has meant to so many in need, particularly my cousin, Ben Roberts, and his mother, Naomi Roberts. Their often heroic struggles with mental illness reflect a pattern sometimes seen at the Farm. Ben came to Gould Farm as a volunteer in the early 1970s, after recovering from an initial bout of depression following open-heart surgery. This would later change into a diagnosis of schizophrenia, at which point he became a Gould Farm "guest" (the Farm's term for those at the Farm for assistance). Ben would later leave the Farm, be hospitalized, disappear for weeks, then eventually settle down, finding a subsidized apartment near his parents. He died of cardiac arrest in 2002. Naomi, always a fierce advocate for society's underprivileged, began advocating on behalf of those afflicted with mental illness, founding a chapter of the National Alliance on Mental Illness (NAMI) in a small town in Virginia's Rockingham County. She would later help found a short-lived, but Gould Farm-inspired, community in the Shenandoah Valley. She died in 2009.

The aim of this Reader is not to display an imaginary, idealized past to which the Farm should return, but simply to introduce aspects of Gould Farm for the first time to the unfamiliar and to reacquaint Gould Farmers—or maybe introduce them, too, for the first time—to a grand tradition to which they belong. The selections in this Reader, I hope, beckon the Farm to move forward, unencumbered but informed by the best tradition has to offer: a base from which to be creative.

While as of this writing I sit on Gould Farm's Board of Directors, neither I nor co-editor, Terry Beitzel, speak for the Farm's Board or its administration, nor any population, past or present, associated with the Farm. Nor does the Board or its administration necessarily share our impressions, views, selection bias, or attitude. Any errors of historical, therapeutic, or philosophical interpretation are ours. Those interested in a history of Gould Farm, through the early 1990s, should see William J. McKee's *Gould Farm: A Life of Sharing* (1994).

Steven K. Smith

Notes

1. Smith, Steven K. "Growing up on Gould Farm: Generational Reflections on Community, Change, and Tradition". Unpub., c. 2004. 11.
2. Infield, Henrik. *The American Intentional Communities: Study on the Sociology of Cooperation.* Glen Gardner, NJ: Glen Gardner Community Press, 1955. 79.

ACKNOWLEDGEMENTS

We thank the following who provided advice, encouragement, and, at times, access to many of the documents herein included: Claudette Callahan, Christy Dunkle, Ed Dunlop, Isabelle Felici, Emily S. Jackson, Bill McKee, Janet McKee, Katie McKee Mendelsohn, Charles A. Miller, Professor Timothy Miller, John Otenasek, Bob Rausch, Calvin W. Redekop, Alex Tinari, Phyllis Vine.

For digital access to documents, many of which are included herein, we thank Ron Coleman, Reference Librarian, United States Holocaust Memorial Museum; Violet Lutz, Ph.D., Special Collections Librarian, German Society of Pennsylvania; Susan Malsburg, Manuscripts Specialist, and Tal Nadan, Reference Archivist, New York Public Library; Dawn L. Nyce, Hartzler Library, Eastern Mennonite University; Christy Regenhardt, The Eleanor Roosevelt Papers Project, George Washington University; Rev. Bruce Southworth, Senior Minister, The Community Church of New York-Unitarian Universalist; Amanda Strauss, Radcliffe Institute, Schlesinger Library, Cambridge Massachusetts.

We also thank Deborah Kelley-Milburn, Research Librarian and Virtual Reference Coordinator, Harvard College Library, for assistance with copyright matters.

Our University Press of America Acquisitions Editor, Laura Espinoza, provided valuable assistance in the production of this document.

Finally, we are indebted to Andrea Sabet, whose copyediting, layout skills, and innate sense of what this project was about, were indispensible.

- - - - -

Awkward or incorrect syntax, spelling, and phraseology have been kept as close to the original, but changed when necessary to avoid ambiguity.

INTRODUCTION

The psychiatrist and author, Erich Fromm, during a late night discussion at Gould Farm, was once asked: "You are a widely read author in many countries, a writer on psychiatry, on social-ethical questions, on international relations...and many people seek your counsel. Now for my question: I want to ask you, what makes you tick?" Harvard Professor and Gould Farm Board member James Luther Adams' question surprised Fromm, who replied:

> I think I know. What makes me tick I learned from the Old Testament prophets—that the meaning of life is the struggle for justice and humanity against injustice and inhumanity. That is one reason I wanted to visit Gould Farm, for (the Farm) is in that struggle.[1]

Gould Farm (often referred to here as "the Farm"), a rural residential psychiatric community in western Massachusetts, entered that "struggle" in 1913.[2] Founders William J. Gould and his wife, Agnes Goodyear Gould, along with a small group of family members, first assisted mostly inner-city boys from New York and those with situational difficulties. Increasingly, the Farm would serve adults with persistent mental illness, including those with what we would call a dual diagnosis.

The Farm now celebrates its centenary in a very different era and context. Understandings of mental illness, addiction, leadership, therapy, and community have changed over the past 100 years. This Reader reflects, through the use of primary sources, these changes. As we approach its centenary we reflect upon Gould Farm's present, future—and past.

The Farm was founded in a cultural context beginning to challenge traditional assumptions of institutionalization and treatment with which, in part, Gould Farm has been sympathetic. Beginning in the late 1890s, psychiatrists, belonging to a profession affiliated with asylums, slowly began moving toward a biologically-based view of mental illness. This would in time shift emphasis away from the social context in which those with mental illness lived, to "curing" the individual, viewed outside a larger social context. Psychiatrists were distancing themselves from the asylum preferring, instead, roles outside these institutions.[3] Many psychiatrists, echoing the Progressive Movement, also believed in the "possibility of creating a new rational social and moral order that would eliminate existing flaws and alleviate human suffering."[4]

While the emphasis on biologically-based origins would have sweeping effects, especially with the introduction of psychotropic medications in the mid-

1950s, psychiatrists in the early twentieth century would later tend to overlook the distinctive emotional and social needs of the mentally ill who often require social structure and community support.[5] As Oliver Sacks wrote in 2009:

> The last fifteen years or so have seen a new generation of antipsychotic drugs, with better therapeutic effects and fewer side effects, but the too exclusive an emphasis on 'chemical' models of schizophrenia, and on the purely pharmacological approaches to treatment, may leave the central human and social experience of being mentally ill untouched.[6]

This over-emphasis on a chemical cure preceded the deinstitutionalization of those with mental illness in the 1960s and 1970s. Major cutbacks in funding mental health services in the 1980s exacerbated the plight of many of those de-institutionalized, but mitigated in part by the development of "club houses" and other similar social networks. Today's emphasis on "recovery" may be challenging traditional notions of both a chemical cure and institutionalization. Gould Farm avoided these treatment excesses, synthesizing professional medical treatment within a supportive social context.

Wider political and treatment trends aside, the Farm defies easy community and therapeutic categorization. Its beginnings followed the utopian socialist experiments of the 1840s but predated the communal endeavors of the 1960s. Informed by Christianity that was neither sectarian nor doctrinaire, yet steeped in the Sermon on the Mount, the Farm has never required religious, political, or ideological tests for membership, required by many communal endeavors; an individual's private property, though sometimes shared, was never held in common. The Farm, apart from basic daycare services, never schooled its young people, who usually attended local secondary schools. Respect for oneself, others, and for the community, were and are the only "requirements." In fact, the Farm's formula seems to be so simple as to avoid detection. But a family atmosphere of kindness and expectation of community participation, work, service to others, are part of this formula.

Comparisons between the Gould Farm and other residential treatment communities might further clarify the Farm's role. Unlike the Camphill communities, which work with those with developmental disabilities and, in some instances, the elderly, Gould Farm focuses on those with persistent mental illness. As Virgil Stucker notes below, Gould Farm has inspired many psychiatric residential facilities now in existence, like CooperRiis in North Carolina, Hopewell in Ohio, and Rose Hill in Michigan, all of which, to varying degrees, are based on the Farm's program of meaningful work and community. The chronicity of the client population at each of these communities may differ, too, at any given time. Unlike clubhouses such as Fountain House in New York City, both the Farm's patients ("guests") and staff live on the Farm's premises.

Those acquainted with Gould Farm have likely found it difficult to explain what actually happens there. Gould Farmers participate in the seemingly mundane tasks of daily life, such as milking cows, gardening, tapping trees for maple syrup, and mopping floors. But, somehow, these activities, along with others, such as communal dining, the celebration of holidays, and meaningful work, have transformed lives.

Gould Farm has also resisted embracing mono-therapeutic agendas often dictated more by fad than by experience and intuition. But the Farm has incorporated treatment understandings when so required without largely jeopardizing the tenor of its family, community atmosphere. The Farm and what happens therein is, indeed, the "therapy." It incorporates all single "therapies" into a lifestyle of kindness, community demands, traditionally motivated by non-sectarian religious impulses of service. These words of a former executive director, we believe, still hold the "secret" of Gould Farm's success today:

> The mode of our life together is "working with," "playing with," "celebrating with," "eating with," "sharing with," "suffering with"—all of the things that happen when a number of people live in close proximity. We do not see ourselves as therapists, but we consider our life together "therapeutic" in the deepest sense of the word—tending toward healing and new and independent life. We do not have work-therapy, but we work; we do not have occupational-therapy, but we make things and learn skills; we do not have music therapy, but we sing and play instruments; we do not have drama-therapy, but we produce plays; we do not have recreational-therapy, but we have parties, dances, games, sports, and community celebrations. We do not have therapies as compartmentalized activities, but—by intention at least—the whole life of the community encapsulates what is meant by the term *therapy*.[7]

This integrated approach, along with the Charter's admonition to "develop a community devoted to social service, which shall be controlled by the principle of disinterested cooperation both among its own members and its practical relations with the world,"[8] has given the Farm insight and programmatic flexibility to improve and expand its services. From the above quote, it appears, the unintended consequences of living intentionally, in community, serving others, provides a window into the Farm and, perhaps, may also help answer the questions: "What is Gould Farm?" and "What happens at Gould Farm?"

The Farm's fidelity to its Charter may help answer these questions. Consistent with its Charter, the Farm, throughout its history, has expanded its mission beyond the assistance of those who come here as guests and staff. The Farm's roughly 600 acres of mostly wooded land welcomed German Jewish refugees in the 1940s, Civil Rights workers in the 1950s, and Vietnamese refugees in the 1970s. In the early 1980s, the Farm's staff and Board of Directors discussed corporate support of a nuclear freeze resolution and, in 1981, hosted 19 African-American children to escape the horrors of what became known as the Atlanta Child Murders. In addition, the Farm through the decades has assisted its neighbors, including a battered wife, a run-away child, and a family whose restaurant was destroyed by fire. More recently, it hosted a family from the Boston area who lost a loved one in the Iraq War.

This expansion of mission may also have led certain prominent individuals to seek the Farm, inspired by the Farm's innovative program and dedicated, often cosmopolitan, leadership. Thornton Wilder; FDR grandson and United Nation's Official, Curtis Roosevelt; Mrs. Daniel Chester French; women's rights activists Louise Marion Bosworth and Rosika Schwimmer; journalist Angela Morgan; Dr. Richard C. Cabot; and Rev. Henry Sloane Coffin all visited the Farm. Thomas A. Watson, of Alexander Graham Bell fame, visited as did, decades later in the 1980s, Playwright William Gibson. Perhaps it is no coincidence that these individuals, to varying degrees, were social activists, promoting the rights of women, world peace, or the dignity of those with mental illness.

Gould Farm's staff has included both independent and church-affiliated volunteers, most notably from Brethren Volunteer Service (the service arm of the Church of the Brethren). The historic "Peace Churches," (Brethren, Quaker, and Mennonite) have been well represented on the Farm's staff. Both Antioch College and a German volunteer agency sent volunteers to the Farm in the 1970s and 1980s. Its early supporters included professors of theology from Harvard Divinity School and Unitarian-Universalist theological schools, including Meadville Seminary and Andover-Newton.

The Farm's "practical relations with the world," may have helped prevent the Farm from becoming too self-absorbed. Will Gould believed that earlier communal endeavors like Brook Farm failed "chiefly because of their intense inner absorption."[9] (Gould himself disliked the thought of a self-absorbed group set apart from society.) It is to the Farm's credit that its leaders have engaged the Farm, not as existing to perpetuate community for its own sake—which often becomes self-centered—but to fulfill the Farm's mission in a context that happens to be, due to historic and geographic circumstance, communal. Involvement in community, of course, happens to have great therapeutic value for all involved. Gould envisioned a community that served those in need; it was his hope that similar communities would develop and model after Gould Farm. This has happened to varying degrees, as summarized by Virgil Stucker.[10]

Gould Farm has survived many challenges. Its survival, however, is not inevitable. The pressures and challenges following the worst economic downturn since incorporation have challenged the Farm to consider its future in this centenary year, and beyond. Gone are the days of religious optimism and group solidarity focused around a founding, charismatic leader. An elder population, many of whom had direct contact with the founders and whose wisdom guided generations of leaders into the 2000s, has largely disappeared. One might then ask if the Farm is moving toward a "post-communal culture"[11] where individuality and freedom usurp communal commitment. I don't think it has. The Farm now, as it has throughout its history, has wrestled with competing definitions of "community" and even therapy. The Farm, throughout its history, has successfully addressed economic hardships, has synthesized differing visions of the Farm, and reconciled tensions between the individual and collective responsibility.

The selections in this Reader echo these tensions, chronicling a communal way of life that has changed since its founding. Though diverse in both topic and date, the readings point toward an inter-faith, humanistic, communal endeavor which strove to reflect, in Will Gould's words, the "Kingdom of God Here and Now."

Many of the selections also reflect, in addition to cultural change, features of Gould Farm which simply do not change. Some may chronicle the "mundane" and may be, in themselves, rather quaint. They range from client referral letters to the Goulds from social workers Harry L. Hopkins (later to become Franklin Delano Roosevelt's principle architect of the New Deal) and Henry Street Settlement's Lillian Wald, to correspondence between Agnes Gould and Eleanor Roosevelt addressing post-War relief efforts in Europe. There are other selections that may not be as "quaint," a chapter excerpt from a 2005 Harvard College Bachelor's thesis, a letter by Rosemary Antin, Neurologist Oliver Sacks' brief but significant mention of the Farm in the *New York Review of Books*. As such, this may be a "bibliographic history" of the Farm. The selections guide the reader through multiple definitions and meanings of the Farm, and pose and, perhaps answer, the above-noted questions: "What is Gould Farm?" and "What happens at Gould Farm?"

William J. Gould, the Farm's early pioneers, and those today associated with the Farm may not have been, or are, as explicit as Fromm anchoring the Farm in a struggle for "justice" against "injustice." But quietly, mostly in relative obscurity, in times of internal division, solidarity, poverty, and abundance, the Farm has given hope, insight, coping, living, and social skills to those who had few, if any, of what so many take for granted. Its dedicated community members, both short- and long-term, children and elders, professionals and recent college graduates, have made this possible.

It is our hope that these selections provide such insight for interested observers, scholars, medical professionals, practitioners of community, and all those addressing innovative forms of assisting those with mental illness. As such, this book may also be a record, since the Farm's founding, of the "struggles" of those marginalized in society—and those restored to a sense of well-being through a "life of sharing" within the Gould Farm community. In doing so, this manuscript may explain how the Farm has survived for 100 years, hoping its existence continues long into the future.

Informed by social and political theory, Terry Beitzel's concluding chapter examines the issue of justice and its relation to intentional community, specifically Gould Farm. The Editors do not claim to speak for the Farm nor do our views necessarily represent those of the Farm's Board of Directors or administration. We write about and reflect on the Farm from personal experience and study. Steve Smith grew up on the Farm where his parents lived and worked. He now sits on the Farm's Board of Directors. Terry Beitzel has followed Gould Farm more remotely and indirectly for 25 years.

Steven K. Smith

Notes

1. Fromm, Erich. "VIP Visitors at Gould Farm" from "Gould Farm News," Vol. 43, No. 2. Summer 1976.

2. Definitions of "community" and "intentional community" are vast as is the literature, a survey of which is beyond the scope of this Reader. See Donald E. Pitzer's *America's Communal Utopias* (1997), Timothy Miller's *The Quest for Utopia in Twentieth Century America* (1998), Yaacov Oved's *Two-hunderd Years of American Communes* (1987), and Rosabeth Moss Kanter's *Community and Commitment* (1972).

3. Grob, Gerald. *The Mad Among Us: A History of the Care of America's Mentally Ill.* New York: The Free Press, 1994. 130.

4. Ibid. 141.

5. Ibid. 140.

6. Sacks, Oliver. "The Lost Virtues of the Asylum." *The New York Review of Books.* Vol. 56, No. 14. September 24, 2009.

7. Smith, Kent D. "Gould Farm: Rehabilitation Through Intentional Community." Paper presented at the International Association of Psycho-Social Rehabilitation. May 29, 1981.

8. See Chapter Two for the entire text of the charter.

9. McKee, William J. *Gould Farm: A Life of Sharing.* Monterey: William J. Gould & Associates, 1994. 72.

10. See Chapter Eight.

11. Rieff, Philip. *The Triumph of the Therapeutic: Uses of Faith after Freud.* New York: Harper & Row, Publishers, 1966. 11.

Chapter One

A Vision: In the Words of the Founder

Gould Farm founder, William J. Gould (1867-1925), wrote the first two pieces in this chapter. Here he envisions, informed by a "Protestant social idealism of the Progressive era," the work which would later be performed at Gould Farm in Monterey.[1] (Between 1894 and 1911, Gould and his family started nine such endeavors before settling in Monterey.) Gould's reported charisma and dedication to serving others are revealed in these writings, attributes that attracted people of all faiths, and those of none.

As a boy and young man, William J. Gould was prone to depression, like his father, David Hill Gould, who died when Will was five years old. Will Gould had a driving need to address his family's poverty and, from a childhood vision, felt led to carry out the teachings of Jesus through service to others. This led, at first, to assisting boys from the city (inspired by a childhood story his mother told him about a generous but poverty-stricken child named "Tim"), then later to those with other situational difficulties, and finally accepting those that became "guests" suffering from a wide variety of problems, both situational and mental-health. His independent spirit rejected the idea of incorporating one experiment, in Becket, Massachusetts, in about 1902, which many saw as a successful residential camp for troubled boys.[2]

An excerpt from the second selection echoes Gould's striving, throughout his life, to close the chasm between belief and action:

(Religion) is worth while because though perfect in its ideal, its principles are yet so fundamental and so simple that they can be applied to every exigency of life... because it has taught me that in place of personal ambition that can never be satisfied may come the joy of loving service...[3]

The third piece, a sermon given by Will Gould just months before his death, was recorded by the Russian-born novelist, Mary Antin (1881-1949). Best known for her autobiography, *The Promised Land* (1912), Antin was a lecturer

1

and women's and immigrant rights activist. Born into a Jewish family in Plotzk, Russia, she arrived at Gould Farm in 1923. Antin was a Zionist but endorsed assimilation. She endorsed the Progressive movement's platform and supported the unsuccessful Progressive presidential candidacy of Charles Evans Hughes. Antin suffered from mental illness following her separation, in about 1917, from her husband, paleontologist and Columbia University professor Amadeus Grabau. Antin referred to her illness at various times as "a nervous breakdown," "a psycho-neurosis," and "a deep soul sickness."[4] Unable to lecture and experiencing financial difficulties in New York, Antin moved in with a sister in Winchester, Massachusetts. By the early 1920s she became a patient at Austin Riggs, a psychiatric center in Stockbridge, Massachusetts, later moving to Gould Farm. Antin became attached to the Goulds and became interested in anthroposophy and other forms of spiritualism and mysticism. Antin left the Farm to meet and live by the mystic, Meher Baba, then returned to the Farm in the mid 1930s.

THE SELECTIONS

The following is an excerpt from a letter from Will Gould to his family, dated October 18, 1896, while at a seminary in Bangor, Maine. At age 28, through the efforts of a minister in Gould's hometown of Schroon, New York, Gould applied for and was accepted into the Theological Seminary in Bangor. Rose McKee further writes that Gould never finished his studies, finding himself ill-suited to the ministry and his studies "irksome." He was also older than most of the students, with a different life experience. McKee notes that Gould felt that every Christian is committed to complete consecration of himself; he disliked the thought of a group set apart from others. Wherever Gould later lived, McKee observed, he was asked to preach, finding his seminary training was a great help to him.[5]

> I think I have got along with my studies the best this week that I have at all, which is very encouraging to me. But my dear people you mustn't think that your "illustrious son" will ever make much of a mark in the world intellectually or as a scholar. It is too late for that, if I ever could, so you mustn't expect great things, although for your sakes I should like to be more brilliant. It grows upon me more and more that I have a special work to do, and the more I meet with other men, the more I feel that mine has been a peculiar preparation. I have learned certain things in my close association with nature, with plenty of time for meditation, that never will be gotten in a Theological Seminary.[6]

Gould and his wife began experimenting with the type of social work Gould had in mind. The Goulds and their family, in 1910, moved to near Delanson, New York, and rented a house which Agnes Gould called a "gathering of people in the home." The Goulds took in people with "serious emotional problems" including homeless, several children, and a niece of Mrs. Gould's. After about 18 months here, the Goulds settled in Winsted, Connecticut, their final stop before arriving in Monterey.

In Winsted, the Goulds worked with convalescent men and boys. They worked with drug addictions but found this required long-term care for which Winsted eventually proved inappropriate. The Goulds received patients from medical and surgical wards in New York City. Hannah Josephi, chief of social service at New York Hospital, and Amelia Massopust, child of social service at Bellevue Hospital, became the Goulds' collaborators and friends. These contacts likely served as contacts for referrals in Monterey.

Gould wrote the following piece for a contest sponsored by *The Congregationalist and Christian World* in 1910, for which he won second prize.

LAYMEN DECLARE THEMSELVES IN PRIZE CONTEST

The question, What makes the Christian religion worth while to any man? is answered in each of the following brief articles. While preparing for this Men and Religion Number of The Congregationalist, which is especially for men, we wished to secure some definite, practical expression from the men themselves as to what they had found in the Christian religion that would be helpful to other men. So we asked the question and offered prizes for the best answers. The contest was limited to laymen, which restricted the number of those who might have replied. The answers came from many sections of the United States, to the number of about thirty-five, and most of them were from business and professional men, who spoke strongly and to the point from their own experience. The conditions of the contest limited answers to 350 words. One of the best had to be thrown out because it was too long. Seven of the best answers, including the two prize winners, have been selected for publication. We regret that the limitations of space prevent printing others.—Editors.

Gould's entry:

THE MORE ABUNDANT LIFE

The Christian religion is worth while to any man because it embodies a perfect ideal, an ideal that when applied to a human life raises that life to its highest power.

It is worth while because of its teaching that well-being is based on love and service and because of the glorious opportunity it gives to inspire others with this principle.

It is worth while because though perfect in its ideal, its principles are yet so fundamental and so simple that they can be applied to every exigency of life, from the soul's greatest need to the smallest detail of everyday living, and when so applied being a fullness of joy compared with which nothing else is worth while.

The Christian religion is worth while to me because it has opened the door of possibilities and given me a glimpse of what life may become if actuated by the spirit of the Founder.

It is worth while because it has taught me that in place of personal ambition that can never be satisfied may come the joy of loving service which is the very secret of the more abundant life; because it helps me to see the possibilities of the lives of those men who are down and out, who have tried every way to happiness and have found each one to fail; that in spite of all the past there is still the way of life for them, and that the Master may use me to bring them to the joy that is mine through his power.

Lastly, it is worth while because it gives to my soul a more vital grasp of the thought that true life is everlasting life, and the Master's words, "He that liveth and believeth in me shall never die," have become a part of the joyous faith that moves all life which expresses the Christian religion worth while to any man.—W. J. Gould, Delanson, N. Y.

Mary Antin recorded the following sermon by Will Gould, on Thursday evening, November 24th, 1924, six months before Gould's death.

W. J. comes in like a ship with tugging sails; appearance, voice, and manner more than usually energetic. Opening remarks very impressively spoken. Reading more explosively emphatic than usual. Half a dozen hymns called for from the congregation opened the meeting. From the Windsor chair in which he always sat, Brother Will started speaking as follows:

"Well, children, I've got a great subject tonight. I've got such a great subject that I shan't have much to say about it. I'll only read it. The words that I am about to read are those of a man who spent forty years studying and then forty years more in business, applying his studies. During these second forty years, I suppose he was still chewing on these studies. And then, after eighty years of study and application, he gives us his experience in a speech that takes about five minutes to read.

"I've been doing a lot of chewing myself today. Some days things come that make you think. Most days seem so alike, and then comes a day when somehow we catch an inspiration, we don't know how or why. Such a day I've had today. Today, somehow, I've seen this work of ours as if from the outside, as if I wasn't a part of it at all. As I thought how I can put to the family what I want to say, I felt as if I couldn't—I didn't know how. Then I thought of Moses and felt as if to him I'd have to turn, in him I'd find the words. Here's his summing up of his years of experience at the moment when he felt that his work was over, when he turns it over to the people:

"'See, I have set before thee this day life and good, and death and evil; In that I command thee this day to love the Lord thy God, to walk in His ways and to keep His commandments and His statutes and His judgments, that thou mayest live and multiply; and the Lord thy God shall bless thee in the land whither thou goest to possess it. But if thine heart turn away, so that thou wilt not hear, but shalt be drawn away, and worship other gods, and serve them; I denounce unto you this day, that ye shall surely perish, and that ye shall not prolong your days upon the land, whither thou passest over Jordan to go to possess it. I call heaven and earth to record this day against you, that I have set before you life and death, blessing and cursing: therefore choose life, that both thou and thy seed may live.'

"I wonder if there was ever a farewell message from any leader finer than this, the most magnificent summing up of a leader to his people, of a general to his army, of a patriot to his country, that was ever penned. Right in the midst of a mass of petty details he bursts into this lofty appeal: Choose ye this day between life and death. The decision is not for the future, it's not conditioned by circumstances—when this thing or that thing has worked out the way we hoped; the decision can be made now.

"Moses had been one hundred twenty years getting ready for this moment. And then all of a sudden he realizes that it is this day they could be free. He had been promising them all sorts of blessings when they should get to the promised land: the victories over their enemies, lands, wells of water, increase of flocks, all the good things they were hungry for, but they must first get hold of the land beyond the Jordan. But suddenly it wasn't so: it was now, not by and by.

"And today it came to me with tremendous force that we haven't got to wait to round this thing out before we can have what we mean by Gould Farm. Moses put it to them as a choice between the blessing and the curse. Now we don't want the harsh word curse, but perhaps we'd better realize it belongs, because unless today we do choose the blessing, what is left is a curse.

"And I felt today how we've wanted to carry out our plans at Gould Farm, wanted to see this or that rounded out, some finish on the things we've begun. And here we are, so many unfinished things on our hands. We keep getting raw recruits—we're most of us so raw. We feel the strain, the pressure of the error of the world, we feel how little we can do to change all that.

"Here's Mr. Call [our earnest, full-time carpenter]. He was saying to me today: 'But what can we do to make things over? We can't touch it—it's the whole world that's queered.' It was a cry from a man's inmost soul. But we mustn't let this feeling of helpless despair creep into our ranks. Choose ye this day what ye shall be, what you yourselves shall be. Have ye got to wait till all the world is sound before we are sound? Till all the world is unselfish before we are unselfish? Till all the world has peace before we have peace? Till all the world has joy before we have joy?

"The world isn't preventing us. The enemy we have to fear is the enemy of our own strain and stress, our own selfishness, meanness, despondency. He shall deliver you from your enemies—whenever you choose. Today you can be free and safe. Hold out your hand, what is it you want? The healing is yours, instantly, the moment your will merges with the will of the Lord. We say, O Lord, when? when? We think it's tomorrow, tomorrow; yet we only have to accept it now. Accept the blessing, enter into the promised land. We can *choose* the blessing now."[7]

Notes and Permissions

1. McKee, William J. *Gould Farm: A Life of Sharing*. Monterey: The William J. Gould Associates, Inc., 1994. x.

2. McKee, Rose L. *Brother Will and the Founding of Gould Farm*. Monterey: The William J. Gould Associates, Inc., [1963], 1975. 17-20.

3. Gould, William J. From "The More Abundant Life." *The Congregationalist and Christian World*. September 23, 1911. Contribution to a prize contest on: "What makes the Christian Religion worth while to any Man?" Page number unknown. Every effort has been made to trace copyright for this piece reprinted on page 3. Proper credit will be included in any future printings upon receipt of written notice.

4. Salz, Evelyn, Ed. *Selected Letters of Mary Antin*. Syracuse: Syracuse University Press, 2000. 87.

5. McKee, Rose L. *op cit.* 15.
6. Ibid. 13-14. Reprinted with permission: The William J. Gould Associates, Inc.
7. Ibid. 46-48. Reprinted with permission: The William J. Gould Associates, Inc.

Chapter Two

A Vision Realized

This chapter leads with the Introduction from Rose L. McKee's book, *Brother Will and the Founding of Gould Farm*. Rose McKee arrived at the Farm in her early 20s, in 1918, and lived and worked at the Farm until she died in 1985. She writes:

> New England has known many ventures in community living, some of which have been doctrinaire or at the edge of odd ways in thought or behavior. There is, in contrast, nothing peculiar or theoretical in the basis of Gould Farm. Practical and moderate, it seems in consonance with its physical setting, at the same time, drawing strength for its pioneering work in the field of religious social service from its geographical association with earlier New England traditions.[1]

This piece is an inspiring description of the Farm, which includes an account of the frontier existence of the Farm's founders.

Also included are selections from promotional brochures, dating from 1929 through 2012. Written especially for parents of prospective patients (the Farm uses the term "guest"), they present matter-of-fact details about the Farm's therapeutic programs. One sees, in their entirety, an evolution of programmatic emphasis at Gould Farm, which reflects, and sometimes transcends, contemporary practices, and anticipates what would later become encouraged in psychosocial rehabilitation.

The last piece in this chapter is from former Executive Director, Kent D. Smith, who wrote this about the Farm's therapeutic approach:

> The mode of our life together is "working with," "playing with," "celebrating with," "eating with," "sharing with," "suffering with"—all of the things that happen when a number of people live in close proximity. We do not see ourselves as therapists, but we consider our life together "therapeutic" in the deepest sense of the word—tending toward healing and new and independent life. We do not have work-therapy, but we work; we do not have occupational-

7

therapy, but we make things and learn skills; we do not have music-therapy, but we sing and play instruments... We do not have therapies as compartmentalized activities, but—by intention at least—the whole life of the community encapsulates what is meant by the term *therapy*.[2]

THE SELECTIONS

The following excerpt is the "Introduction" from Rose L. McKee's *Brother Will and the Founding of Gould Farm* (1963). Rose Le Vino (1897-1985) came to the Farm in 1920 after working for a Jewish welfare agency. She served, among other roles, as Gould Farm social worker. She was an original associate and served on the Farm's Board of Directors. In 1927 she married Sidney McKee (1882-1971) a Presbyterian then Congregational minister who came to the Farm in 1922 after serving as a teacher-social worker in Shanghai. Mr. McKee served as the Farm's pastor and in positions of managerial responsibility. Like Rose, Sidney was an original associate and served on the Farm's Board of Directors.[3]

INTRODUCTION

The natural beauty of Gould Farm holds the interest of the most casual visitor. Low, softly rounded hills—the Massachusetts Berkshires—encompass it. Hard and soft maples mingle with pine, hemlock, birch and laurel in quiet woods and on the slopes back of the main houses. A brook, which flows from a series of falls two miles to the south, crosses the property and flows down to meet a smaller branch coming from the village of Monterey, two miles to the east. Thence it forms the Konkapot River, bounding the original tract along the main highway and turning south again toward the United States Fish Hatchery, which, with its wide expanse of thickly wooded hills, is the Farm's neighbor to the southwest. The hill air is clear and dry, the summers usually cool, the winters cold and brisk. This is a health-giving climate, challenging and severe at times, but for the most part enjoyable and stimulating.

New England has known many ventures in community living, some of which have been doctrinaire or at the edge of odd ways in thought or behavior. There is, in contrast, nothing peculiar or theoretical in the basis of Gould Farm. Practical and moderate, it seems in consonance with its physical setting, at the same time drawing strength for its pioneering work in the field of religious social service from its geographical association with earlier New England traditions.

In location, Gould Farm has the advantages both of isolation and of accessibility. Nine miles from the nearest railroad and town, it can easily be reached both from New York City and from Boston. Interested observers could manage, even in the earliest days of its history, to seek it out if they would. Guests could find it for short or longer stays, and residents could turn to the cities to study and develop the Farm's particular possibilities of service.

In the fifty years of its existence, the kinds of people coming to Gould Farm have not changed very much. They hold in common their sense of need,—need of rest and change, of companionship, of comfort and guidance, of a sense of purpose in life. If the Goulds opened their doors wide to meet these and other kinds of need, the social service they accomplished was incidental to their purpose. Their aim was no less than to make the spirit flesh and to raise the level of every-day living to a level of fulfillment and joy as recorded in the Christian gospels.

William Jonathan Gould, born October 19, 1867, was the third child and only son of a Congregational minister in upper New York State. The years of boyhood and early manhood as the main support of his widowed mother and four sisters were a discipline of poverty and hard work. Yet the farm home at Schroon Lake was a happy one, the family life deeply rooted in an outgoing Christian faith. Will Gould was the product of this home, carrying with him always the skills, the strength and the ideals it had given him.

In maturity, Will Gould was of medium height and stature, strong and sturdy. He had regular features, a firm chin, dark, wavy hair and a clear, fair complexion. His voice, a baritone, was often raised in song as he hurried about his work. His manner was forthright, but gentle and tactful. Those meeting him for the first time felt an immediate sense of his integrity and of his radiance of spirit.

George Brooks, a life-long friend of Will Gould, once said, "There's not one in a thousand could walk such a straight road as Will." Indeed the clarity of his purpose was always bright. From a boyhood vision while still at Schroon, his outstanding thought was to demonstrate that life carried out according to the teachings of Jesus was not only a practicable possibility but the richest and most joyous life a human being could know. Through years of experiment, the form developed for his demonstration was that of an enlarged family group, each one using his capacities to the full for the benefit of the others. The simple home setting at Schroon was transferred to Monterey and there adapted to the needs of those who sought it out.

When William Gould and Agnes Goodyear met, he was thirty-five and she was thirty-three. She had been brought up in a cosmopolitan and well-to-do family. Both her father and her grandfather were successful inventors; and although, by the time of her marriage, her family had lost its money, she had behind her a background of travel and culture. Religious commitment, as strong in the Goodyear family as in the Goulds, was a vital element in common.

One of the qualities people recall first about Agnes Gould is her graciousness. She had the air and demeanor of a great lady, which seemed to have become a part of her personality. In addition to her cosmopolitan background, Agnes Goodyear brought to her married life a talent for understanding all kinds of people and a warm and generous outreach toward them which went well with Will's deepest concerns. With this strong sense of dedication held in common, it became possible for their very different and distinctive personalities to grow together and to benefit in their daily lives from all that mattered most to each of them.

In the first twelve years at Gould Farm, Will and Agnes Gould worked together, he acting as practical innovator and prophetic guide, she as a warm-hearted and devoted assistant. With Will Gould's death in 1925, Agnes was called upon to play a more decisive role. During the final year of his life, Will Gould remarked in private more than once that, successful as it might seem in the eyes of the general public and as it undoubtedly was in terms of actual accomplishment, his work had nevertheless failed in establishing itself in a form that could be carried on after his death. He had always maintained that the strength of the Farm lay in its firm basis in the teachings of Jesus and not in identification with his own personality; and yet in those last months he sought in vain for a way of transferring to others the responsibilities which he knew he could not long continue to carry. To most of those who knew Gould Farm at that time, its future apart from him was inconceivable.

That he and they were proved wrong was the achievement first of all of Agnes Gould. Lacking her husband's physical stamina, lacking the possibility of leading a family in farm labor, lacking Will Gould's capacity for experimental accomplishment, she nonetheless kept his spirit and ideals alive and essentially in the form which he had given them. As Will Gould had perceived, Gould Farm required a practical and a spiritual leader. Through devotion to his vision—his dream, as she would say—she called upon hitherto unknown reserves of imaginative and executive talent to provide this leadership for the remaining thirty-three years of her life.

And when at last, in her eighty-ninth year, her earthly life ended, Gould Farm had sunk its roots so deep and stretched them forth so wide that the necessity of continuing it was self-evident. Gould Farm has proved strong enough to adapt itself to change without changing the quality of spirit which identifies it.[4]

With concern, Agnes Gould decided to incorporate what was known as Social Service Farm in 1929, four years after Gould's death. Mrs. Gould feared incorporation would jeopardize the Farm's independence. However, she was persuaded to incorporate for, among other reasons, fund-raising purposes. The charter was written by Agnes' sister, Caroline Goodyear (1868-1962), who left a job in New York City to join the Goulds in 1916.[5]

"The original charter of purpose," wrote Rose McKee, herself an original Associate and signatory Charter, "...although based upon scientific experience, was deliberately vague and general in its wording. After all, the Associates agreed, how could they then be certain what turn of events might occur that would cause them to broaden out in new and unforeseen ways?"[6] Here is the charter:

1929

THE COMMONWEALTH OF MASSACHUSETTS

Be it known that whereas Agnes C. Gould, Caroline Goodyear, Rose L. McKee, Sidney McKee, Faith Blake Colt, Howard F. Colt, Jane Eleanor Goodyear, Minnie W. LeClear, Antoinette H. Tuttle, Henrietta S. Tuttle, Florence May Scovill and Mather Lamont Brown have associated themselves with the intention of forming a corporation under the name of The William J. Gould Associates, Inc.

For the purpose of the following: To develop and perpetuate the work generally known as Gould Farm, in accordance with the ideals of its founder; in other words, to develop a community devoted to social service, which community shall be controlled by the principle of disinterested co-operation both among its own members and in its practical relations with the world at large, and shall at the same time be as nearly as possible self-supporting. The beneficiaries may be drawn from any or all walks of life, and may be of any race or creed, but are preferably those who, because of special personal circumstances or conditions, have difficulty in finding elsewhere the care or opportunity they need. They may contribute according to their ability towards the costs of maintenance, but no minimum rate shall be fixed by the management. Beneficiaries may be assisted away from the community. The object of the associates shall be to secure for the beneficiaries a greater degree of physical, mental and spiritual well-being. It is a further purpose of the associates to foster according to their ability and opportunities other out-growing enterprises having special social value, whether eleemosynary, educational, therapeutic or industrial. Such enterprises may be self-directing and free to develop into independent organizations as soon as they desire and are able to do so. Generally the associates propose to do any work not engaged in for financial profit to its members as individuals in so far as the same now is or may hereafter be authorized by chapter 180 of the General Laws or any amendment thereof or addition thereto, excepting only powers, the exercise of which require especial regulation by the government; and have complied with the provisions of the Statutes of this Commonwealth in such case made and provided, as appears from the certificate of the Proper Officers of said corporation, duly approved by the Commissioner of Corporations.

Caroline Goodyear (1868-1962), Agnes Gould's sister, was an original associate and the first Vice President of the Gould Farm Board of Directors. Before moving to Gould Farm in 1916, she was a social worker in New York City where her work and contacts at the Charity Organization Society led to patient referrals to the Farm. The following is from a pamphlet she wrote around 1936.

THE STORY OF GOULD FARM

Physically, Gould Farm consists of 555 acres, mostly upland meadows and wooded hills, in the heart of the beautiful Southern Berkshires, at an elevation of 1400 feet. A lovely brook runs through it, waterfalls are nearby, and two picturesque lakes are within easy reach. Two of the highest peaks in Massachusetts are only a few miles away, and famous trails (including the Appalachian) are all about. Besides a main house of about forty rooms, there are over 25 other buildings, nine of them heated cottages, and 21 in all that are occupied during the summer.

Gould Farm has been described as "not an institution, but a way of life." The inception of the idea came to William J. Gould in his early boyhood, while at work on the farm of his widowed mother, in Schroon Lake, N.Y. It came to him definitely on a certain never-to-be forgotten day, in the form of an illuminating vision of a world transfigured, spiritually and materially, by Christ's spirit of brotherly love. By it he felt himself called and consecrated to a life of practical service, and throughout his career he looked back upon it as the source of his inspiration, and forward to it as the ideal and goal to be attained, not by his individual personality, but by the redemption of society.

History

Always an idealist and something of a mystic, the necessity of working the little farm for the support of his mother and four sisters (a mother who was one of the deepest inspirations of his life, and sisters whose loyal support later more than repaid these early labors) forbade his boyish dream of pulpit oratory and developed the practical side of his nature. Sound economics was one of his enthusiasms and no project which had not a firm basis in this respect could pass muster with him. The strength and integrity of his character made him a recognized power in every community where, even for a brief period, he made his dwelling.

There developed in his early manhood the determination to "preach the Gospel" by devoting *his home* to human service, and he found a wife whose ideals were in complete harmony with his own. After several experimental beginnings elsewhere, he reached, on the eve of Thanksgiving Day, 1913, the present location of Gould Farm, convinced that in this beautiful setting he was to establish his permanent abiding place. He bought the long-abandoned boarding-house with borrowed money, and energetically set about making it habitable. The guiding vision remained undimmed, and from the very day of their arrival his doors were opened to guests who most needed what he had to offer—a share in the spirit of the home, and a share too, in the dramatic pioneering vicissitudes which lend many a thrill to the story of their early struggle for a foothold. Joy was throughout the dominant note, as service was the underlying motive.

Substituting faith in God and man, neighborliness, skill, and sagacity, for more common forms of wealth, the remaining twelve years of William Gould's life effected a transfiguration of the old place which seems positively miraculous, even in the eyes of those who saw it in process. Observers of his work were inspired to give aid—without which these achievements would have been impossible—but in his mind and purpose material progress was always subordinate to the advancement of the Kingdom of Heaven on earth.

Under the corporate title of "The William J. Gould Associates, Inc.," his fellow workers are striving to carry on, without deviating in spirit from the lines which he laid down. More than eleven years have elapsed since he passed from sight, yet the work goes on unchanged in its essential features.

Methods

From the moment they enter the doors, guests sense the atmosphere of *home*— to many, the only real home they know. The absence of formality, the companionable way in which the routine work is shared, the complete democracy of the social life, even the simplicity of the appointments and the absence of "hired help," contribute to make the newcomer feel at ease; and rapidly, though by impalpable degrees, a change comes over him. Relaxation replaces strain; opportunities for friendly help to others who are still less fortunate than himself, as well as to have a hand in making the Farm itself a success, revive interest and incentive; and the sense that he is, himself, an object of interest and concern restores his courage and brings realization of his true place in God's world.

Types of Guests

Guests are referred by physicians, clinics, social agencies, or come by personal application. They may represent any race, creed, or social station; and the interest and spice of the family life on the Farm arise largely from the variety of its constituents and the unexpected combinations and alliances which often develop, as well as from the genuine personal contributions of skill or art to be garnered by sympathetic yet critical appreciation from so heterogeneous a group.

The reasons which bring guests to the Farm are various, ranging from the need of a few days' rest and change to deep-seated difficulties occasioned by maladjustment, friction, worry or bereavement. Some, on the other hand, are drawn by recognition of opportunities for service, and come to give as they are able of their means, strength, or skill. Social workers and others are welcomed for week-ends or longer rest-periods, and former guest-patients frequently return year after year for vacations.

The Newcomer's First Day

No attempt is made to schedule the time of a newly-arriving guest, but his day takes shape unconsciously. His neighbor is usually one who will make him feel at ease. Dish-drying after the meal gives opportunity for making further acquaintances; then someone offers to show him the weaving room, the music studio, the carpenter shop or the brook, or suggests a hike later in the day. After a brief period of mutual observation and acquaintance he usually finds or makes for himself a niche, and time seldom hangs heavy on his hands.

Getting Beneath the Surface

This easy-going fellowship in itself works like magic in many cases, but with the majority the trouble lies deeper, and no pains are spared to meet it with understanding sympathy and intelligent guidance. Family difficulties have often been healed, frictions lubricated, maladjustments remedied in a practical way, self-centeredness enlightened, incentive and courage restored. (It is a fact that nearly all the members of the Farm's own staff have been recruited from the ranks of the guest-patients.)

Co-operation

Cordial and active co-operation is maintained with social agencies, physicians, and relatives, and cases too deep-seated for the Farm's informal and non-technical methods are often helped to find such further care or treatment as may be indicated.

Finances

First—the Farm has recognized its obligation, as a matter of self-respect, to obtain from each applicant, or from the group individually interested in the applicant, at least the amount of the per capita cost of about $10 a week, if that is possible. Guests who can afford to do so are asked to pay $12 to $15 a week.

Second—strict economy is practiced.

Third—there is no salaried service except for some of the larger farm operations and in a few instances where small stipends permit full-time attention to duties. Lighter forms of routine work, discharged in the spirit of team play, have been changed from a financial drain to a measure of actual therapeutic value.

Fourth—the balance is provided by the voluntary gifts of friends here and there, who have seen or heard what is being done. Other friends have recognized special needs and have provided for them.

The foundations are already laid for the central portion of a new building, which, when completed, will afford increased accommodations and other advantages.

Woodworking and Weaving

Aside from the vital benefit to guests which lies in voluntary sharing in the outdoor and indoor activities of the place, the main opportunities for busying oneself agreeably and beneficially are to be found in Woodworking and Weaving. The Woodworking Shop, equipped with several thousand dollars' worth of power machines, and under skilled and sympathetic supervision, produces children's play blocks, which are sold to kindergartens, day nurseries, parents, etc., at a small profit, in the hope of making this department at least self-supporting. Friends of the Farm are invited to send for our illustrated price list of blocks and similar products of the Woodworking Shop.

The Weaving Shop has an enviable record for giving fascinating employment, on the same volunteer, unpaid basis, to those who wish to try their hands at weaving rugs, curtains, handbags, scarves, etc., either for the Farm itself, for sale by the Farm, or—if they pay the bare cost of materials—for themselves, or as gifts to friends. Men as well as women have quickly developed a real knack for weaving. This shop usually has a small supply of articles on hand for sale, and we shall be glad to correspond as to prices, special orders, etc.

Music and Languages

Exceptionally competent and friendly instruction—without charge—is usually available in vocal and piano music, English, and one or two other languages. Drawing, block-printing, and similar classes are held from time to time for those interested.

Plays and other home talent entertainments are frequently given, and choruses sometimes formed. Volley-ball is a favorite warm weather game, and table tennis a winter recreation. Group hikes are almost a daily diversion at all seasons; and Great Barrington has a very good motion picture theater.

Transportation

Gould Farm is nine miles from the railway and bus stations in Great Barrington. We are therefore obliged to charge—including driver's time—$1.00 for the special 18-mile round trip for arriving and departing guests; two more persons, 50 cents each. Word of the day and hour of arrival—unless wired—should be timed to reach us at least 24 hours in advance, as our one daily mail comes late in the afternoon.

Applications

No formal application is necessary, but a personal reference, a physician's certificate of health and freedom from communicable disease, and enough general information to enable us to judge of the Farm's ability to supply what is needed, are required in the case of all personal applications. We have no resident physician, and are not equipped to supply special diets or to give any sort of technical care or supervision.[7]

Grace Elliston (1881-1950), the author of the following 1940s pamphlet, was a retired actress who lived in Stockbridge, Massachusetts, and who raised money for Gould Farm. She debuted in a series of Frank Daniels musicals. Her role as Shirley Rossmore in Charles Klein's play, "The Lion and the Mouse" (1905) had more than 500 performances at the Lyceum Theater, New York City.[8]

GOULD FARM
EXCERPTS FROM LETTERS

From MISS IDA CANNON, Chief of Social Service Department, Massachusetts General Hospital, Boston, Massachusetts.

"There is a growing feeling among the scientific medical men that there are aspects of treatment far beyond the scope of science that have deep healing power, and I feel that Mrs. Gould should be classed among those who are practicing the art of medicine. One of the rare characteristics of Mrs. Gould is that she sees that the science of medicine must have due recognition in such cases as it is required. I have seen demonstrations of this cooperation in which the art and science of medicine were made possible for the patient in a suitable balance of service."

From MISS MARY A. TOBIN, Director Social Service, City of New York, Department of Hospitals, Coney Island Hospital, Brooklyn, N.Y.

"The Gould Farm offers a unique service, very much their own and also the type of health service which we feel we get nowhere else...My only criticism is that I am so often unable to have patients admitted because of the lack of a bed."

From MISS MAY F. CLEAVER, Director Social Service Department, St. Luke's Hospital, Amsterdam Avenue and 113th Street, New York City.

"We appreciate more than we can say, the intelligent and beautifully thoughtful work which they do with these individuals. There are so few places where people with very moderate means and many with no means at all, can go and be refitted to enter in a fairly normal manner, ordinary life. We are very happy to express our appreciation to you of the work of Gould Farm."

From REV. S. M. SHOEMAKER, JR., Calvary Rectory, 61 Gramercy Park, North, New York City.

"I do not think there is any word of commendation from me that can do justice to what I feel about the Gould Farm at Great Barrington. I have visited it twice and the spirit of the place seems to me to be filled with the healing which touches people's fundamental attitudes. I think it one of the most impressive communities I have ever been in, and I count it always a privilege to renew my contact with Mrs. Gould and with Gould Farm."

From DR. AUSTEN FOX RIGGS, Stockbridge, Mass.

"It has been my experience that people who have gotten their values of life

all twisted or who are discouraged with the difficulties of the struggle for existence and for whom the machinery of civilization or the business world have
proved too much, find in Mrs. Gould and her staff and the life at Gould Farm a
demonstration of what really counts and what is really important in life; how
simple these essentials are and how the byproduct of happiness depends upon
taking advantage of their immediate opportunities."

From DR. JOHN A. P. MILLET, 770 Park Ave., New York City.

"The cost of care at Gould Farm is lower than any reconstruction center in
the country. This fact is of course one of greatest importance at the present
time. The chance for an individual who needs spiritual inspiration, friendly interest and wholesome country life during a period of temporary disability and
to obtain all these at the extremely low cost made possible through Mrs.
Gould's idealism, is one that cannot be duplicated, to the best of my
knowledge, anywhere."

From REV. ANSON PHELPS STOKES, D.D., Lenox, Mass.

"Gould Farm seems to me to be helping great numbers of people who
need rest, relaxation and help in making life adjustments. Its beautiful location
in the Berkshire Hills, its emphasis on the cooperation by guests in the work of
the farm and the home, its cooperation from leaders of the medical profession,
and its remarkable Christian spirit all make it exceptionally well qualified to
meet the need of those looking for a quiet home at minimum charges, for recuperation from illness or heavy strain."

Gould Farm lies tucked away in a beautiful part of the Berkshires near
Monterey, overlooking the country with valleys and hills in the distance. The
main house and twenty-one smaller ones are set in the midst of woodland,
enough of which is under cultivation to provide vegetables for a family varying
from sixty to one hundred people and provender for cattle and poultry. It is not
an institution, nor a sanitarium, nor a hospital. It is "Just Gould Farm," "A Haven set apart," but isolated only in the physical sense, in order that it may make
its contribution to the outer world. What this contribution is I shall try to tell.
Yet as I saw, heard and read of the Farm and Mr. Gould's work I realized more
and more upon what delicate ground I was treading. One would have to be possessed of a most sensitive psychic instrument to register accurately the workings of the forces there, appertaining to the inner experience of man. Nevertheless, I shall try to tell you something of the life at the Farm and its founder,
William J. Gould, who gave his life for it, literally. He died May eighth, 1925,
fighting a grass fire that threatened the main house on the Farm. His work is
now being carried on by his wife, Agnes C. Gould and her co-workers, all consecrated to preserve the ideals of its founder...

What I found was an experiment in living that is so simple that most of us
have grown away from it in the complexity of our modern urban life, but to
which we seem forced to return when disaster and trouble beset us. It would
seem that anything that has gone on for twenty-seven years, is no longer an
"experiment," but perhaps we may call it that inasmuch as twenty-seven years
is a short span when we reckon for the future.

The main house, with its ells and built-on third story, stands battered and worn from constant use of a small army of people; over six thousand in twenty-seven years! Yet it seems to reach out to its visitors with dignity and gracious hospitality...Any visitor who stays there long enough may be surprised at the number of distinguished people who find their way there. Shortly before his death Dr. Richard C. Cabot made a memorable visit. Angela Morgan, Albert Spalding, Rosika Schwimmer, and Henry Sloane Coffin have been more recent guests. During the winter there are occasional dances at the "big house," while outside are winter sports; and in the summer, picnics for the less active ones, and hiking and bathing for the young people...

Gould Farm flings its doors open wide to those from every walk of life, from every land, race and creed, who need what the Farm has to offer. Those are welcomed who are trying to recover from a serious illness or operation and need more than anything else the association of sympathetic, kind friends, under simple conditions of living, in order to regain their strength. Others who have been beaten down by life and lost their perspective are helped to regain the more precious values. Here they find friendship with something else thrown in,—"Loving kindness," as one woman said, who had been in a fashionable sanitarium...

It is more un-institutional, more inclusive, more alive, than what we think of as a convalescent home. There are no doctors, no specific medicines. People go there to cure themselves and experience a greater regeneration than any institution could give them.

Gould Farm has no time limit. Young men and women do not go back to their jobs, or their homes, until they are completely cured or better able to adapt themselves. Those who have stayed there have almost always been benefitted (in so far as they were able to enter into the community life on the Farm) and they have become better human beings, better citizens...

Carlyle says, "As the highest Gospel was a Biography, so is the life of every good man an indubitable gospel, and preaches to the eye and heart and whole man." Without exaggeration this might be applied to William Gould's life from boyhood up.

He was born October nineteenth, 1867 in Essex County, New York, the only son of a country minister, David Gould, and Mary Calkins Gould. William was five years old when his father died. The young widow was left with five small children, the little homestead, and a modest life insurance.

William from early boyhood began to count as the man in the family. At sixteen he could hold his own with any of his neighbors in a day's work, and became later a practical, skillful farmer.

Even so he was not always a match for the severe Adirondack climate and the primitive farm methods imposed by poverty. He had fits of discouragement and revolt. Out of these however he was lifted by the watchful mother, whose courage and religious fervor communicated themselves to him. She drilled her children in conscientious economies of matches, basting threads, and candle ends; though they came to a supper consisting mostly of milk and home grown popcorn, this meagerness was somehow redeemed from meanness, and dreariness never touched her household.

Will Gould had little formal schooling. Occasional attendance at the district school did not satisfy his hunger for education, so he made the most of his father's library. At the end of a day's work, he huddled in his bed, in a frozen

room, determinedly keeping himself awake, for hours of candlelight reading!...
He found flesh and blood heroes; Saint Paul and Abraham Lincoln, Horace
Bushnell, Lyman Abbot, Dwight L. Moody, Henry Drummond, and Phillips
Brooks were among his formative influences of his early manhood.

It had been expected, from early days, that he would be a minister. It was
like the end of the world to him when at the age of nineteen, he suddenly realized that he could not get away to fit himself for the pulpit. It would be desert-
ing his mothers and sisters...However, his mother rose to his need, and suggested that the Gospel might be preached from the hayfields...He threw
himself into the task of improving the family situation, while watching for opportunities beyond the family circle. At last, at twenty-nine he did enter the
Theological Seminary at Bangor, Maine. It was too late! His character and ideals had taken on that strong individuality which made religious dogmas and
conventions foreign to him...

His first activity outside the home had been as Christian Endeavor leader,
and as lay assistant in the church at Whately. Now after a year's experience at
the George Junior Republic, for several seasons he operated, with the aid of his
three sisters, under the auspices of the People's Home Church of New York, a
fresh air camp for boys near Becket, Massachusetts, on a farm loaned for the
purpose. "Boy Work" was in its beginning. He developed great skill with adolescents.

So far he had no permanent allies except his faithful sisters. They shared
his every aspiration; gave of themselves with devotion, to their common cause.
In 1905, however, he married Agnes Cortelyou Goodyear, a granddaughter of
Charles Goodyear, the inventor. No single act of his life was more important to
his work than his choice of a mate...

There followed seven years of experimentation. Five different times in different localities, he made a fresh start. There were times when he was homeless, when his wife stayed with relatives, while he slept at twenty-five cent
lodging houses.

The boy problem, meanwhile, was rapidly becoming a pet concern with
social agencies, and presently the field was well covered. Then Gould discovered a totally neglected field—the convalescent care of male adults. An elderly
relative contributed a few hundred dollars with which he obtained title to a
small farm in Winsted, Connecticut.

From Winsted he went to New York to ask for "guests" for his new home.
"I have the farm," he said, "I know I can help those who have let themselves
'slip into the shadows.' I have figured it out that for $3.50 a week per person
we can get along. It doesn't cost much if everybody turns in and
works."...Some tents used by a fresh air organization were lent to him... That
summer sixty people were cared for without a single servant or hired man. His
success with free-hand methods of his own that rode right over standardized
treatments presently brought down on him more guests than the farm could accommodate, and after two years he was on the lookout for a larger place.

In November 1913 he found the present location at Monterey, Massachusetts, an abandoned farm, once used as a boarding house...Gould's eyes took in
the splendid view of valleys and hills; then he went to the cellar and struck the
blade of his pen knife into a girder to see if the underpinnings were sound.
They were...His wife, her mother and cousin, his two sisters and others were to
stay in the comfortable Winsted home, while he went ahead to make Monterey

house fit for occupancy...

No money, no influence, just a man with a vision facing the wilderness and a New England winter—but he did not get to Monterey alone! His "women folk" overruled him and they came along. A little black horse and wagon brought food and a few winter vegetables. The furniture was not enough to go around. They brought two "guests."...Buckets were placed to catch the rain from the leaking roof...

Mr. Gould experimented with the worst social risks—drug addicts, alcoholics, neurasthenics, at four dollars a week, at three, at nothing. Many times a guest who couldn't pay was taken in preference to another who could easily afford it, because his need was greater. Gould had the conviction of Dr. R. H. Stafford of Boston that "Man at his lowest deserves and will repay interested effort in his behalf." Extreme cases of mental disorders were barred by the state, and contagious disease could not be dealt with.

Someone asked Mr. Gould why he took such burden upon himself. He answered, "Did you ever see a beautiful sunset or flower, and call your friends to see it? Well, I have found that which is most glorious of all—a way of life that I want to share with everyone I possibly can."

He took people without time limit. He took over whole families, the care of which had required the combined efforts of numerous public agencies, and women and girls were added to the group...(Gould Farm's) success with nervous cases brought forth the comment from a celebrated psychiatrist, "Gould Farm—where they do the things the rest of us are talking about." This recognition was flatter but not quite what Gould was after. Not what he did but the secret by which he did it, was what he wanted to pass on.

Through the work with nervous cases his "secret" was more and more easily revealed. He believed that the cure of nervous cases was based on reconstruction of the personality. This reconstruction of the personality had been his method right along, but hitherto the fact had been obscured. His success with boys and different kinds of invalids had been ascribed to country life and his personal influence; everything, it was supposed, depended on his continued presence. "Then I have failed," he said, "for my conviction has been that this principle of life is larger than any one personality, independent of any single embodiment..."

Joy was the dominant note of his life. He loved play as he loved work and gave himself up to it with the same abandon. Laughter was as much a part of his religion as prayer. No matter how tired or disheartened the newcomers were, they were soon absorbed into the industrious community, conscious of being a necessary part...

Seated at the great dining-room tables of bare scrubbed boards, were janitors waited on by college professors; broken down laundresses entertained specialists of note, while the family spirit showed in the talk.

No compulsion of any kind was, or is exercised. No one is asked to do any work until he has shown a desire to do so. No religious training or talks about it are offered (except at the three weekly services) and the guest goes or not to these as his inclination leads him. But he cannot be there long without realizing something of the spiritual forces at work. He senses them in the song of the brook, in the blueness of the shadows on the hills and in his daily contacts. Before he realizes it, he is responding to these in ways of help toward others, in work and in play. He sees others so much worse off than himself that he is ashamed to voice his woes, and seeing others busy in this human hive, he soon finds a job of his own.

Every manner of activity is open to him. The "occupational therapy" is founded on a natural, non-institutional procedure. The activities center in and about the HOME, starting from the time the guest gets up, wakened by the big bell on the top of the main house. He may do out of door work on the Farm, or indoor work in the house—cooking, baking, scrubbing, dish-washing, sewing. If he works in the Weave Shop, it is usually that rugs or runners may beautify the home, or scarf its wearer. Even since the destruction by fire three years ago of a well-equipped Carpenter Shop, woodworking has started by anew with donated machinery, and interesting articles are being produced with the hope of establishing a self-supported unit. In the Music Studio piano and voice culture are taught, that talent may be uncovered and music provided for the entertainment of the family. Teachers fall from Heaven as it were, and young people find someone equipped to tutor them in different subjects. Other needs are being constantly filled by persons whom fortune provides, and gifts that fall from the skies. If a cow is needed, somehow, from somewhere it arrives. One came recently from Pennsylvania. No steam heat until 1934, but then it came! A new home properly equipped will rise from the old. Additional stock and farming possibilities will be developed with other needed improvements.

The Farm struggled along for years with "guests" paying $2.50 to $3.50 a week. As the budget mounted with heat, electricity and improvements made, it became necessary to ask more. Gould Farm now is self-supporting in the summer when one hundred people are cared for—but not in winter, when only forty or fifty people can be accommodated owing to the lack of heat in the smaller houses.

Will Gould's life from boyhood up, was a continued mastery of the art of poverty. He opened his mortgaged home to the needy and assumed responsibility for any deficit. He accepted gladly any voluntary gifts that came from those in sympathy with the work he was doing (and Mrs. Gould speaks with heartfelt gratitude of those generous people who helped them at times when it was so needed). He conducted his work as a business and kept it a solvent business. His credit expanded with the extension of his undertakings. He bought up farms near by and remodeled houses to add to his plant.

His vision was of many such social service centers, started by others who had caught fire from the Gould Farm idea, that would offset the dangers of modern progress. He realized that our development of physical science was far in advance of our knowledge of how to handle it. As we review his life work, we realize that he was a statesman as well as a prophet. He grasped the principles of political and social reform, as well as those of spiritual growth. Today the Farm is recognized as a place where the secret of individual and national recovery has been at work for years.

By Mr. Gould's death, his achievement was more fully revealed. Many had looked upon Gould Farm as a one-man performance, that would stand or fall with its founder. To the surprise of all onlookers, the work was carried on without a break by a staff of workers devoted to his ideals and trained in his peculiar technique. They had gathered around him slowly through the years, for the most part from the ranks of patients, working without remuneration, after the example of their leader; and they are looking into the future with the same confidence that he had, trusting in the permanent value of the principles underlying the work, rather than the leadership of any one personality.

Whatever be true of the "world" in general, here on this back-country farm in the Berkshires, the secret of the completely socialized life had been discovered and was in daily, hourly operation. It was not in "Brother Will" alone; it was in all those who formed the working family—in his wife, in his kin and hers, in their associates, in the guests, of whom it would be difficult to say whether they were there to be ministered to or to minister. Brother Will was the vital, beating heart of it all, yes; the secret looked out from his eyes, thrilled in his voice, was felt in his handclasp. In him was life, abundant, rich, life-giving. And then, swiftly, in a moment busy at accustomed toil, he passed. But the life that was in him did not pass; it pulses as creatively in the group as it did when he led them. In other words he lives on. Death has not brought him to an end, nor his work to a stop. There has never for a moment been a question of its continuance and growth. That is his victory; that is the sign and seal of his success.

The following pamphlet, from the 1960s, incorporates terminology, such as "milieu therapy," that reflects the medical culture of the time.

REHABILITATION CENTER
OFFERING MILIEU THERAPY
REST – CARE – WORK – COUNSELING

TO HELP TROUBLED PERSONS
REGAIN PHYSICAL WELL-BEING
SELF-RELIANCE
PEACE OF MIND

Rev. Hampton E. Price, Executive Director

What and Where is Gould Farm?
Gould Farm is a small, family-type community situated in the Berkshire Hills of Western Massachusetts about 1300 feet above sea level and near the village of Monterey. It was established in 1913 by the late Will Gould, a New England farmer and dedicated minister to his fellowmen, to provide a sheltered environment in which God's healing gifts of work, recreation and fellowship can be extended to those in trouble.

The Farm property comprises 550 acres of varied terrain including evergreens and white birch forests, mountain streams, and a 100-acre working farm. The large Main House, where "Brother Will" as he was called, first set up the Farm, has accommodations for 37 guests. Greatly expanded since 1913, it also contains a commodious living room for meetings and religious services; a communal dining room with a modern kitchen; a TV room; and executive offices. A wing, Rhinelander Hall, affords space for lectures, dancing and movies.

Largely Self-Sustaining
In 1958 a one-story building with 16 sleeping rooms, known as East House, was erected opposite Main House. Using rooms in several adjacent cottages which have been winterized, a total of 75 guests can be accommodated all year round, while more guests can be housed during the summer in a number of cot-

tages not winterized. The Farm staff and their families occupy year-round houses in the vicinity of Main House. When all facilities are taken, Gould Farm has a total population of 150 people, with retreat and camping accommodations for forty more. Barns, a sheep-fold, piggery, hen-houses, a sap-house, a craft shop, a weaving studio and two pump-houses comprise the rest of the Farm's 46 buildings. To a high degree Gould Farm is a self-sustaining community.

Who May Come to the Farm?

Men and women, and young people of every creed, race and nationality may come to Gould Farm for recuperation. While the range of problems is widely varied, we find that those within the following categories can profit the most:

1. Persons suffering from bereavement, broken home, divorce, emotional shock of various kinds; change of life; debility and depression following an operation or illness;

2. Those needing respite from situations causing emotional and physical tension; needing support in breaking off detrimental habits; requiring time to make crucial decisions; or simply needing to learn how to get along in normal group contacts (sic).

Narcotic addicts, advanced alcoholics, retarded individuals, those with brain damage, acute psychosis or active suicidal tendencies are not accepted.

Requirements for Admissions

Applicants may be referred to the Farm by physicians, psychiatrists, hospitals, social workers, church representatives, family, friends, and former associates of Gould Farm. Each applicant must present a completed application form, furnished by the Farm. This includes a physician's diagnoses; a certificate of freedom from communicable diseases; a social summary; a statement by the applicant as to his financial means; and a personal reference. In other words, enough information is required to enable the Farm to judge whether it can meet the applicant's needs. It is recommended to visit the Farm in advance.

As there is no resident physician and the Farm routine is permissive, a guest must not be in need of special care or close supervision. He must be able to take care of his room, come to meals, and participate in the daily life of the Farm. The nursing staff gives supervision, administers medications and covers emergencies. When physical or mental examinations or tests are required, these may be arranged at Pittsfield or Great Barrington hospitals or clinics or the guest may call on his own physician.

Rates Are Adjustable

Giving according to ability and receiving according to need was basic in Will Gould's philosophy and still obtains today at the Farm. Guests are expected to pay the full rate of $540 per month (this was crossed out and stamped "Rates are Now $140 per week"—Ed). However, applicants will always find the Farm ready to discuss necessary adjustments. Rates include three meals a day served family style. No extra charges are made for any services except transportation, medication and telephone.

Length of Stay

Guests may come for a short rest or a longer period of recuperation, depending upon their needs. The length of stay is determined by the rate of improvement and signs of ability to cope with normal activity and environment.

The Farm does not take persons seeking a permanent home.

Work A Main Healing Factor

Most people are happiest and make the best recovery when busy one way or another, indoors and out. Since the Farm operates with a small paid staff, every guest is expected to keep his room in order and take part in service at meals.

In Summer, the flower and vegetable gardens invite volunteers with potential "green thumbs."

In Winter, there are chores for amateur carpenters, painters and mechanics in repairing and sprucing up the various cottages under the guidance of an all-round carpenter on the Farm staff. In late February and March more than 100 sugar maple tress are tapped and the sap is collected and boiled down to syrup for Farm consumption. Throughout the year, volunteers can help with many farm chores, including the care of poultry and animals, and the equipment, under the supervision of the Farm director. There is a weaving studio where one can learn to weave and hook rugs, crochet, knit or sew with aid from a competent teacher, and a craft studio where many skills are taught. Or one can learn to play the autoharp or recorder, instructed by a professional musician. Mid-morning coffee breaks and afternoon tea bring guests together for sociability.

Entertainment

For entertainment there is a week's schedule of movies, square dancing, and recorded music concerts with interpretation. A choral group enjoys folk singing. On Wednesday evenings, a religious service is held with audience discussion. In Winter, parties are organized for skating, skiing, and bowling. In Summer, there are nature walks, camp-fire breakfast and lunch picnics, and swimming parties in nearby lakes. Three saddled horses and a pony are available for riding the forest trails. Parties are organized for Tanglewood concerts, the Berkshire Summer Theatre, the Ballet and Dance Festival at Jacob's Pillow, all within a 20-mile radius. Groups may be formed for study of poetry, creative writing, current events, and other special interests. Ping-pong, bridge, chess, pool, and other table games afford evening diversion.

A Healing Environment

The therapy of Gould Farm lies in working toward a human environment in which healing can take place. Under the guidance of a psychologist, who has a Ph.D. in psychology and counseling, a program of therapy is being developed which seeks to use all the human resources on the Farm. Group therapy sessions are held twice weekly. Guests frequently discover in these sessions other persons who can help them come to grips with their own problems. Current experiences and relationships are used to help in aiding self-understanding and growth.

Individual counseling is an important part of the program. A guest may need to talk problems out with an objective and sympathetic person of broad experience. In addition, the Farm family which includes nurses, hostesses and the executive director may be called on. A continuing study of how to use human relationships more effectively as a means of healing is going on at Gould Farm.

Help When Leaving the Farm

When it is time for a guest to leave, hopefully he is ready to go with renewed self-reliance. He may pick up his former situation with greater confidence. On the other hand he may seek a new direction in life.

A basic part of Farm counseling is focused on helping guests plan for a better adjustment. Consultations with family, friends, employment services and vocational rehabilitation facilities are frequently of great help.

[This short note was inserted in the original pamphlet:]

"No Cars—We believe persons stand to gain a great deal more from their experience on the Farm if their attention is not divided.

"NOTE: New Policy—Guests are not permitted to bring motor vehicles."

Below is a Gould Farm pamphlet from the 1980s.

GOULD FARM
A Residential Rehabilitation Center in the Berkshires
Kent D. Smith
Executive Director

In November, 1913, Will Gould—New England farmer, humanitarian, and man of deep religious faith—purchased an abandoned farm property near the village of Monterey in the calm and peaceful Berkshire Hills of western Massachusetts. Here, in the years that followed, this remarkable man fulfilled his life-long dream and established a secluded retreat that offered emotionally exhausted and disturbed human beings the healing fellowship of a "family" community.

Today, Gould Farm is well-known and highly respected, a non-sectarian and inter-racial recuperation center offering a healing milieu—care, work, rest, counseling—and accommodating 40 guests. Our full time staff number over 35. Our 600 acres include a 100-acre working farm, high hills, a brook with swimming in summer, miles of hiking trails through beautiful woods, New England stone walls.

Here individuals suffering from mental illness, anxiety, depression, situational difficulties, and fatigue have found help in community living, in work, in the friendship of another human being, in quiet places of natural beauty. Each guest has a private room.

Who May Come to Gould Farm

Most of our guests are between 19 and 40. We occasionally take one as young as 17 but do not provide a high school program. We are also open to middle-aged or older people who can adapt to community living and participate in our program. We accept men and women of all creeds and races. Many of our guests have been under psychiatric care and some have been hospitalized at one time or another. But we also welcome those experiencing marital difficulties, the strain of living in our complex society, anxiety, and grief—and needing a temporary change in life style, responsibilities, and opportunities.

We are unable to accept those who are retarded, have brain damage, are assaultive or suicidal, or are addicted to alcohol or illicit drugs. We do accept those who have suffered the major psychoses, but only those who are in a reasonably good state of remission. We do not offer a permanent home to any guest, nor do we keep those who become acutely psychotic, present serious behavioral problems, or who resume the use of alcohol or illicit drugs.

Requirements for Admission

The applicant's psychiatrist—if he has none, another physician—must complete our medical referral form. The applicant who appears to be eligible will then be invited to the Farm for a twenty-four hour trial visit for which there is a fee. (Applicants should bring their own medications, an alarm clock if needed, and clothes suitable for outdoor work.) If the applicant wishes to come and is accepted by our admissions committee, placement is generally possible within a relatively short time.

Rates

No one is ever turned away from Gould Farm for lack of money—if the applicant and family are willing to pay a fee appropriate to their income and resources. Families unable to pay the full rate may apply for a reduced rate or no fee at all. These arrangements are approved before admission by the director. Our fee includes everything except personal spending money, physician's fees, medication, and special transportation.

Program

Most basic to our program is provision of a warm and friendly caring atmosphere in which the healing process can take place. We have both group and individual counseling. Guests frequently discover others at the Farm who through insight or from personal experience can help them come to grips with their own problems. Many of our staff are well qualified to discuss personal and interpersonal problems with guests. The services of a full-time registered nurse and a social worker are provided. A psychiatrist spends one full day a week on the Farm, consulting with staff and seeing individual guests on a private-fee basis.

The necessary work of a community and farm are at the center of our program. Each guest is expected to take care of his or her own room, participate in common chores such as helping with meals and dishes, and for several hours each day assist staff in such varied work activities as farming, green house and gardening, making maple syrup, clearing trails, splitting wood, shoveling snow, raking leaves, house-cleaning, cooking, baking , and many more.

We balance work with recreation and community events: square dances, discussions, coffee houses, parties, swimming and a sauna, ice skating, tennis, softball, volleyball, table games, picnics. We have trips to movies, concerts, the Friendly Ice Cream store, and in summer to Tanglewood and Jacob's Pillow, according to interest. In winter there are trips to nearby resorts for swimming and skiing. There is a weaving studio and a craft shop with special instruction provided from time to time. We have daily trips to the village store and post office as well as a shopping trip each Saturday afternoon. Guests do most of the work on the Farm Yarn, a Farm newspaper. There is tea each afternoon. Those who wish may attend a nondenominational vesper service each Sunday evening. Trips are provided to local religious services.

Our social worker assists each guest in planning for his or her future. Advice and some assistance are given in seeking housing, jobs, and needed support for the guest going out on his own—often for the first time. Many former guests maintain contact with us by letter or by phone...

Boston Program

Gould Farm operates Farrington House, a residence in Lincoln, Massachusetts, near Boston. It is a large house on over 70 acres of land in a safe and quiet community, but close to train and bus connections with other outlying towns, Cambridge and Boston. It houses twenty residents in ten double rooms. Competent staff live in the building.

Those who have been guests at Gould Farm, at least briefly, are eligible for the program. Farrington House is open to those of our guests who have demonstrated their ability to be cooperative, to follow medical advice, to work well on our program, to socialize adequately with others, and who have the potential for finding a forty-hour-a-week program outside the House.

The staff provide a congenial and homelike atmosphere, support to those who occasionally have difficult days, transportation as needed to bus and train stops and for medical services, some guidance in preparing of common meals and caring for living areas, and help in finding jobs and working out an approved program. Staff do not act as therapists, however. We have an affiliation with a psychiatrist who lives close to the House, is on call, and sees residents as desired on a private basis.

Most residents of Farrington House have lived at Gould Farm. Some "graduate" to Farrington House after longer periods of time here; others who feel ready for such a setting come to the Farm for a brief screening period. Those who get paying jobs are expected to contribute toward the fee from their pay.

No further application procedures are necessary for the transfer from Gould Farm to Farrington House. The possibility and the timing of the transfer are worked out informally among the guest himself, his family, and the Gould Farm staff.

If the person moves to Farrington House, but does not live up to the relatively high expectations for those living there, transfers back to Gould Farm may be worked out with families without further formal application procedures.

Our Boston program also includes eight apartments where residents live independently but are seen regularly by a staff member who lives in one apartment. There is also someone on call. Residents of the apartments maintain full time jobs, shop and cook for themselves, manage their own finances, and participate in community activities outside our program.

For information or application contact Kent Smith at Gould Farm Office.

The latest Gould Farm pamphlet (2012), as of this writing, follows.

"Gould Farm is a unique and pioneering refuge for people with mental disorders...a place where respect and relationship, work and friends are central to the healing process." Oliver Sacks, M.D.—Neurologist and Author.

The Gould Farm Story

In the year 1900, William J. Gould, visionary and pioneer in social reform, conceived of a plan for emotional rehabilitation based on the principles of respectful discipline, wholesome work, and unstinting kindness. Thirteen years later, "Brother Will" and his wife Agnes purchased a farm in the Berkshire Hills, giving birth to the nation's oldest therapeutic community.

Nearly a century later, Gould Farm's success continues to stem from the truth that a society is healthiest when its most vulnerable members are enabled to thrive. The Farm provides psychosocial rehabilitation in a nurturing and non-institutional environment for adults (ages 18 and over) coping with mental health conditions such as schizophrenia, bipolar and schizoaffective disorder. Gould Farm is a diverse community of guest (our clients) and staff and their families.

Housing and Meals

Each guest has a private bedroom and a shared bathroom facility in one of the three residential houses. Experienced residential advisors support guests in the evening hours and organize special activities. We offer hearty farm meals including vegetarian and vegan options and can accommodate special diets. Meals often feature some of Gould Farm's products such as milk, cheeses and maple syrup. The 4PM gather for tea and snack at the end of the afternoon's work is one of the many Gould Farm traditions.

Continuum of Care

Guests typically stay at Gould Farm for 9 to 18 months with the average stay of 11 months, depending on individual needs and goals. Many guests move on to the Boston-area program "Fellside," located in Medford, when they reach a sustainable level of readiness, self administration of medication, daily living and work skills and time management. Individuals typically return to school or work while receiving the support of continued community living.

This phase of the program can also serve as a good preparation for those who may return home or continue residential care in another setting. The maximum length of stay at Monterey and Fellside is three years. Residents are encouraged to move into their own homes and build adequate outside supports when they are thriving.

Clients who have completed the transition to more independent living can transfer to the Extended Community Program. This program is available on a long-term basis to clients who have settled in the Boston area and whose families wish to secure continuity of Gould Farm's unique service and connection.

Admissions

A phone call is the best first step to begin the Admissions process. We will be happy to answer your questions about our program. The admissions forms are available online at www.gouldfarm.org or we would gladly send them to you. Once the forms and documents are received, a tour, interview or a two-week exploratory visit can be arranged.

Cost & Financial Aid

Financial aid is available to qualifying families. Please call for information.

The Program

Through active participation in community work, recreation and therapy in Gould Farm's deliberately eclectic environment, guests find opportunities and strength to transcend their mental health challenges and move forward in an in-

dividual recovery process. Work is one of the many rewarding activities that
community members engage in together, supporting and encouraging one another.

Celebration and play are most therapeutic when they evolve naturally out
of the community's long history and spontaneous imagination, affirming what
is most hopeful in each member. Diverse holiday traditions, music, drama,
sports, coffee-houses, dances and quiet evenings by the fire draw newcomers
into the circle.

Gould Farm's clinical staff and work team leaders support each guest's
individual treatment plan. Clinical supports include psychiatric evaluation, individual counseling, registered nurses, medication monitoring and education,
and medical referrals as needed.

Kent D. Smith (b. 1935) was Gould Farm's Executive Director from 1972 to
1990. Trained in Clinical Pastoral Education at St. Elizabeth's Hospital, Smith
later became director of CPE at Lancaster General Hospital and Lecturer at Lancaster Theological Seminary. Smith conducted trainings in and worked at various federal and state psychiatric institutions and, for the State of Delaware, administered chaplaincy programs within the Department of Mental Health. Two
years before moving to Gould Farm the Smith family joined a communal venture, with two other families, near Lancaster, Pennsylvania.

The following is revised from a presentation Smith gave at the International
Association for Psycho-Social Rehabilitation Services, Washington, D.C., May
29, 1981. In a way, it incorporates the Farm's communal, therapeutic, and cultural changes seen successively in each of the above pamphlets.

GOULD FARM
By
Kent D. Smith
Executive Director

Gould Farm has a small but unique place in the history of psychiatric rehabilitation. Providing for only a tiny fraction of those tens of thousands who need
rehabilitation services, the Farm's leadership and experimentation have been
not insignificant forces in the field. We expect to continue to learn much from
other models and styles of rehabilitation services; we hope that others continue
to learn from us.

Gould Farm is located in Monterey, in the Berkshire Hills of western Massachusetts, about 130 miles from both Boston and New York with direct bus
service from each. We are not a farm but rather a kind of intentional community. As one of our projects, we do operate a small working farm on about 100 of
our six hundred acres. Three buildings house a total of forty residents in single
rooms. A houseparent lives in a small apartment in each building. The Main
House, in addition to guest rooms, has living and recreational spaces, central
dining room and kitchen, offices, and rooms for single staff. There are close to
forty buildings in all, the others including houses and cottages for single and
married staff, a weaving studio, a sugar house for making maple syrup, a
woodworking shop, wood sheds, barns, garages, and a greenhouse. Most of our

land is wild and rugged with some beautiful trails. We are currently intensifying our forest management program. A brook runs through our property. A sauna is situated near its bank in a lovely wooded area. In summer we swim in our brook as well as in a river formed by it and another stream.

Gould Farm was founded in 1913. Actually it moved to Monterey from Winsted, Connecticut, in that year, having operated successfully in Winsted for the two previous years. Even before Winsted, the founders, Will and Agnes Gould, had attempted community living with the purpose of serving those with all kinds of disabilities in seven other locations, none of them ultimately successful. But by 1913, the work was going well; a property with potential for expansion was needed and was purchased on faith and with the most meager of resources. The Gould Farm community has served disabled people without interruption for over seventy years. Although it has always served individuals who today would be diagnosed as schizophrenic or manic-depressive, in earlier years it also served many with situational difficulties, depressions, and multiple disabilities. Since the introduction of psychotropic medications in 1955, the Farm has gradually moved toward a resident population composed primarily of young adults with chronic schizophrenic illness. It is limited to those in a reasonable state of remission and with some degree of potential toward rehabilitation and independent living. We accept those with other psychiatric diagnoses and a few with non-psychiatric difficulties.

The founder died fighting a woods fire in 1925. The Farm then being Mrs. Gould's personal property, and she, having no children or heirs interested in continuing the work, had the Farm incorporated in 1929 as The William J. Gould Associates, the original trustees being the adult members of the community who had been associated with the strong and loving figure, Will Gould, affectionately known as Brother Will. (For details, see BROTHER WILL and the Founding of Gould Farm, by Rose L. McKee, privately printed, 1963.) Our present corporation, still bearing the same name, consists of sixty members, a number of whom are in residence on the Farm. The Board of Directors consists of twenty-five men and women and a representative of the Pittsfield Area Council of Churches. Mrs. Gould was president of the corporation until her death in 1958. Since 1960 the Board has appointed an executive director who, under the direction of the Board and in consultation with staff and members of the community, is responsible for the welfare of each resident of the Farm.

Gould Farm has some of the marks of other classic intentional communities. It had a somewhat charismatic founder and early leader. Its early members demonstrated genuine loyalty to the founder, shared the conviction that the community had a clear purpose and mission which should be an example to others, and worked for little more than room, food, and the dedication to an exciting cause. Early members made long-term, often lifetime, commitments to the work. Eleanor Goodyear, a founding member of the community, remained with us until her death in February, 1981. Faith Colt and Rose McKee, who came to the Farm in 1916 and 1920 respectively, are still active members of the community. Others who have since died or moved away, served the Farm for many decades. Like other intentional communities, Gould Farm has religious roots. Yet the founder was neither dogmatic nor authoritarian; he was very strong but very caring, deeply spiritual, but deeply ecumenical, open to people of all faiths or with none, as long as they did not threaten the integrity of the community.

Nor was Gould Farm a community for the sake of being a community; it was not intended to establish or perpetuate any utopian view of society. It was a community meant to serve others in the spirit of Christ as exemplified in the Sermon on the Mount, not the dogmas of the church. The founder believed that the community would endure only as it was centered on service. Never an egalitarian community, the Farm is even less so today. Guided by an outside Board of Directors, administered by an executive director under contract to the Board, the director having authority to hire and fire, staffed by individuals on salary and covered by a pension plan, it has marks of a psychiatric facility as well as a community. But it is indeed a community in that all staff, many with families, live on the premises in houses and cottages belonging to the Farm. Beyond their required hours of work and specific job descriptions, they generally share concern and caring for our *guests,* the term *we* apply to residents who come for recuperation and rehabilitation. All staff participate to some extent in common meals and the common recreational activities and celebrations of the community. Very few staff have been professional mental health workers. Most staff come rather with specific skills in farming, gardening, maintenance, athletics, recreation, cooking; and they, with our guests, do all the work that a community with over a hundred members on six hundred acres requires.

The mode of our life together is "working with," "playing with," "celebrating with," "eating with," "sharing with," "suffering with"—all of the things that happen when a number of people live in close proximity. We do not see ourselves as therapists, but we consider our life together "therapeutic" in the deepest sense of the word—tending toward healing and new and independent life. We do not have work-therapy, but we work; we do not have occupational-therapy, but we make things and learn skills; we do not have music therapy, but we sing and play instruments; we do not have drama-therapy, but we produce plays; we do not have recreational-therapy, but we have parties, dances, games, sports, and community celebrations. We do not have therapies as compart-mentalized activities, but—by intention at least—the whole life of the community encapsulates what is meant by the term *therapy.* In living together, individuals deal implicitly and explicitly with anxieties and depressions, hopes and fears, struggles with authority, resistance to change, manipulation of people and situations, acceptance of disabilities and the need for medications, gaining realistic expectations and making appropriate plans for the future. We do not ignore exacerbations of psychiatric symptoms, sexual acting-out, inappropriate behavioral patterns, or unwillingness to take needed medication. But we do deal with them in personal encounters and *ad hoc* groups rather than in formal group therapy.

We are *not* anti-professional or anti-medical. At present on the Farm, we have a Master of Social Work and a registered nurse. In addition we have a consulting psychiatrist who visits the Farm and sees many of our guests on a private-practice basis. We encourage guests to accept and understand their disabilities, and to cooperate with psychiatrist and nurse in finding the proper medications which will permit them to be optimally functional. We have no problem with the *medical model,* that favorite whipping boy of some in our field; although our medical model is not a Freudian-analytic one, but rather an understanding that much major psychiatric illness is probably biochemical in origin and that chemotherapy is absolutely essential to many of our guests' participation in our program.

Above and beyond our medical understanding of schizophrenia and manic-depressive illness, we consider our guests as human beings with all of the human needs and problems and joys in which all people participate. Thus, we not only determine that guests are receiving adequate medical care including medications, we also attempt to respond to the total range of human needs in a supportive, but directive, way. Since our average guest has been ill since age eighteen and is now age twenty-four, we often find great gaps in work and social skills resulting from years spent at home or in hospitals. The Farm community exists to help guests learn or re-learn these skills in a setting that is real and somewhat demanding. The guest is asked to work with staff at jobs that have to be done. The guest is not treated as a patient but as a fellow worker. We do not excuse lateness, wandering away, refusing to work, unwillingness to follow orders or to work cooperatively with others as symptoms (although we recognize that they may be so to some extent), but as learning problems that can be overcome by effort of the guest and by the right combination of understanding and firmness by staff. The work expectation is non-negotiable: guests too sick to work are too sick to be here. But only rarely is anyone asked to leave. Most guests, however disabled or discouraged, move quickly into the work routine, although with a wide range of levels of productivity. Many guests who have never worked soon learn to be productive, and move on eventually to independent jobs.

We also see the Farm as an excellent place to socialize. It is unlike some guests' family homes in that there is an expectation and demand that people move quickly toward acceptable socialization. It is unlike hospitals where patients relate only to other patients and to professional and non-professional staff. It is unlike some halfway houses or community residences, often located in hostile or impersonal and often deteriorating neighborhoods, with residents usually having no real interaction with the surrounding community. The Farm provides an ongoing community of "normal" people of all ages (recently the range was 1 to 95) who are neither professional mental health workers nor suspicious and angry neighbors. The sixty or so members of the permanent community, including children, wives, of working staff members, volunteers, and semi-retired staff, not to ignore the many pets and all the farm animals, give each guest an extremely wide range of individuals with whom to relate.

Guests who have problems, for instance, with peer and with authority relationships can work them through with staff of their own age and with administrative staff. Such staff, by living in the same community with guests and participating in all levels of activities, can become even better role models than commuting staff who come and go, often leaving their private lives unknown and mysterious to patients. Living together in a community setting, staff cannot hide behind professional roles or long conceal their basic humanity and obvious weaknesses. Like guests, staff sooner or later lose their tempers, forget something important that needs to be done, vent their frustrations. Unlike some mental health workers, they are not trying to play roles of junior psychotherapists, they do not analyze each behavior according to some academic model; they are as much concerned about getting the job done as about how the guests feel (which often, although not always, is good for the guests). Generally staff do not plan recreation *for the guests*; rather guests and staff plan recreation that all will enjoy together, or at least staff plan recreation that they, too, will enjoy.

It should be said, however, that without staff leadership and initiative, activities would tend to dwindle away; without staff encouragement, many guests would avoid all but the required activities. Nor are all guest-to-staff relationships healthy and helpful. Some staff do lack adequate understanding of human psychology and of therapeutic approach, although we try to help them grow and learn on the job. Gould Farm is not a hothouse environment for human growth; there are risks for both guests and staff, although minimized by the responsibility and understanding of some longer-term members. Clearly, we do not permit proselytizing by staff for any religious or psychological reasons, nor do we permit sexual relations between staff and guest or any kind of emotional exploitation of guests by staff.

Believing that guests could profit from an even wider range of learning experiences, we have developed two new projects in recent years. We bought a small local business—a country store with lunch counter, gas pumps, and a modest line of groceries and supplies. The Roadside Store is open seven days a week. Usually one staff member and two or three guests operate the store on a given day or work period. Guests who have learned to work well in the somewhat sheltered atmosphere of the Farm, doing actual farm work, maintenance, gardening, care of grounds, forest management, making of maple syrup, cooking, and housekeeping, now add to these demands the necessity of meeting the public, both local citizens and tourists, who demand good service and do not always treat guests with the respect they receive from their work leaders. Guests who do well in the Store usually do well in holding competitive jobs after leaving the Farm.

In January, 1978, we opened the first facility away from Gould Farm. Farrington House in Lincoln, Massachusetts, near Boston, houses up to twenty residents, most of whom are ex-guests of Gould Farm. With rare exceptions, guests at Farrington House are expected to find and keep full-time, often entry-level, but at least minimum-wage jobs, using the House as a supportive residence until feeling ready for completely independent living. The need for Farrington House grew out of our awareness that many of our guests, having achieved a very high level of working and socializing, and feeling ready to move on, returned to their parents' homes with all good intentions of finding jobs and moving into their own rooms or apartments. We believe that the parents of our guests and their homes are not much different from the general run of parents and homes, except for the impact that a psychiatrically disabled son or daughter has made on the home and family. But we found that returning home often leads to the guest's enjoying the comforts of home, losing his motivation toward independence, suffering frustrations in job-hunting, and eventually becoming depressed and apathetic, going off medications, and returning to the hospital where the whole vicious circle begins again.

Rather, those who move to Farrington House from the Farm lose little or no momentum, find themselves in an area where jobs are readily available for people with some limitations, are encouraged by job offers within the first few days, and begin employment in a setting where it is the norm for peers to get up early, get off to a job, and come back tired after a full day's work. Peer support and some direction from a small staff have now kept many of our transfers moving ahead for several years.

Those who leave Farrington House for independent living are still encouraged to visit for talks, sharing, and meals according to need. A local psychiatrist consults with Farrington staff and sees current and ex-residents, using an approach highly compatible with our general philosophy.

Early in 1983 Gould Farm acquired a building in Newton and one in Waltham, each with four apartments. This constitutes for us a supportive apartment program for those who are employed, can benefit from public transportation, and do not need live-in supervision. Residents of the apartments will have regular visits from our staff who will also be available on an on-call basis. [Paragraph originally at end of publication.]

We are frequently asked about psychotherapy at the Farm and at Farrington House. Given the probably bio-chemical basis for schizophrenia and the negligible results of psychotherapy in the treatment of those diagnosed as schizophrenic, we do not see formal psychotherapy as a useful approach. We see psychoanalytic therapy, if not damaging, at least contra-indicated in terms of our approach of encouraging guests not to wallow in the past, but to deal honestly and realistically with the present and to plan with realism and hope for the future.

We do not believe, and we discourage guests from believing, that years of psychotherapy will—or even might—cure their schizophrenia. We discourage them from believing that there is an unconscious cause in their psyches for their illnesses, the *cause* which—if uncovered—would allow their illness to go away. We discourage them and their parents from believing that parents did something wrong that must have caused the illness. Some problems may need to be worked through with families, but we discourage the kind of family therapy that seems interminable and may simply recreate the emotional binds which for many are better left alone. We encourage guests to stop blaming their families (although not to ignore their real weaknesses and faults), usually by distancing themselves from their parents by not too frequent visits and by not returning home after leaving the Farm, and by hoping for an eventual adult-to-adult relationship with parents, after parents have given up their guilt feelings and guests having given up blaming their parents.

Although not claiming to have the final word on the etiology of schizophrenia, we do know that parents who do not blame themselves for their children's illnesses are both less rejecting and less indulgent and thus are more mature in their relations with sons and daughters, and that few guests can afford or can tolerate depth therapy, and that those who do become totally involved to the exclusion of effective movement toward independence in the here and now.

Yet guests do need to see our psychiatrist long enough and frequently enough for proper evaluation and regulation of medications. And, like other persons, they often profit from counseling which deals with medical, sexual, interpersonal, financial and vocational problems.

This description of Gould Farm still misses the essence of what it is and has been. Although there is little evidence of religiosity on the part of our staff, although only some of us have outside religious involvements, and although we are clearly nonsectarian, most of us would see Gould Farm as something of a "spiritual community" as over against a secular organization or facility. By this we do not refer to any required religious observance or any indoctrination of residents (which is in fact forbidden), but to a quality of caring that is shown in different ways by each of us but which collectively seems to permeate our life together.

Our staff includes individuals of all religious faiths as well as those who profess none. We have had on our staff Protestant clergymen; representatives of the peace churches including Friends, Mennonites, and Brethren; members of the Catholic and Jewish faiths; and those who present themselves as non-believers. The only religious requirement for joining our staff is that one will neither disparage others' beliefs nor attempt to indoctrinate them. But the vision which created Gould Farm seventy years ago, although to some extent it waxes and wanes, seems to remain alive and to be perceived by staff, guests and visitors. Sometimes it is recognized only in retrospect, after a person has come, struggled, and left. The vision is not dogmatic, not authoritarian, and not pietistic. It is not mentioned often, nor are any of us expert at articulating it. It is exemplified in the stipulation of the founder that there should be no minimum fee that would exclude the very poor. It is exemplified in the charter which states that it must always be a community providing social service. It is seen in the many who have served for one year or for a lifetime with minimal compensation and sacrificial giving of their human resources. It is even seen in our present ability and willingness to provide modest compensation and reasonable hours and time off for staff. Not all of us are unusually loving and caring persons, but together we provide that undergirding of loving and caring presence toward our guests which allows many of them to see the Farm as "home" long after they leave, to continue writing to some of us, to visit the Farm in health and success, or to return for another stay when things go wrong.

We have no common creed. We do not necessarily share a body of psychiatric or psychological theories in which people are trained in some facilities. We are a very heterogeneous group in almost every way, including age, education, previous experience, or even length and depth of commitment to our community life and work. But living and working together we are grasped by a vision that gives continuity and depth to our endeavor.[9]

Notes and Permissions

1. McKee, Rose L. *Brother Will and the Founding of Gould Farm.* Monterey: The William J. Gould Associates, Inc., [1963], 1975. viii.

2. Smith, Kent D. From a presentation at the International Association for Psycho-Social Rehabilitation Services, Washington, D.C. May 29, 1981. Used with author's permission.

3. McKee, William J. *Gould Farm: A Life of Sharing.* Monterey: The William J. Gould Associates, Inc., 1994. 48, 289.

4. McKee, Rose L. *op cit.* viii-x.

5. McKee, William J. *op cit.* 46.

6. McKee, Rose L. *op cit.* 77.

7. Goodyear, Caroline. "The Story of Gould Farm." 1936.

8. McKee, William J. Personal correspondence with Steven K. Smith. See also Bordman, Gerald and Hischak, Thomas S. *The Oxford Companion to American Theater.* Oxford University Press, 2004, 389.

9. Smith, Kent D. op cit.

Unless otherwise indicated, all selections reprinted in this chapter used with permission, The William J. Gould Associates, Inc.

Chapter Three

What is Gould Farm?

Gould Farm has had countless visitors, guests, staff, and those related to these and others acquainted with Gould Farm. Each has likely taken away something different from that experience. As I wrote in an unpublished essay:

> What Gould Farm *is*—or what people think the Farm *was*—varies for each person associated with the Farm. Common understandings of the Farm, beyond its stated goals, are elusive. For some, the Farm is the embodiment of a long-sought ideal community. For others, illusions of "community" are shattered when the Farm fails certain communal or therapeutic expectations. Such expectations have led at times to institutional eruptions or, more frequently, discontent, which have triggered departures. Patterns of enthusiasm and disillusionment repeat throughout the Farm's history, a phenomenon familiar to those acquainted with community dynamics.[1]

Arguably, the days of collective optimism and enthusiasm, present during the Farm's early years may not be as visible now. Or, perhaps, they are manifested in less visible ways.

Gould Farm was listed as a residence for both women and men in a 1921 "Directory of Convalescent Houses for New York City."[2] Identified as a "year round" residence for men, the Farm was described as follows: "Admission, write direct. 15 beds, 30 in summer, no surgical dressings, country home convalescence, nervous cases do well, private rooms, small rates." And for women: "Admission direct. 15 beds year round, 30 in summer. Convalescent, fatigued and nervous people. Private rooms, small rates. Women and children."[3] But Gould Farm was never a "convalescent" home as such and, depending on need and medical trends, has at various times emphasized particular diagnoses or needs.

The following pieces were written by friends of the Farm, but who were never permanent members, nor guests, nor staff. The first piece, from the New York Times, reflects this early optimism, as do the selections by Clayton Bowen, a Meadville Theological School professor and close friend of the Goulds.

They also provide interpretations about the work, program, and people of Gould Farm.

While the Farm's founders were of deep faith informed by the Sermon on the Mount, it was nonsectarian, non-doctrinaire. The Farm from its beginnings welcomed those of all faiths, and those professing none. Bill McKee relates a story of one of the first Gould Farm guests, an Orthodox Jew who, within 24 hours of arriving at the Farm, planned to leave after hearing grace sung at a communal meal. He was reassured by the Goulds that no one would proselytize him, and Beck stayed.[4] Charles H. Joseph's entry in *The Jewish Criterion* reflects this openness.

This chapter concludes with two letters from Appalachian Trail founder, Benton MacKaye, in which he describes the therapeutic nature of the outdoors, and proper land stewardship. MacKaye's sister was a guest at Gould Farm in the late 1920s.

THE SELECTIONS

Four years after arriving in Monterey, the Goulds wanted to establish closer contacts in New York City. Sometime during the winter of 1917-1918, Gould closed the Farm leaving a man in Monterey in charge of the property. They moved to Brooklyn and stayed with Henrietta and Nettie Tuttle, two elderly sisters who had lived at Gould Farm.

The Goulds worked as volunteers in wards at the Neurological Institute and at Bellevue Hospital, becoming "accepted as team members and advisors" to social workers there. Gould worked two hours a day in Belleview Hospital's drug ward. While there he experimented with rug weaving as a kind of occupational therapy. This effort, however, proved unsuccessful because those with addiction issues failed to keep up the work when Gould was not present. It was in New York where the Goulds established contacts who would later send guests to Gould Farm.

It may have been from his experience in New York and at the Farm during this time that Gould realized that the best cure for those with addiction and others was through what Bill McKee called "real work with a sufficiently strong motive of unselfish service behind it."

The following is an article about Gould's work, from a 1921 issue of *The New York Times*.[5]

FARM OF NEW HOPE

This is a story of a unique idea that came to a man as he plowed fields of the Adirondacks behind a team of horses and a plow. It was an idea on how to regenerate people who had lost all desire of and faith in life. Today social agencies in New York are making every effort to have this work duplicated and enlarged.

Gould Farm at Great Barrington, Mass., is the place where every year something like seventy people, gathered from all walks of life, find new purposes and encouragement in living. The man who dreamed of the possibilities of such work over twenty years ago is the guiding factor of the home. William Gould's father was a Congregational minister. (He) fell ill and the family was forced to move up into the Adirondack Mountains and conserve his strength. Up there the sick man hoped to combine the duties of a farmer and minister. In the Winter of that year he died and the family, consisting of the widowed mother and five children, the oldest of whom was the boy William, was left almost destitute. They decided, however, to stay there and till the soil which they had acquired.

From the very beginning it had been planned to let the oldest son follow in the footsteps of his father.

With this in view the boy under the direction of his mother had devoted himself in the hours after the day's work to the study of theology. Things, however, were not going as well on the farm as they might have. One day while driving a plow through the fields it suddenly came to the nineteen-year-old boy that a college education was out of the question for him. The financial state of the family couldn't warrant it. It was then, as he put it, that the great truth came to him. "The pulpit is not the only place that the Gospel can be preached. It can be preached in these fields which I am now plowing."

Years ago, when he had been a child, his mother had comforted him in his work by telling him that after all he had the woods and the fields and the wide places in which to toil, whereas the poor in the city had not only had their physical battles for existence to fight but had besides to live with their spirits cooped up between the walls. The boy decided then what he would do would be to bring to the country those who were most in need of its help.

For a number of years he worked with the boys of New York—urchins who made their homes in the alleys and docks and doorways of the city. Before very long, however, New York's social conscience awoke, and there was a definite well-directed movement to take care of the boy problem. For a time Mr. Gould worked with one of these groups, but dissatisfaction with the results made him decide there were other fields as yet untouched where help was needed for human beings in distress.

An intimate knowledge of social institutions and social agencies in the city showed him that there was little or any help needed for physical ills. There were places to cure every conceivable physical illness where the very poorest might get relief, but there were comparatively few places where the man or woman who had suffered a mental or nervous let-down could be restored. What he wanted to do was to bring back the desire of living and working to those who had lost it through loss of faith in themselves and mankind.

William Gould became convinced that his idea was right and, what's more, that it was practicable. He had his own little farm on which he lived with his family. He had no money. Nevertheless, he felt the thing he wanted to do was what the city needed. He came to New York to borrow some money to start the plan. He met a number of people whom he had known in his social service days with boys and told them what he intended to do.

"I have the farm," he said. "I know I can be of help to the people who have let themselves slip into the shadows. I have figured it out that for $3.50 a week a person we can get along. It doesn't cost more if everybody turns in and works." So clear was his conviction and so apparent his power, that the money was lent him.

The first thing he did was to go to a ten-cent store and buy a stock of "silverware." Then he bought a bale of unbleached cotton. Some tents used by a fresh air organization were loaned him. The barn turned into a dining room. The chairs and benches were made out of hemlock trees cut in the woods.

That Summer sixty people were sent to him for care and treatment. Those sixty people were cared for without a single servant or hired man. They were a big family living together, and everybody did his work and her share of the work. Here be it noted that nothing was ever assigned to anybody; each man or woman was permitted to remain idle as long as he or she chose to. The point is, however, that it was not long before each took a personal interest in the completion of the work of the farm.

"What I wanted most," said Mr. Gould, "was to bring them to a point where they would believe that work was not a curse that was laid upon mankind by God. I wanted them to come to an appreciation that it was a blessing. 'Consider the lilies of the field, how they grow.' Too often has that passage been misapplied. The emphasis has been placed on the wrong meaning. What was intended there, was to impress upon humankind the wonder of 'growing.' 'How they grow.' It is that which is worthy of thought."

Mr. Gould went on to say that too often, also, had the mistake been made of taking people out to the country and leaving them there in the hope that just the change of environment would work a miraculous cure. What people needed, especially those who were mentally unhappy and depressed, was to have the country interpreted to them by showing them where they fitted into the scheme of things.

This work has been going on now for eight years. It has grown intensively and extensively. Improvements have been added to the farm. Patients, or, rather, now members of this family, are sent up during all seasons of the year and they stay, according to Mr. Gould, as long as they need to. The rate they pay runs from nothing a week to $10 a week. At the present, there are seventy people who are learning once more that life is worth living and fighting for.

Not the least interesting development of the work is the kind of people who are sent there. It started originally to be a sort of department of the hospitals and social welfare agencies dealing with the derelicts of the streets of New York. It is still that but in addition some of the people who are sent there are wealthy patients of well-known nerve specialists. So crowded is the place that very often, a choice has to be made between a woman of wealth and a man who has been picked up in the slums of the city. After one has spoken with William Gould, it is easy to understand that all things being equal, it is the latter who will be taken in.

One of the Goulds' closest friends, Clayton R. Bowen (1877-1934), was Professor of New Testament at the Meadville Theological School (later to affiliate with the University of Chicago). Seeking a place of recuperation for his wife, Bowen learned about Gould Farm through a minister in Maine, who had earlier visited Gould Farm. Gould would eventually visit Meadville in 1920 at Dr. Bowen's invitation. (Efforts to find a transcript or any record of this talk have been futile.)

The following is an excerpt from a longer article by Bowen, titled "The Work of Gould Farm," which appeared in the journal *Hospital Social Service* in

1923. The Hospital Social Service Association of New York (not related to the current Hospital Association of New York State) published this journal.[6]

In December, 1920, William J. Gould did something unprecedented in his career. He gave a lecture. To his own amazement he found himself speaking on the Ballou Foundation for Christian Sociology before the students of the Meadville Theological School. His subject was: Country Co-operation with City Social Service. What he talked of was the subject of this article, the work of Gould Farm. He told the students that the city is not socially sufficient unto itself, any more than it is economically sufficient unto itself. The city creates its vast congeries of social problems which it cannot solve alone; to many of these the country must be the answer. Particularly is this true of problems arising out of broken physical and mental health. The hospital is not the last word. The city cannot heal the wounds of body and spirit which itself has inflicted. The open spaces, the forests, the meadows, the simplicity of life, the touch with the elemental foundations of civilization—all these are restorative as the huge process of the city cannot be. Everyone realizes that. The rich and the privileged know it, and take their holiday at seashore or mountains, or maintain luxurious country estates. The poor know it, and sigh for these things as for something needful yet unattainable. The doctors know it, and cursorily order their patients "three months rest in the country," when they might sometimes as well order three months quiet in the moon. Social workers know it, and fresh air camps, boys' farm schools, country vacation homes for working girls and innumerable similar philanthropies dot the landscape. The need is felt, and response is made, but the need is never even remotely met. Philanthropies, institutions, homes, sanitariums, schools; these do work of incalculable and increasing value. There is a work they cannot do. Will Gould's fine social sense detected that need and his finer ethical sense would not let him rest until he had singlehandedly attempted to meet it.

The thing began very simply. A devoted over-worked Congregational minister broke down in health. With wife and five children to be supported, bread must still be earned. He found a tiny parish among the Catskills, a stony hillside farm, the healing mountain winds, toil and hardship and poverty, but continued life and joy in the primitive spaces and unspoiled beauties of that paradise of lakes and splendid hills. The children grew amid it all, learning to love and trust the infinite bounty and resourcefulness of Nature. The father died. Will, the only son, made the rocky farm support his mother and sisters. Hopes of education had to be given up; never could he, as from childhood he had dreamed of doing, follow his father through college and seminary into the pulpit. Ploughing on the hillside one day, pondering these things, he threw down the reins and went to the homely, homey farmhouse where his mother was preparing the frugal supper. Very simply he told her that his mind was made up. He could not gain an education, he could not become a minister of religion, but he could do one thing and that he would do while he lived. He would be a minister of Nature and country life. This great, free, wholesome, simple living in the open places close to the sources of life, which could be had without money and without price, this thing which was such a passionately prized boon to himself, he could help to make the portion of others less fortunate. The mother put the supper on the table; it was popcorn and milk. "There are thousands who are supping worse in the city tonight," thought the boy, "and while I have a roof and a bed and a bowl of popcorn and milk, they shall be shared."

The mother died, the farm was sold; the young farmer made a new home for his sisters nearer the great city, and scarcely was the table spread for the first meal when he felt the challenge of the empty chairs. He went to New York, to the Social Service Agencies of those days, (I do not know the correct titles of these societies, the reader can readily supply them) and asked if there were not patients ready to come out of the hospitals who needed a period of recreative convalescence in the country before going back to the city's toil. If there were any such! There were only too many! Will Gould had hardly reached his home before his guests began to arrive; all he had asked for, and more. The change was a godsend to them; they grew well and strong on their simple fare, their plain surroundings, the atmosphere of genial friendliness which surrounded them, taking them as brothers and sisters in need and asking no questions. If these profited, more ought to profit; the roomy barn could be made to house the new-comers and the milk and vegetables and home made bread could somehow be made to go around. The cost of all this was not great; it was all so simple. The largest part of it did not demand money. Will Gould, assisted by his guests as they were able, could make the fields and gardens produce a large share of the food. His sisters could manage the cooking and simple housekeeping. The actual cost per person was little and this the social service agencies were glad to supply. Nowhere else could so much be found for so little outlay.

Will Gould's ambition to serve grew by what it fed on. This earliest home gave place to others, each of greater capacity for service. Among the earliest guests were boys from New York, weak, anemic, sometimes only just from the hospital. To these their host's heart especially went out. He determined to learn all he could about helping boys. He spent a year at the George Junior Republic as an unpaid assistant, accompanied by one of his sisters with a vision and a desire like his own. Profiting by all such an institution could teach him and by extended service as a conductor of summer camps for "fresh-air boys," he settled on a farm in the Berkshire Hills, and opened his home to a group of twenty boys from the city. Scarcely was this venture well established when the house and its entire contents were destroyed by fire. With never a moment's loss of courage or enthusiasm he began again on a new site. Again came a destructive fire, and yet again in a succeeding home. Through these and other exchanges, the scope and possibilities of the work grew. Nine or ten years ago he settled in his present location, and Gould Farm, as we know it, began to be. It was a small and painful beginning. The farmhouse was dilapidated and without any improvement. He had some twenty guests and no one save himself to do the outside work of the place. But he had recently married Agnes Goodyear, daughter and granddaughter of two of the most eminent inventors of modern times, and in her had the perfect sharer and helper in his enterprise. Neither one could bring any money at all to the work; Will Gould never worked for pay or enjoyed an income of any sort, and the Goodyear fortune, such as it was, had passed entirely out of Goodyear hands. But both brought an identical social vision, an identical passion to serve. Little by little, from the first incredibly hard winter, Gould Farm took shape. It has never been much of a farm, in the large sense, for Mr. Gould has had to do most of the farming, with such desultory assistance as his guests could from time to time render. Men from the cities rarely make good farmers. But some of them have developed unexpected talents, and willingness and zeal have counted for much. Somehow the gardens and fields have been made to feed the increasing family; the dairy has grown until a great new barn for fifty cows has just been finished as a simple necessity. Alongside the barn is rising a cottage for the man who tends the stock; a new road of hand crushed rock built as the Romans built and to last as long, leads up to the home place crowning the hill. And that home place! It is not the ruinous farm-house of a decade since. It is a broad, hospitable, white painted dwelling, in the midst of a spacious lawn with great shading maples. About the house are broad terraces of cement, where the less robust guests take the bracing air or "walk the deck" as on an ocean liner. Within, simplicity, spaciousness, beauty of an austere and yet appealing kind. The great living room with huge fireplace and grand piano, books galore, a few good pictures, hosts of windows to welcome the floods of Berkshire sunshine. Then the dining room, where a hundred people may eat in comfort, as one family; with one side mainly glass, fronting the sun. Two huge kitchens, one for the cooking, one for washing-up. Pantries, laundry, storage, sheds in plenty. And upstairs, forty or more bed rooms, very tiny, but very clean and very charming. That is the home place. All about are the fields and the woods and the hills of glorious views. Here and there are cottages, nearly a dozen now, where families may go, or those who need greater retirement. There is a dormitory for women. There is a sleeping porch, a sugar bush, a swimming pool, a haymow and all the things you expect at a farm. But these are all very plain, of the real old-fashioned farm sort. The home place has grown to an area of some six hundred acres, some of it with valuable timber, and most of it capable of great productiveness under cultivation. During the last year the "family" on the farm place has varied from ninety during the summer months to thirty or forty during the winter. That is the maximum expansion of which this original home is capable. But applications for admission have increased to such a degree that two new units are in preparation, and the locations have already been secured. Sunset Farm, with a spacious house in excellent condition, will soon be ready for use—it-is a mile from the original house. A little farther away is Hyde Farm, which will take more reconstruction, but which has great possibilities. It is more retired and has more natural beauty, including a remarkable ravine with fine waterfalls.

This then, is the plant of Gould Farm. It lies tucked away in the heart of the Berkshire Hills, nine miles from the railway station at Great Barrington, Massachusetts, with which constant connection is maintained by automobile. New York is four hours away by through train, Boston a little farther. Lenox, Stockbridge, Pittsfield and Williamstown are close by. The section is among the most healthful in the country; the climate, winter and summer, is stimulating and delightful. There is health for mind and body in the clear air and the bright sunshine, in the abundant wholesome country food, in the quiet peace that brings long hours of deep sleep. Above all, there is recreating power in the atmosphere of friendliness, and goodwill that makes the place a home to everyone that comes. (One does not come as a "boarder" or as a "patient;" one comes as a member of the family.) It must be remembered that Gould Farm is not a sanitarium; there are no doctors or nurses or medical treatment. It ministers primarily to those who have graduated from the hospital and the direct medical care and need only a wholesome environment for complete convalescence. It ministers also to those whom such a period of rest and invigoration may save from the need of a hospital and the physician.

It is an experiment in social service, and a very daring experiment. It was begun without the faintest financial resource; it was simply Will Gould making a home for himself which he could share with others. Neither he nor any of his workers has ever had any salary or income beyond the living which they share with every one of their guests. Some of these helpers are trained social workers, others are grateful guests who have elected to stay and serve. Altogether they are an extraordinarily efficient group. As to the guests, they are of every sort. Rich and poor, educated and ill-schooled, Jew, Gentile, Catholic, Protestant or no church at all—if they are only human beings and need what the Farm can give. The majority, no doubt, come through the mediation of some social service agency, mainly those of New York City. Through the Association for Improving the Condition of the Poor, through the various Social Service Associations, the American Red Cross, or others, and through individual workers, the contact is made. Many, of course, come independently, having heard of the Farm through friends. For some the social service agencies contribute, some make their own contributions. But at the Farm no one knows or cares which, there is complete democracy and family unity. The financial support of the Farm comes from these contributions by or for the guests, and through occasional gifts from interested friends. The place is made so far as possible self-supporting, expense is kept at a minimum, all share as they are able in the work that supports the common life, there are no salaries to pay, and so the home goes on and expands. There is no incorporation or organization whatever, nowhere is there any suggestion of the "institution." It is just a great home, whose moving spirits are "Brother Will" and "Sister Agnes," where the money side is kept in the background, where broken and discouraged lives may come back again to faith and hope and the will to work with regained strength.

And that is just why it is so hard to tell anything about cases. There are no "cases" on the place at all; there are only our brothers and sisters, about whose problems and troubles we cannot talk in public. The confidences of this family intimacy may not be violated. But one remembers how there came to the farm some of distraught and troubled mind, on the verge of mental illness, perhaps of the most serious sort, and how these under the influence of peaceful good cheer, under the stimulus of the incentive to serve rather than to be served, came back to normal mental poise, to enter again, as new born, into the world's work. One remembers those who came seeking and finding escape from pathological alcoholism. Others there were with recurrent illness, that would be cured only to come again, who found in the wholesome and happy life of the Farm, strength to throw it off permanently. One thinks of some friendless and homeless, with nowhere to turn, who found here home and family and kin, and so came to find again the world a place wherein life could be happy. Some who came have grown permanently into the family life; the majority come for a period of weeks or of months, and go back to the world's life refreshed and renewed, not only in body, but in spirit and ideals.

There is no reason why such homes should not multiply, and the country everywhere be made to minister largely to the city's distresses. Yes, there is one reason. It cannot be done as it is done at Gould Farm without such wise and gracious personalities as make Gould Farm what it is. Given such personalities, the thing can be done with ease. The money cost is reduced to a minimum; the really important factors are those which money does not and cannot provide.

Gould Farm needs money; the financial responsibility which Will Gould is carrying is a staggering one, of which he should be at once relieved. But, in its continued work of ministration to men and women, its greatest elements of success will be what they have always been, unselfish friendship for the service of all who need. Gould Farm is a kind of co-operating country social service unit. It is a home for convalescents; it is a rest cure; it is a great many things to a great many people, but in the last analysis it is a unique experiment station in the art of completely socialized living.

The *Christian Register* was the leading Unitarian weekly journal, published between 1821 and 1957 when, as its contents focused less on Christianity, it changed its name to *The Unitarian Register*. The paper, after merging with *The Universalist Leader*, is published today as *UU World*. Here is another article by Professor Bowen, which appeared in a 1922 issue of *The Christian Register*.[7]

WHAT IS GOULD FARM?: IT SOUNDS LIKE THE KINGDOM OF HEAVEN

I LONG TO MAKE my fellow-readers of The Christian Register acquainted with Gould Farm, but how shall I describe it? For years I have lectured to classes about the kingdom of God, the rule of whose life is set forth in the words of Jesus in the Gospels. After I had been at Gould Farm for a week I said, "This is it." I have now a concrete embodiment of the great principles announced in Galilee, which helps me to realize their significance and to make it real to students. I talked to one of our scholarly ministers, who is also a university teacher, of the way we live at the Farm. "Why," he said, "that sounds like the kingdom of heaven." When Mr. Gould visited our school at Meadville and talked with the students he did not talk about the New Testament, but what he said made it vastly easier for the professor to make the New Testament intelligible to his classes.

What is Gould Farm? It is just Gould's farm, without a capital letter. It is most emphatically not an institution of any kind: it has no charter, officers, trustees. It is not a hospital, sanatorium, "home" (but it is a home!), or country boarding-house. It is just where William J. Gould lives, with his family about him. It is a large family. About forty, as I write, are at home; many of us are away from home, at various employments in the world. In July and August there were seventy-five or eighty in the household. Some are related to William Gould by blood, as his gifted maters; some by marriage—his wife, who was Agnes Goodyear, and others of that notable Goodyear family, including beloved "Aunt Clara," the last surviving child of Charles Goodyear, one of the great benefactors of mankind by his invention of the process that made rubber a practical commercial product. Most of his living immediate descendants are at the Farm. They have no money at all; though their name is blazoned on every garage and shoe-store in the country, not a cent of the millions that Charles Goodyear's invention is making for other people comes to them. They have something better than money—personalities. But most of the family who call its head "Brother Will" are related by affection only to this really great man. His father was a Congregational minister. He wanted to be the same, but the opportunity of training was denied him; he had to be a tiller of the soil. For years he took city boys on his farm in the summer, he worked with the George

Junior Republic, but his farm and his opportunity were never so large as his heart. He simply must share the peace and strength of his country life. Losses came—twice his buildings were destroyed by fire—but never a moment of discouragement. Eight years ago he took his present home, an abandoned farm in the town of Monterey, Mass., nine miles from the station of Great Barrington, in the most beautiful section of the Berkshire Hills. He patched the roof, put glass in the windows, and said, "Come!" They came, and they have come in increasing numbers ever since.

Who are they? They are people of all sorts—men and women and occasionally children, Americans and Europeans, Jews, Gentiles, Catholics, Protestants, educated and untrained, rich and poor. There are the physically or mentally ill, the weary, worn with the strain of mistakes, of toil, or of sorrow, the homeless, the friendless; there are also the eager, the strong, ready to help. No one is in too desperate need to be received (always remembering that the Farm is no hospital or sanatorium, it has no doctors or nurses); no one is so hearty or happy as to be debarred.

What do we get there? We get, of course, the wonderful invigoration of country life, in the stimulating Berkshire climate (it is one of the most healthful sections in America); we get fresh air and an abundance of wholesome country food; we get rest and quiet and deep sleep, and, according to our wish and our strength, the opportunity of useful labor. But these things may be had elsewhere. What we get primarily, the thing that helps and re-creates us, that makes broken lives whole, ready to go back into the world's activity as new-born— that is the personal influence of William and Agnes Gould and of the family life which centers about them. I said that people of all sorts come; people of only one sort stay. In twenty-four hours new-comers are amalgamated into a spiritual unity with the group by an indescribable charm. Nowhere have I seen anything even approaching the absolute democracy and family spirit that is here the unconscious law. Its violation seems so incongruous as scarcely to enter the mind. We are one. Every one helps every one as he can, as he needs. The service that carries on the life of the home is freely rendered by all; there is no "hired help." Will Gould (I can't call him Mister) has no salary. He has not even an income; he has never had an income in his life. He has his food and lodging like the rest of the family. The whole place has been created and supported mainly by his prodigious, unremitted, untiring physical labor. I have never seen an individual accomplishment to equal it.

Of course the guests contribute, if they can. The majority probably contribute five dollars a week toward the maintenance of the home. Some contribute more, some less, or nothing. No one knows or cares which is which. All contribute service, as they can, not of compulsion, but of spontaneous desire. One can chop wood, another can tend the garden; another, perhaps, can keep our modest wardrobes in repair or can uplift us with music. Another can contribute a brave smile and a cherry word that makes us all more efficient. One of the most useful of our family is a girl who is completely deaf, dumb, and blind; the home would be vastly poorer without her.

Healing comes at the Farm, physical and mental; cases that seem like the Biblical miracles are becoming more and more numerous in its annals. Of these I cannot publicly speak. Peace comes there, and courage to take up life again. Comfort comes there to what seemed like hopeless sorrow. Many have been reminded of Robert Herrick's "Master of the Inn," but there is no evidence that

Herrick ever knew of our Farm. One secret of the place, of course, is the fact that religion is real there. It is absolutely un-sectarian, but it is real religion, of the sort familiar and dear to Register readers. It is the brotherhood of man and the leadership of Jesus and salvation by character. It is about us all the time, never obtrusive, but like the air we breathe. There is health in it. But there is no theory or "ism." It is not Christian Science or New Thought; it is not Socialism or Communism. It is the Golden Rule and glorified common sense. There is a good deal of song, there are informal services of common worship once or twice a week. But better than all is the peace and the joy of the home life.

Applications to be received into the home come ever more thick and fast. At present about one applicant in ten can be taken, owing to the physical limitations of space and equipment. Will Gould can enlarge his home no further. The dilapidated farmhouse of eight years ago is now a comfortable rambling dwelling of forty rooms. There is a women's dormitory; there are six or eight cottages; there is electric light and steam heat and complete plumbing. There are open fires and broad piazzas and a sleeping-porch. Such improvements have come slowly; they represent mainly the incredible toil of Brother Will.

Every one asks, How has the place been financed? That, too, is a kind of miracle. No one knows exactly, least of all, perhaps, Will Gould himself. Much of the work he and members of the family have done in person. There have been desultory contributions, of no great amount; but nowhere in the world does a little money go so far. There have been two or three loans, to cover in part the cost of the land. These are secured by mortgages, which are not pressed, but which entail the payment of interest and are a charge against the home. If it were turned into an incorporated institution, an endowment could easily be secured, but every one who knows the place urges Brother Will not to do this. It would wholly change the spirit of the Farm and destroy precisely its distinctive dynamic. For years this great-hearted man has single-handed borne the entire responsibility; it still weighs heavily upon him. Let me say that he should be relieved of it. A large public should make him its agent in this most efficient of benevolences. His personal influence in the help of those who come to him is too important for him to have to spend his time longer in physical toil, as he has done for all these years. The hundreds of men and women who belong to the "family" by virtue of longer or shorter residence want to help, and do help as they can. But they are seldom of those who can give materially. It has been suggested that one thousand people become honorary members of this family by contributing ten dollars each. That would enable the five hundred acres of land now belonging to the Farm to be developed so as to support an almost indefinite number of people in need of this help. At present most of the land is undeveloped, waiting for the means to make it fruitful. A considerable number of people are contributing members, giving five dollars a year. These attempts at financial assistance are being made, I need hardly say, not by Will Gould, but by his friends. The writer of these lines is one of an informal committee to receive and forward such contributions, of whatever sums, or to furnish information about the Farm and its work. Do you want to help? Do you want to go there to be helped? Do you know any one who should help or be helped? If so, communicate with me or directly with William J. Gould, Great Barrington, Mass.

Among those who have been at the Farm are President and Mrs. Bouthworth of Meadville, and its work is well known to Dr. Howard N. Brown of

King's Chapel. These inadequate words about a great spiritual enterprise are written out of a deep and grateful enthusiasm, admiration, affection.

The following is an except from a sermon preached by Dr. Bowen at Gould Farm on August 23, 1925, three months after Will Gould's death.[8]

To us all now and then life seems to lose all sense and meaning—it becomes a huge puzzle or riddle—and our whole thought becomes one repeated why? The great whirling world with all its rushing noisy activities gets too much for us— we lose our grasp of it and go to pieces-as we say. We need to get away from it all for a little while, in such serene place as this, to recover our vision and our poise. It all *has* meaning, something intelligible is going on, the work of the world is being done, but we can't see it until we recover first something of our vision of God.

It is just what Gould Farm is meant to do for us. That is why religion is such a vital, indispensable element of our life here, why we have these Sunday and Thursday meetings, our daily graces and prayers and hymns. Just good air and good food and wholesome work and jolly good times, important as they all are, would not of themselves alone do the real thing that is done here. I often think of it as I watch our work here. A stranger who should come in just after Mrs. Gould has rung the bell to clear the table for dessert might think the din-ing-room a scene of the wildest confusion, as people rush hither and thither with dishes clean and dirty, with plates and food; and to go into the kitchens af-ter the close of the meal would seem to enter wilder confusion still. And yet it is not really confusion—there is system and meaning in it—there is a living spirit in the midst of the wheels, and out of it all comes our ordered, whole-some, happy family life. We who have been here long enough to understand (and we all know it doesn't take long) see that and are untroubled by the seem-ing confusion. And it is very significant that in the morning before these dis-tracting duties of kitchen and shed and garden begin, we gather about the piano for a hymn. This might seem again to the stranger the maddest thing possible— with all that work waiting, to stop and sing hymns. But then, if the hymn has no meaning, the work has none. If the spirit of religion of which the hymn is the expression is all a folly and delusion, then all that we do the rest of the day is the maddest thing in the world. Why should we scrub pots and pans and wash dishes and chop wood and hoe corn and pitch hay and all these things that the dictionary calls drudgery? We don't have to. Few if any of us is compelled to do this work. We might be staying somewhere else, in easier, more comfortable surroundings, having all sorts of pleasures. We do these things and find joy in doing them because the thing the hymn is about is real, because religion is true, because there is a great God who is the Father of us all, making us all brothers and sisters of one family, because His Spirit, which is love, lives in us all and makes us want to serve others. That's the reason we would rather come here and wash pots and pans or dig potatoes than to go to the seashore or the sum-mer hotel or to Europe and be waited on by hired servants and try to have a good time. We wouldn't have it there; we do have it here. Once proven to me that religion and all great ideals are untrue, and you can wash your own pots and pans. There would no longer be any sense in service or in anything except selfishness. But thank God, religion is true, God is real, not a notion in pious people's heads, but the Father of every one of us. You are my brothers and sisters, love is not a sentimental delusion, service is sense, life has meaning; and we can go on with our happy work together, each for all and all for each, without danger of being reproved for foolishness. The secret of life becomes clear when we glimpse the secret of the Lord. To be sure, even we, in these unusually favorable surroundings, may miss it now and again—when things go wrong, when some other people seem stupid or thoughtless, when the water supply is low or the weather is bad; but if we do, we can get it back again by entering wholeheartedly into these things which we do together, into these services, and the song services, or into our common daily tasks. The living spirit is in the midst of the wheels. We may easily miss it if we stay on the sidelines and merely look on.

I am sure that most of us feel this, that I am only saying the commonplace thing about Gould Farm which is in all your minds. Here where we live is Holy Land! Here is Galilee and Gethsemane and Calvary, and here an open tomb! Here a new and living way has been opened for many of us into the presence of God and we have learned to know—as Whittier puts it in one of our favorite hymns—our common daily life divine, and every land a Palestine. It is holy life that makes holy land; in itself Palestine is no more holy than New Jersey, nor Jerusalem than Chicago. But the place where men and women have seen God, where heroic lives have been lived and the spirit of service has found final expression in triumphant death—this place is forever hallowed. As we walk about these fields and gardens and lawns, we may well say: Put off thy shoes from off thy feet for the place whereon thou standest is holy ground.

Living here, we are on a kind of mount of vision, where it is easier to see and understand. People, as we meet them here, become individuals, persons, brothers, sisters, as they do not out in the world. In a great city like New York, I always feel that the thousands of men and women who rush up and down about me are just a great mass of human stuff; I find it very hard to realize the brotherhood of man. I might as well look over one of our meadows and try to realize the beauty of the separate blades of grass or the tiny flowering plants. They are beautiful, if you look at them individually. There is a story which illustrates very well what our life together here does for us. The story, in brief, is about a shepherd who met in his pasture a man with a microscope who was studying plant life. After looking through the microscope, the shepherd commented, "To think that I've crushed thousands of them beneath my clumsy feet!"

Just so, in a family life like this, we are all under the microscope, not that our faults and failings are magnified, but we are seen as we really are, as human beings, with personal lives and characters, with individual significance. Thousands such as you and I are crushed under the clumsy feet of the world, but here we are tender with one another, because we see and know one another. We open our eyes and see the meaning of life. What we are doing is not just washing dishes or making a path or cutting the grass—it is a larger and more noble thing. It is building, it is creation...

The Jewish Criterion, a proponent of Reform Judaism, was a weekly newspaper published in Pittsburgh, PA, from 1895 through 1962. The author of the note below, Charles H. Joseph, was the paper's associate editor in 1901, a position he held until 1927. The quote is from an anonymous reader, which appeared in a 1927 issue of this weekly.[9]

Well, here's great news indeed! There are actually *Christians* living in this country! The other day, in commenting on a statement of Dr. Samuel Parkes Cadman, I took occasion to say that if one were to square his life according to the teachings of Jesus, he would be considered "peculiar." But here comes a reader from Rochester, New York—a prominent Jew, by the way—who writes this:

"You will find at the Gould Farm, near Great Barrington, Mass., a group of people who are actually squaring their lives with the teachings of Jesus, and are not considered 'queer' by the believing Jews, Catholics, and Protestants who have been fortunate enough to come into contact with them. This is not a sect or a cult, or fanatical experiment. Some have called it communism. I believe it good Judaism, and also believe that whatever the sources of their spiritual inspiration, people can live practically by adhering to these teachings which as you and I know are neither original nor unique. Vide our prophets!"

I certainly am going to take a run out or up or down to Great Barrington. It may be that a group of Christians may be segregating themselves approximate a Christian life without being viewed with suspicion. But I am still of the opinion that the world at large will consider them a wee bit queer.

Benton MacKaye (1879-1975) was a forester, planner, and conservationist who helped found the Wilderness Society and conceived the idea, in the early 1920s, of the Appalachian Trail.

In November 1928, after months suffering from various maladies, his sister Hazel moved to Gould Farm where she lived for about 10 years. MacKaye visited Hazel there regularly during her stay, especially during the Christmas season.[10] By the spring of 1937 Gould Farm was unable to accommodate Hazel due to the severity of a reported "nerve attack."[11] With the financial assistance from Lewis Mumford, among others, MacKaye placed his sister in Green Farms, Connecticut. Gould Farm volunteer and Unitarian minister, Samuel Spaulding, wrote this about Hazel MacKaye long after Hazel had left the Farm: "(She) herself was exceptionally charming and accomplished, having been an actress, and a writer and director of pageants...She played the piano exceptionally well, gave recitals (at Gould Farm), and gave piano lessons to many Gould Farmers."[12]

Below is a letter from MacKaye to Agnes Gould:[13]

Gould Farm
May 29, 1945

Memorandum for Mrs. Gould
Concerning the Gould Farm Woodland
    Having in mind a letter from you written some months ago about your fuel and woodland problems, I have, since arriving here the other day, been giving the matter some attention. Yesterday I made two trips into the woods—one

with Raymond Olds and the other with William Gilchrist. I am now recording for your information some ideas drawn from my conversations with these two men.

The Farm property, as I understand, covers some 500 acres, of which at least half may properly be classed as permanent woodland. This is a typical mixture of white pine and hardwood (largely paper birch) in various stages of growth. What I have seen is in fairly good condition except for the need of thinning, of cutting out dead and damaged trees, and of brush clearing here and there.

Your immediate and constant need is fuel wood—from 100 to 125 cords a year, I'm told. This should be forthcoming from the damaged trees just noted and (under suitable management) from the normal growth of thinnings throughout the total woodland areas. Hence there is no necessity apparently for clearing off (or cutting clean) any substantial patch or patches of land. Thus you can, if you wish, preserve your forest intact, in short—*have* it and *use* it too.

This brings us to the basic question before yourself (or any other proprietor)—just what is it that you *wish*.

Two quite definite and opposing policies may be set up. Between these a definite choice should be made and held to, unless there is to be incessant confusion and misunderstanding between proprietor and woods' boss. Such has been my own observation covering forty years of forestry experience. The policies aforesaid seek the following objectives.

1) *Maximum yield of lumber.* This requires letting the best trees grow to financial maturity (when annual growth begins to lag) and then cutting them all down. This means (usually but not always) cutting an area absolutely clean and preparing it for a second crop. It means cutting holes in the forest rather than keeping it intact.

2) *Optimum psychological influence.* This may sound like a fancy term. But it has in forestry a definite technical meaning. There are two opposing outward influences at work on the human mind. One is that of the city street—of subway, electric sign, and radio. The other is that of the forest path—or of unmolested nature. Each has its use. For purposes of psychological rehabilitation, the forest influence is uppermost. It is the environment of calm as against that of confusion. To obtain this fully on any given acreage of woodland requires keeping the forest canopy intact and letting the best trees grow to their climax in old age.

In each case, (1) and (2), thinnings and improvement cuttings can and should be made. Theoretically, the time would come when no more thinnings could be had. On Gould Farm this would not be for many years. Meanwhile, you could reasonably depend on getting your needed yearly fuel supply.

For the purpose of Gould Farm I should suppose that policy (2)—not policy (1)— would be most appropriate. Properly developed it could be made the basis of a therapy all its own. Methods of woodcraft and kindred pursuits, to fit the temperament of art or science, have been well worked out and tested. For such activity of body and mind I am unacquainted with any better opportunity than the one afforded by the natural setup of Gould Farm.

On these matters you appear to have good counsel near at hand. I am impressed with the keen sense and high appreciation exhibited by our friends Olds and Gilchrist. They tell me that you have available also the good advice of the

State District Forester, Harold Green, with headquarters in Swan Forest.

With these various advantages I should think that an interesting forest program could be developed and made a valuable asset. Operations should be planned in advance and laid out on an accurate map of the Farm property. Careful records should be kept.

All woods' work should be under thorough supervision. Where possible, trees should be marked for cutting by a competent woodsman. Brush should be disposed of so as to preclude all fire hazard. No brush burning should be started except under special care and under a permit, as required by law, from the Town Fire Warden. A system of fire protection trails should be established. For psychological as well as practical ends the Farm might well promote an extended "Forest Mindedness."

I am newly impressed with the vital possibilities herein sketched. Such assistance on my part as may be possible awaits, of course, your call.

> With High Esteem,
> Benton MacKaye

Ethel Phelps Stokes Hoyt (1877-1952) raised funds for Gould Farm in the 1920s and 1930s and was likely the one who first made contact between the Goulds and the Rockefeller family. She was a leader of the pastoral counseling movement.[14] Here is a letter, dated March 10, 1932, that MacKaye wrote to her.[15]

My dear Mrs. Hoyt:

Mrs. Gould has asked me to write you my impression of Gould Farm, in Monterey, Massachusetts, with which I understand you are already familiar. My sister (Miss Hazel MacKaye) went to the Farm in November 1927 suffering from a nervous breakdown, and I have since then made repeated and extended visits there. During my stays I have made the close acquaintance of most of the Farm people, especially Mrs. Gould and the others on her staff; and I have watched closely the life going on. So it pleases me to have the chance of presenting what are to my mind some of the possibilities of that institution.

Is Gould Farm an "institution?" That is the first question which presents itself. It will take a whole letter to answer this question; and to do it justice it will be a long letter. I might be brief and say merely that I consider the Farm an unique place—with able leadership, that it seems guided by a rare spirit of helpfulness and buoyant cheer, that it is "going back home" to visit there, and that I personally feel deeply beholden to its leaders from returning my sister to health. All this is true. But the Farm seems too vital to public life to be thus privately disposed of. So I should like to present not an encomium of actual accomplishment (the record gives that) but an analysis of possibilities.

I see things from the background of a regional planner and a forester (I was for twelve years in the United States Forest Service). So I can best tell what (to my mind) Gould Farm *is* by stating what I see it to be potentially. It is not a sanatorium nor a hospital nor a boarding house, though people are cured and well fed there. I see Gould Farm as a school in the *art of living.*

To explain let me define:

Living consists of work and play, industry and culture.

Industry in essence consists in converting natural resources into food, clothing, and shelter ("shelter" including warmth and equipment as well as roofing). In our modern mechanistic world we lose sight of the essential process, and thereby lose our sense of the means of livelihood. One of our greatest public needs is to restore that sense, especially in periods like the present. The old time New England farm was an industrial microcosm: its garden, its hand loom, its woodlot, its shop pointed to the roots for obtaining, out of the soil and forest, our food and clothing and warmth and household equipment.

Gould Farm is, or could be, such a microcosm: its summer garden and springtime maple orchard, its hand loom in the upper studio, its woodland on the hillside being cut on lines of forestry, its furniture shop, these represent in their entirety the four corners of the Nation's industry. By applying to these simple beginnings a little conscious educative effort the great total process could itself, I think, be in a sense unfolded.

Culture in essence comes down to art and science. Music (especially singing) is part of the Gould Farm life, a part which is being furthered and extended through the recently established music studio. Dramatic art and reading aloud (around the open fire)—these form another important Farm activity. The scientific study of outdoor nature might be more vigorously furthered, and a world of opportunity lies at the door. The blazing and cutting of wood paths and the establishment of "nature trails" make the readiest approach to this line of outdoor culture.

Here then in these activities appear to be the ingredients for molding a real art of balanced living—the value of which as a restorative measure cannot I think be overestimated. But "ingredients" alone are not enough. They must be *integrated*—even as the flour and the yeast. In no place that I know of has this been done; certainly in no conventional school of learning. To do this would seem to be Gould Farm's special function—possibly its biggest service in a bewildered world and country suffering from confusion as to the means and ends of life. Indeed to purge this confusion, in the mind of any individual, makes a mental treatment in itself.

How to achieve this synthesis of simple purposeful activity (in contrast to the aimless chaos of complex mechanistic life)? This makes too long a story to enter here (some informal but systematic study might be the thread to bring the parts together). But I believe that Gould Farm, through its tradition and its present tendencies, through the keeping alive of the ideas of its great founder, blended with increasing scrutiny of the present forces working in the outside world, is capable of doing this big thing. A school of living such as I can see would make an *institution* in itself—one which apparently has not quite come to pass within this country.

And now I am prepared to give my own answer to the question put at the beginning of this letter— *is* Gould Farm an "institution?" My answer is *no*; but it seems to be the seed of the thing which I have attempted to describe.

Severe handicaps may prevent this consummation. I am impressed by the heavy load of the daily household routine. Whether this could be lightened within the present plant I am not prepared to say. Without question a new building is needed urgently—not alone to lighten daily burdens but for downright safety. The danger from one source alone—that of the use of kerosene stoves—is enough to condemn the present equipment.

I have written thus at length not merely from a sense of personal obligation for a profound service rendered but because as a planner, and a would-be revealer of the possible, I see this modest effort as something of very deep importance. Gould Farm has gone far in the direction of the goal herein set up— so far indeed that I think it should go farther. Gould Farm is no mere "charity"—it is a potent social force.

I am very happy, as stated at the start, to be given this opportunity of writing you on a matter so much within my thoughts.

Very sincerely yours,
Benton MacKaye

Notes and Permissions

1. Smith, Steven K. "Growing up on Gould Farm: Generational Reflections on Community, Change and Tradition." Unpub. 2004.

2. In addition to appearing in contemporary directories for service providers, Gould Farm has been listed in directories for the general public and academics. See entries in Robert P. Sutton's *Modern American Communes: A Dictionary* (2005), Morris and Kross' *Historical Dictionary of Utopianism* (2004), and Timothy Miller's *The Quest for Utopia in Twentieth-Century America* (1998). I thank Timothy Miller for this observation.

3. From "Directory of Convalescent Homes for New York City." New York: Sturgis Research Fund of the Burke Foundation, 1921.

4. McKee, William J. *Gould Farm: A Life of Sharing*. Monterey: The William J. Gould Associates, Inc., 1994. 28.

5. Public Domain. *The New York Times*. Sept. 18, 1921. "Farm of New Hope." 7.

6. Every effort has been made to trace copyright for this piece. Proper credit will be included in any future printings upon receipt of written notice.

7. Bowen, Clayton R. *The Christian Register*. Jan. 12, 1922. "What is Gould Farm? It Sounds like the Kingdom of Heaven." Used with permission from UUA Publications, Skinner House.

8. From R. McKee. (1963 [1975]). *Brother Will and the Founding of Gould Farm*. 60-62. Used with permission: The William J. Gould Associates, Inc.

9. Joseph, Charles H. "Random Thoughts." *The Jewish Criterion, A*ugust 19, 1927, 6. http://diva.library.cmu.edu/pjn/search-results.jsp?ssf=Gould=Farm&typ=s. Accessed February 28, 2012. The Pittsburgh Jewish Newspaper Project, Carnegie Mellon University Libraries. Used with permission.

10. Anderson, Larry. *Benton MacKaye: Conservationist, Planner, and Creator of the Appalachian Trail*. Baltimore: The Johns Hopkins University Press, 2002. 259.

11. Ibid. 288.

12. Spaulding, Samuel. "Gould Farm Personalities." N.d.

13. Used with permission from the Trustees of Dartmouth College and The William J. Gould Associates, Inc.

14. McKee, William J. *op cit.* 288.

15. Used with permission from the Trustees of Dartmouth College and The William J. Gould Associates, Inc.

Chapter Four

Work

The idea, practice, and attitude toward work were born from necessity at Gould Farm. At the same time, the Farm's founders saw work not as a burden to avoid, but as a challenge, participation in which helped integrate all members in the community.

In addition to fulfilling a practical need, the therapeutic potential of work was not lost on the Goulds who anticipated, more than half a century later, the practice of psychosocial rehabilitation. A notice in the Hospital Information Bureau's Directory of Convalescent Homes, for New York City, described the Farm's approach as "Work on social rather than medical lines. Mental and physical convalescence incidental only."[1]

These selections, including one by the late Quaker theologian and Haverford College Professor, Douglas Steere (1901-1995), explore the therapeutic, spiritual, and social dimensions of work, as practiced and emphasized on Gould Farm. Work is the Farm's principal "therapy." Duhon's piece, excerpted from her Harvard Bachelor's thesis, examines, in part, work from the perspective of the guests yet has broader theoretical significance. The excerpt by Trelawny-Ross takes qualitative data and measures the importance of work on a guest's "recovery," work often being a tool for guests to gain insight into their illnesses.

THE SELECTIONS

This chapter opens with the following essay, excerpted from Steere's *Work and Contemplation* (1957).[2] Steere frequently quotes his interviews with Harold Winchester (1892-1966) who, among other roles, was a member of the Farm's board of directors, edited the Farms newsletter, served as a volunteer adviser to the Farm, and was active in the Society of Friends.

GOULD FARM: A CASE STUDY OF THE ROLE OF WORK IN A THERAPEUTIC COMMUNITY

Gould Farm, near Great Barrington, Massachusetts, is an example of one of these intentional communities. It is so admirably suited to illustrate this two-way interplay of the community framing the work and the manual work exercising its therapeutic effect on the community, that I have chosen it as a kind of case study.

Gould Farm is a convalescent community for persons who are suffering from some form of mental distress. Some of the guest clientele of the farm are people who have come directly from mental hospitals but are not yet ready to meet the rigors of our fiercely competitive society. The only requirement is that they be well enough so that they are not in need of nursing care. Others have come to the farm from their homes or from occupational situations where they have been driven beyond their powers of adjustment and have been unable to go on. Others have come with heavy inner problems to solve and because they needed a time and a place away from the thick of things in order to balance the budget and to sort themselves out.

As long as the farm can manage, guests are taken irrespective of their capacity to pay. There is no state aid involved. All are expected to come as near as they can to meeting the bare cost of their being there. The venture was undertaken and is maintained by a staff of deeply committed persons who are there in no small part because of religious motivation. I mean to quote generously from a short description of the work of Gould Farm which one of their principal counselors, Harold Winchester, has been good enough to prepare for me, and here and there to break into it in order to add comments.

"Ever since its inception in 1913 Gould Farm, under the leadership of the dynamic Will Gould, has emphasized the value of work for its guests as an important part of the therapeutic process. Having taken over an old run-down property and farm, there was of course the urgent necessity to make repairs, to get the farm going again, to maintain the household functions for the growing number of those who were invited to come and join the Gould family for recuperative purposes. It was a place where, as Mrs. Gould recently put it, 'people with a complexity of thoughts are met by the simplicity of the Christian life.' Guests seemed glad to pitch in and found it was a wonderful change to follow Will Gould to the farm for helping with planting and weeding, to the woodlot for hewing firewood, to the chicken coops to gather eggs for breakfast. Those less suited to the more strenuous work helped Mrs. Gould in the kitchen, set the table, washed the dishes, assisted in the laundry, put up the sheets on the line and tidied their own rooms.

"As the family increased, the custom developed of calling out for volunteers for various projects in the living room where all had gathered for morning devotions. Then leaders would be assigned to the projects and off the groups would go singing to their work. As the years have gone by, the Farm of 550 acres with its 22 buildings, cottages, barns, studios, and shops has built up a tradition of work for all its guests, no matter what rate they pay and no matter how short or long their stay.

"In the forty-odd years that the Farm has been operated, it has become evident that the medical profession, particularly its psychiatric section, has wholeheartedly swung over to the supreme importance of work as prime therapy for those in the convalescent stages of mental illness."

Harold Winchester goes on to relate the process of involving these patients in manual work, and the chasm that separates the isolation of the mentally ill from the sense of belonging to a vital and necessary work community is forcefully described in this forthright account. In recruiting guests for the necessary work on this hard-bitten farm, he continues, they have "always emphasized the permissive system. There is no initial pressure to work. The guest is allowed to seek to help out in his or her own time. It is hoped that the example set by so many of the other guests busily occupied in the necessary daily tasks will become contagious, as it frequently does. Naturally, a small start in this direction is given from the first day by the necessity to remove one's own dishes, to carry in the food, and of course to make one's own bed and clean one's room. If the guest is a young person, he is soon included in a young persons' group which is working on some field project. He is asked to accompany them to the gardens where he can sit and watch. If he has any sense of group responsibility, he will soon make some effort to join in, even if only for a short period. The next day he will work longer and if he has enjoyed the work, it will be no time before he is doing his full share along with the group.

"One guest who came to the Farm after a severe emotional illness and who was not ready to help out with the work, was approached to assist in filling the little cream jugs for one of the meals. Later, in her evaluation of what the Farm had done for her, she singled out this incident as the starting point of her rapid recovery. She said that she had approached this work with great insecurity and then was surprised when she had been told, 'You do it so well.' The fact that something that she did was appreciated proved extremely helpful to her then.

"Another guest, who sat around during his first week feeling a kind of lost and helpless stranger, was asked to give a quick hand with a large limb of a tree, partially split off during a heavy storm and endangering the Main House. He responded with some hesitation and then because of the danger of the situation became engrossed in doing his share in the emergency. Later when he was a regular member of a working crew, he confided, 'Why, you feel that you belong as soon as you do something for the place.'

"In essence, it is this feeling of belonging to the group which is so important to restore. So much of mental illness is isolation from the group, a sense of not belonging. It is valuable therapy to work in a group toward a purpose which has an easily recognizable value and of which all in the group are aware."

The focus here on the frame of meaning of the work has about it a familiar ring, and with mentally ill patients there would seem to be a particular sensitivity to the character of the frame. Yet at bottom each of these same elements is yearned for by every man in all of the normal work that he does, and its absence is not unconnected with many of these breakdowns. In a therapeutic community where a guest feels himself to be uncritically and lovingly accepted and where the meaning of his work is clearly visible, the work again redeems and heals and seems to seal his acceptance as being an acceptance not only by men, but by nature, and at heart, by the Creator.

Harold Winchester insists that nothing is so vital at this stage of the work as for the guest "to see that his actions are purposive and contribute directly to the ongoingness of the farm. As they make a further recovery, many resent using up their energies in the daily repetitive actions such as chopping wood for the fireplace, washing dishes, or setting the table. They want to see that their actions have an accumulative result, like the erection of a tool shed, the construction of an incinerator, the start of a library, or the clearing of a section of the forest. This is particularly true of men who are given to thinking in terms of constructive progress. They like to see that their actions are part of a long-term program of change and development.

"Many others develop a permanent affection for the Farm and feel themselves somehow a part of it because they may have planted a tree or set out an asparagus patch or helped construct a building. Only yesterday a city-bred lawyer who had been at the Farm some years ago returned for a short afternoon visit with his bride-to-be, and the first thing he did was to rush her down to the hen house to point out with great pride how he had helped erect it. He had built himself into the Farm in a lifelong way by this creative act.

"Yet it should be pointed out that a policy of recognition of a person's efforts, of judicious praise, of a loving spirit of inclusiveness, must accompany a work program. If a guest feels that the work is compulsory, or that his efforts are exploited or unappreciated, he is likely to develop resentment instead of affection. Although large public institutions like the Hudson River State Hospital or the Passaic Retreat have good work programs, such large and impersonal places seldom develop in their 'graduates' any feeling of loyalty or love or devotion. It is undoubtedly the spirit of loving recognition of the individual's value and his ability to see that the Farm needs his particular service at that time (with no one else to do it if he doesn't) which is the element that produces his sense of belongingness and of personal worth.

"Gould Farm is comparatively small. It is always poor. And it is perennially shorthanded. Any service that a guest renders is genuinely appreciated, and the guest is made to feel this. In a place as hard-pressed as Gould Farm, the long-term needs for repairs and development are so obvious that even the most self-absorbed guest can hardly miss them. In fact, basically the charm and value of the Farm is that it has always retained the family atmosphere with each guest made to feel that he is always one of the important contributing members of it."

It does not take any very profound analysis of this situation to see in it not only those factors that woo men back to health and make them willing to join the normal working community again, but also factors which if present in any work situation would profoundly affect its frame of meaning: the obviousness of their personal contribution's being decisive as to whether the work got done or not, the worth of the work itself, the being consulted and treated as responsible members of a working community, the close touch with those who benefited from the work, the acquiring of new skills; and back of it all, for those who chose to see it, a sense that in every aspect of the community life they were praising a Source of life to whom not only they themselves, but all that they did and the care with which they did it, mattered immeasurably.

A convalescent center for Indian tubercular patients on the edge of Durban in South Africa has been developed along the Gould Farm ideas with a variety of work for all. This work is so graduated that a patient can put in as few or as many hours as his returning strength permits. Facilities are also provided for the patient's family, suitably protected from infection, to live with him in a little cottage. The work has been guided by a remarkable pioneer who knew how to draw out the full capacity and sense of responsibility and worth in people. The result has been not only a vastly improved prospect of a swift recovery but a recovery which, when it was completed, had brought the man to a psychological condition in which he could take his full place in society again. This pattern is being widely studied in Africa and its offspring can be found in many places.

Tamsin Trelawny-Cassity first heard about Gould Farm as an intern with Heifer Project International, United States, before which she worked in community-based social work in the United Kingdom. She moved to the United States to work at the Farm, from 1994 through 1997. She then returned to England to pursue an Masters in Social Work at Oxford University, specializing in adult mental health. After receiving her degree, she returned to the Farm in 1999 to work as a case manager. She and her husband, Lew, a Professor of Philosophy at Antioch College, and their two sons, live in Yellow Springs, Ohio. Tamsin now conducts exit interviews for Gould Farm guests as part of the Farm's annual "outcomes study."

Below is an excerpt from her thesis for Oxford University (1999) titled "The Experience of Mental Illness and the Meaning of Work: 'If I'm just sitting, I don't feel I'm living.'"[3]

CHAPTER FIVE - DISCUSSION AND CONCLUSIONS

The association between work and severe mental illness The experiences of the interview participants illustrate several of the findings presented in the review of the research on the association between mental illness and work. First, participants reflect the general experience of adults with mental illness, regarding the high rates of unemployment and work disruption associated with mental illness (Meltzer 1995, Van Dongen 1998). Prior to Gould Farm, participants had experienced severe disruption to their ability to work, through a combination of factors relating to the illness, disability and environment. All participants experienced significant improvements in work history post-Gould Farm, although symptoms, stigma, financial need, interpersonal difficulties and other work environment-related stresses were still problematic in attaining and maintaining work (alongside intrapersonal factors). However, at this point job terminations were more often due to positive factors, such as seeking more rewarding work or successfully completing a job placement. Participant responses suggested that a key component in this change was their experience of Gould Farm, as shall be discussed below.

Second, the interview responses illustrate the potential role of work in alleviating the clinical, functional, social and psychological consequences of mental illness, and confirm findings on the importance of work to clients (Strong 1998, Leete 1989, Mueser et al 1997). Work was felt by participants to help with self-management of symptoms and overall mental health. It aided in regaining social, prevocational and vocational skills and the confidence to use these skills. Work had a central role in the process of recovery, making the move, both practically and symbolically, from "patient" to "normal adult". Participants identified the importance of integration, pay, control and job permanence, both for the ensuing practical benefits, and for the valued social status these factors implied. Through these multiple processes, work played an important role in preparing participants for reintegration in the wider community and a wider range of employment opportunities, and aided in an improved quality of life and increased independence. These are core goals in the current discourse on mental illness, reflected in statutory legislation on community care, current models of normalisation (Ramon 1991), and the growing consumer movement (Deegan 1992, Leete 1989).

The literature increasingly points to the work environment as key to whether work is beneficial or detrimental (Warr 1987, Mills 1991, Strong 1998). Key factors raised by participants were: working in an integrated environment, interpersonal contact, the ethics of the organisation, levels of responsibility and interest, and the opportunity to use skills. Comments on responsibility illustrated Warr's (1987) model of "additional decrement," whereby responsibility was seen as beneficial to a certain point, and precipitating stress beyond that point. As with Strong's (1998) sample, what was experienced as beneficial within the work environment varied between individuals and for individual participants, as the pattern of illness, disability, skills, and confidence changed.

The use of a wide range of work situations and the different reactions to different environmental factors, illustrates Strong's (1998) and Scheid and Anderson's (1995) recommendation that work needs to be matched to the individual's stage of rehabilitation, recovery, course of illness, and individual interest to be successful in its outcomes. This requires the opportunity to use a range of specialised employment and close attention to the work environment.

Schneider (1998) points to the paucity of specialist employment opportunities in Britain. In contrast, interview participants had access to a relatively wide range of opportunities, reflecting the geographical area but also the services accessed through Gould Farm's Boston programmes, including formal rehabilitation services (state rehabilitation services, club houses, transitional and supported employment, training schemes), local educational establishments, and supportive voluntary positions. While at Gould, individuals had available a range of work opportunities through the work programme, which provided work with varying degrees of responsibility and integration, and requiring different skills.

Work in the rehabilitative process

Participants repeatedly emphasised the importance of Gould Farm's focus on work in making a decision to apply to the programme, and in the subsequent time spent at Gould. Reflecting the client-centred accounts discussed in chapter one, work was important for both the objective and subjective processes experienced; for the "doing" of work, and what that "doing" implied about the self and the illness. Work was important for the clinical, functional and social outcomes, and for the motivation, self-esteem, self-efficacy and status (re)gained.

Important to participants' experience of the work programme were the attitudes, expectations and opportunities encountered, which were opposite to those encountered in social attitudes and previous mental health services used. Neither denying the illness nor allowing it to take over life, and approaching clients as capable, responsible adults, enabled clients to begin the process of renegotiation of the self and self-illness relationship (Strong 1998), including coming to accept the illness and/or disability while rejecting the "disability package plan" (Deegan 1992)—the process of recovery.

Strong (1998) found that clients emphasised issues of recovery and disabling environments rather than hospital recidivism, reflecting the primacy of recovery in the "consumer" movement (Deegan 1992). One implication of this is that providers need to focus their services more on enabling recovery and addressing disabling environments if they wish to engage clients and provide services relevant to clients.

Opportunities and expectations, community and independence

Two complementary themes emerged from the interviews as key to the rehabilitative and recovery potential of work. First, the balance of expectations and responsibilities with opportunities and support; second, the integration of independence and community.

Strong's study (1998) stressed the importance of opportunities and responsibilities in the process of recovery (reflected in the Independent Living Movement, where "recovery" may be rephrased as "empowerment"). Participants in this study likewise stressed the reciprocal importance of the two concepts. Expectations implied respect and a belief in individual ability (to work, take responsibility for oneself and others, change, be in control of one's life). The accompanying opportunities and support enabled fulfillment of these expectations. The dual process of responding to expectations and utilising opportunities was seen as core to (re)gaining the sense of belonging to community and self-sufficiency (where self-sufficiency refers to strengths including skills, responsibility, control and choice; Emerson and Thersky 1996).

This conjunction of self-sufficiency and belonging reflects Dalley's (1988) collective model of community, which incorporates both concepts, in contrast, community care and the individualistic model of community overemphasizes "independence" in the narrower sense of the word: Living in one's own place, owning a car, and having a job is the standard rehabilitation ideal. But the national drive to close institutions and assure independence and self-sufficiency for mental health consumers often neglects the broader human need to belong—to an inclusive group, a church, a family, a neighbourhood (Gould Farm 1994).

Participants contrasted their experience of independence and belonging to their prior experience of dependency and/or isolation—the position many persons with mental illness find themselves in, regardless of (or as a result of) community-based care (Dalley 1988, Ramon 1991). The research on work and mental illness (e.g. Strong 1998, Coughlan 1993) suggests that participation in integrated employment can, as with Gould Farm, shift client experiences of "community care" towards a sense of community belonging and independence.

Therapeutic communities and the "real world"

Therapeutic communities have often evoked a negative response from practitioners for various reasons (reviewed by Kennard 1998), including a reliance on methods that fail to generate the skills required by clients to live in the wider society. Contrasts are drawn between the supportive community and emphasis on intense group process, and the "real world." However, interview participants described a process of successful (to varying degrees) rehabilitation and transition to the broader community, and implicated Gould Farm as significant to this process (other primary factors mentioned were medications, time and religious faith).

Some of the reasons that former clients have given for the efficacy of Gould Farm have been discussed above. Other reasons may be located in some of the features which distinguish Gould Farm from many other forms of therapeutic community.

First, the integration of Gould Farm within the wider community, both geographically and through the significance given to "normalising" roles (specifically, work) and structures, ensures that client experiences at Gould are not divorced from reality. Indeed, study participants stressed the challenge of living and working in community, and the importance of confronting this challenge as a basis for moving onwards.

Second, Gould Farm's view of mental illness reflects the biopsychosocial view of mental illness, which is well supported by evidence (Kavanagh 1992). This view provides a basis for Gould's integration of medical and rehabilitative goals; this is likewise supported by evidence of the improved outcomes gained through integrating treatment and rehabilitation (Becker et al 1998).

Third, Gould Farm provides a continuity of services, from progressive opportunities at Gould Farm through the Boston programmes and into the extended community. The importance of such a "continuity of care" is well-demonstrated and now widely accepted as the ideal in community care (Seymour 1998, Malla et al 1998). Comments made by participants reflect their own perception of rehabilitation/recovery as an ongoing process, started at Gould but continuing after discharge (Deegan 1992).

Given these structural and theoretical parameters, therapeutic communities could play an integral part in the continuum of services for persons with mental illness that should exist within community care, providing a much needed service where neither hospital care nor high levels of independence (or lack of meaningful structure, and/or an isolated living situation) appropriately meet the needs of the individual.

The role of work: the current situation

The literature increasingly points to the potential role of work in the ongoing process of rehabilitation for adults with severe mental illness. The point is reiterated through client views on work, illustrated by the former clients of Gould Farm interviewed for this study. However, as Schneider (1998) points out, opportunities to participate in work—and thence to enjoy its benefits—remain scarce, with rates of unemployment and unsatisfactory job terminations remaining high. Some of the multiple factors contributing to this situation include:

First, inadequacies of current research, in particular in Britain. Most British studies have been conducted in institutional settings several decades ago, or in vocational settings that concentrated on light industrial skills. Thus they do not reflect the current community context or changing market towards service skills (Schneider 1998).

Second, work opportunities are affected by the wider economic situation. In periods of unemployment, opportunities decrease in response to concerns of displacement of more "productive" workers, and the effects of this on the economy (Warner 1995). However, "leaving job placement to market forces ignores the non-economic rewards of employment and the detrimental impact of unemployment on people with mental health problems and on society at large" (Schneider 1998; 90). Not all clients will be able to work in competitive situations, even with accommodations; alternatives that do not prioritise economic efficiency need to be provided, such as social firms.

Third, while many clients want to work, significant work disincentives exist through the welfare system.

Fourth, there is a lack of directive policy, while existing legislation is limited in its impact. For example, legislation on disability discrimination is inadequate without accompanying education, support and training, for both employers and employees (Noble 1998). Employers show continuing reluctance to employ people with mental illness, especially if there is a history of psychotic illness (Schneider 1998).

These do not outweigh the grounds for provision of appropriate work interventions.

First, clients are strongly dissatisfied about not working (Lehman 1995). With increased understanding of the processes of mental illness and disabilities, and improved medications, work is a possibility and/or priority for the majority of clients.

Second, there is increasing evidence of the clinical benefits of work, and of the possibilities of creating beneficial work environments. Research in North America finds that work place "accommodations" (e.g. flexi-time, clear supervision) are proving relatively inexpensive and straightforward, and are often incorporated as good general employer practices (Rehab. Services 1998, Mancuso 1993, Van Dongen 1996, Kirsch 1996, Fabian et al 1993, Scheid and Anderson 1995). There is increasing knowledge of the environmental factors that are beneficial or detrimental, although more research is required.

Third, work is central to the goals of community care and broader human and civil rights, including community integration, the rights of clients to work and live "ordinary" lives, and client empowerment. Work could also be used for policies aimed at risk minimisation through achieving noncustodial supervision, while at the same time promoting therapeutic ends (Schneider 1998).

Fourth, there are fiscal and societal benefits of employing people with mental illness, through reduced use of health services and hospitalisations, and possibly reduced benefit uptake. Studies indicate that following discharge from hospital, people will return at a significantly greater rate if left in the community with no structure or purpose to their daily activity (Coughlan 1993).

For many adults experiencing a severe mental illness, work has a high priority. To move the role of work to a higher priority for policists and service providers requires continued experimentation and evaluation of work interventions, clear policy, and the continued promotion of both accommodations within competitive employment and provision of specialized employment. Through such provision of a range of opportunities, work may maximize its potential for both individual and society.

Anna Duhon grew up on and around Gould Farm, and has always felt a deep connection to the community. She chose to return as an adult to do her undergraduate thesis on Gould Farm in completion of a Bachelor of Arts in Social Anthropology from Harvard University, and fell in love anew with the place, the work, and the community. Her path since then continues to be profoundly shaped by the transformative power of community and agriculture that she experienced at Gould Farm. She completed a Master of Arts in Natural Resources and Peace from the United Nations-mandated University for Peace in Costa Rica, and now lives in rural New York, where she does social and cultural research on the interconnections between people, nature, and agriculture, as part of the Hawthorne Valley Farmscape Ecology Program.

We conclude this chapter with an excerpt from Duhon's Harvard University B.A. thesis.[4]

THE WORK PROGRAM: "I AIN'T GONNA WORK ON GOULD FARM NO MORE"

"Work is for the guests, and to help the guests—it's not for the work itself, even though that's very important. But the work is for us, this place runs by us, to help us overall, that's the main job it has. So this place is only as good as the guests that stay here are."—Thomas, Gould Farm guest (interview, December 5, 2003)

"I ain't gonna work on Maggie's farm no more./No, I ain't gonna work on Maggie's farm no more./Well, I wake in the morning,/Fold my hands and pray for rain./I got a head full of ideas/That are drivin' me insane./It's a shame the way she makes me scrub the floor./I ain't gonna work on Maggie's farm no more.
"I ain't gonna work on Maggie's farm no more./No, I ain't gonna work on Maggie's farm no more./Well, I try my best/To be just like I am,/But everybody wants you/To be just like them./They say sing while you slave and I just get bored./I ain't gonna work on Maggie's farm no more."—Bob Dylan, "Maggie's Farm," verses 1 and 5

The work teams had taken the afternoon off, and much of the Farm was gathered at nearby Benedict Pond for a cookout and "fun day." As usual for Gould Farm gatherings, many people had brought instruments, and a circle of musicians started swapping songs and jamming. Suddenly an improvised version of Bob Dylan's "Maggie's Farm" came to life as "I ain't gonna work on Gould Farm no more." Different people picked up the verses, improvising lyrics about how terrible it was to work at Gould Farm, as everyone laughed. I begin with this scene because it highlights both the joyful flexibility of the work program, in taking time for a "fun day," and the existence of underlying tensions. Work is considered to be the central therapeutic element at Gould Farm, and it is also what enables the community to sustain the way of life that it does. Again, this speaks to the liminal existence of Gould Farm as both a community and a mental health institution. It is in this ambiguous, liminal space that different understandings of the role and purpose of the work program are voiced, discussed and debated.

Work has been central to Gould Farm from its beginning, and since the 1950s work has been increasingly organized into a "work program." The present work program has eight different work departments where staff work leaders and guests join together in teams. Guests begin on the Forestry and Grounds (F&G) team, which combines housekeeping, grounds keeping, forestry and such seasonal tasks as maple sugaring. After guests have worked for a time on F&G, they can petition to switch to other teams. Most of the "work" at Gould Farm pertains directly to the running of the community: the Kitchen team prepares community meals, the Farm and Garden teams largely produce food for the Kitchen, the Childcare team watches over Gould Farm children, and the Maintenance team does a variety of odd jobs necessary to keep the place running. The Farm first extended its work program beyond the community with the 1977 addition of the Roadside Store and Cafe, which is located just across from the beginning of Gould Road, and is run by guests and staff for the general public. The latest addition to the work program has taken form with the recent opening of the Harvest Barn, while I was still at the Farm. The Harvest Barn has a high quality commercial kitchen which is designed to facilitate an increase in the development of Gould Farm products and expand the work opportunities for guests. Like Roadside, the Harvest Barn extends the work program beyond the direct service of the Farm's daily workings.

There are many understandings of the positive benefit and therapeutic value of work. The clinical director explained the importance of work:

"I think an important element to one's healing, and what we offer, what the community creates here, is [to] foster in each person that sense of 'I have something I can give, I have something I can contribute,' and hopefully have enough niches in the community for people to find their way to give..." [interview, December 10, 2003]

He added that healing is fundamentally about relationships, and so "The work is just a forum to create relationships...it would not be sufficient as something that would help people to heal, by itself." [interview, December 10, 2003] The head of the work programs explained that:

"[Work gives] a sense of purpose, a use of energy toward constructive purpose, and shared experience with other people taking raw material and transforming it on some level, a progression from one point to another and I think it's central to the human community to want to have meaning and production and movement from one stage to another. I think that people who are mentally ill are sadly underserved in that regard in that they spend a lot of time and energy on their internal state...Through getting out of your self you become more able to cope..." [interview, October 29, 2003]

A staff member who had spent many years participating in the work program explained, "Work is a way to pull yourself up by your bootstraps, go out there and support yourself and do things that independent people do. I think work is something that people can derive self-worth from. I think in working you transcend your illness." [interview, December 19, 2003] The executive director explained that guests often have led very successful lives, but are no longer able to do the work they could before, which destroys their self-confidence. "Being able to participate in the work program...is a way of restoring that self-confidence." Ultimately, she explained, getting through work at the Farm each day "allows them to envision doing something more independent, outside of the Farm." [interview, December 12, 2003]

Work, in these comments, is not directly valued for its own sake, but indirectly as an activity in which guests can step beyond their illness, build relationships, and discover self-worth and self-confidence through accomplishing tasks that can be seen to contribute to others. In order for these indirect benefits to become manifest, however, work has to also be valued for its own sake. In other words, work has to be real and grounded in necessity. As the head of the work program said, "I think you lose almost everything when you make work that is not necessary." [interview, October 29, 2003] The ever-present challenge for the Farm, therefore, is to balance the necessity of work with its therapeutic purpose. Sometimes, as will be explored, guests and staff don't feel like this balance is being maintained. Ideally, the work program fosters a sense of belonging, connection and ownership in everyone, and that transforms work into a meaningful, therapeutic experience.

Many guests experience and speak of the positive qualities of the work program and the sense of ownership and connection that it fosters. Chloe, a guest, said:

"I think [Gould Farm's] purpose is to take people who have various mental illnesses, and, through work, get them out of their shells...get them out of their total self-involvement, total self-reflection, all of that can just be a downward spiral, and I think that works brilliantly, I think it works all the time, almost all the time..." [interview, January 10, 2004]

Greg, a guest, spoke of the meditative aspect of work, "It focuses you on something;...it can widen your horizons, bring you into the world instead of having pointless...inner dialogues. Anything that increases interaction in a safe environment can help people who have mental problems improve." [interview, December 13, 2003] Jeremy, a guest, expressed:

"When I was having a difficult time with psychosis, work was a very good way to distract myself, but it was also a very difficult time...Anything was better than listening to my thoughts. Now that I'm not psychotic, work is not used as a distraction anymore; it's more like an example of what life can be outside the Farm." [interview, December 13, 2003]

Ralph, a guest, remembered, "I was very impressed in the garden team when I first came and [the team manager] assigned a couple of people to weed cauliflower, without any supervision. You know maybe he doesn't care about the cauliflower it turns out, or it's trust. Which I think is more likely." [interview, August 18, 2003]

Often it is through the relationships that happen in the work program, within a mixed team of guests and staff, that people feel most empowered. Chloe, a guest, described:

"When I went down to the farm team...they gave me a lot of responsibility pretty quickly, which was nice, and kind of gave me the leeway to work by myself when I wanted to, and have people work with me when I wanted, which felt really good...they weren't treating me like a guest, I wasn't delegated to anything...they really treated me with respect...which was really nice, especially since I didn't feel like I was getting it elsewhere on the Farm." [interview, January 10, 2004]

Work environments can be a place where the divisions between guests and staff become less apparent. As a staff member describing the differences between guests and staff commented, "But you know, when we're here on the Farm and we're working in the garden, that guest might pull 10 weeds and I might pull 2 weeds." [interview, December 22, 2003] A guest described his experience on the Farm team, saying "I basically became a staff member, and [staff] would come and ask me what needed to be done...and they would have me assign jobs for everyone because I knew what they could do, and could keep track of it, and I just became responsible for a whole lot of things." [interview, July 31, 2003]

One of the most important aspects of the work program is often seen to be the way it gives people responsibilities. As Henry, a staff member, commented:

"I think one of the things that is Gould Farm's strong point, is that we put responsibility on each other, including guests. So that the guest is doing pasteurizing and they really have to have some amount of responsibility to that. And they can have their hard times and stuff, but I think that's part of what we do and part of what helps people's self-esteem...being willing to lay these responsibilities on people I think is a way of making us all more known to each other and making us more of an integral community." [interview, August 13, 2003]

As Henry describes, work often functions to draw people together as they share responsibilities in the common project of maintaining the community. This is particularly seen when work teams join forces at times to do a particularly large task, like gathering the hay or picking the squash. This sharing of each other's work is often discussed in terms of "energy," such as— "Tomorrow we'll try to direct some energy toward the beans" or "It would be really great if we could get some energy directed out to the Farm crew to help with the haying."

One of the unique aspects of work on Gould Farm is that it is thoroughly integrated with play, home and life in general, and therefore very flexible. On the farm team in particular, I found that work was generally approached in a relaxed and flexible way. Some days we might be so focused on a particular task that we hardly stopped at all, while other days, if the work was under control, we might take off and go swimming in the heat of the day. Farm team breaks were at times legendary in their length, but provided a very important space for people to feel relaxed and at ease with each other, and develop a sense of camaraderie and team identity. Some of the best breaks were Fridays, when the whole farm team went to Roadside, and we were all treated to drinks and Harvest bars on the farm team budget. I remember one particular Friday when we had a lot of work to accomplish, but ended up staying at Roadside longer than usual. After we got back, the head of the farm team said to me that he usually doesn't like to linger so long on such a busy day, but he felt that people particularly needed the space to feel relaxed that day, and didn't want to add any pressure. [personal communication, September 26, 2003] A guest from another team commented:

"I think the farm team has kept on the purest path, because the farm team, in this kind of joking and loving way, has this reputation of being lazy slackers. And I know you're not...yet there's still...this running joke: 'oh, what's the farm team doing?—oh, another coffee break. Look at them all out sunning themselves. Wow, I wish I was on that team.' And to me, it's like 'damn straight, that is therapeutic, in so many ways that you can't even quantify.'" [interview, December 23, 2003]

The integration of work with play and the rest of life often extends well beyond the end of the regular work day at 4:00. This can be perhaps best illustrated by an excerpt from my fieldwork journal describing what happened after the end of the work day one summer evening:

"After milking the cows, Gus decided to make some hay and the rest of the night was quite busy. He raced around getting things ready and gathering a crowd of people to bring in the hay. The softball teams were diverted to the hayfields, and we all ran around picking up hay and throwing it on the wagon in the early evening light. It was a beautiful scene, and great to see how everyone loved to come out from wherever they were to help with the hay. As we passed people on the way there, we would simply stop, communicate that it was haying time, and they'd hop in. We only got one field done before the bailer broke, but no problem. People went back to the softball game, and eventually Gus did as well. After the last inning, I went and got the homemade ice cream and a handful of spoons and put it all down on the grass; it was an instant feeding frenzy. After the game, as dusk was falling, Aaron, Gus, Roger and I went and chased five loose pigs and the cows that had gotten out. I fed the lambs, cleaned up the milking stuff. Took out the cows by myself. Sometimes it is nice to simply be useful and solitary in your work. Also fun to be part of the crew, doing the necessary stuff." [fieldwork journal, July 1, 2003]

As the end of this entry indicates, I found that work often served me in the way that it was ideally supposed to serve guests. After spending a summer engaged, I reflected again in my fieldwork journal:

"We are working for each other. I guess that's the main difference between this and regular society, where people are strangers working for themselves, even if they're doing the things that enable you to get by. It's not a common project. Having a common project is really an amazingly powerful thing. I think it unleashes humanity's greatest potential to do things. We live in a world that makes it hard to have truly common projects because money is most always involved and that puts up a distance between people. At Gould Farm, so many things can happen as if beyond the world of money, even though money comes to play at the level of the board and big decisions. I think people want to give of themselves beyond the taint of money and come together—they just need a structure that enables them to do so." [fieldwork journal, September 20, 2003]

This perspective reflects my own liberated experience of being able to disconnect work from money, as I gladly worked long hours for the joy and necessity of it. Of course, this perspective doesn't actively incorporate the fact that I was also being supported by a Harvard research grant and my parents, and it certainly doesn't address the experience of guests who pay to come to the Farm and be part of the work program.

Many guests are very aware of the fact that they are "paying to work" as it is often phrased. Ralph, a guest, explained, "A big thing is that almost any work here feels like slave labor, really, but you just have to force yourself to think beyond that and realize how many other things are going on." [interview, August 18, 2003] I asked one guest if his sense of connection to the community was any stronger because of how much work responsibility he had taken on. He replied:

"I don't think it made it that much stronger, the fact that I was helping to support the community, because there's always the issue of frustration, it's like...slave labor, because I'm paying to do the work...It keeps some people from getting motivated." [interview, July 31,2003]

At a community meeting early in my time at the Farm, one guest said that even though he understood on the one hand that everyone had elected to enter this kind of program, and believed in it, it was still hard to be working and yet not saving anything up toward being more autonomous, while living in a situation that so severely limits your personal autonomy. [personal communication, July 2, 2003]

Often the tension surrounding the work program is explicitly debated in terms of whether Gould Farm is a community, where everyone has equal status and might be expected to contribute to the work of the Farm, or an institution in service of the mentally ill, where work should exist solely as it benefits guests. Gabe, a guest, expressed it this way, "I see the Farm a lot of the time on a situational basis sort of treats us either on one hand like mental patients, or, [on the other] completely full-grown adults that need to fulfill their obligations—depending on the situation what serves the Farm best." [interview, December 23, 2001] As he further explained:

"Gould Farm takes more liberties than a lot of other places in really asking people to sacrifice things that are sort of endemic and fundamental to a grown adult, but at the same time expects us...to get up when we're supposed to, to make morning meeting at least three times a week or we can't go to town, to do our chore, do our work." [interview, December 23, 2003]

I found variants on this idea—that Gould Farm treats guests in different ways, depending on the circumstances, for the benefit of the Farm (and not the guests)—expressed by several guests. It reflects the fundamental ambiguity of the Farm's approach to being a therapeutic community in general, and the work program specifically. While putting responsibility on people in the work program can be personally meaningful, as some of the earlier comments indicate, it can also be resented if that same responsibility is not extended to other realms, such as guests being able to go swimming alone. And it can also be resented if it's accompanied by a lack of awareness and compassion for the difficulties that someone might be going through.

As a work leader, one of the most difficult things to balance is how much to push people to work. Personally, this was the hardest part of the job for me as I felt profoundly uncomfortable with the power difference implicit in pushing someone else, usually older than I, to do work. I did this in some form nearly every day, however, as my job involved waking people up in the morning who didn't show up at morning meeting, and leading or encouraging the completion of different tasks. I wrote about this in my fieldwork journal:

"It's such a hard thing, to figure out the balance between doing the work of the Farm and the work of helping guests. And it is so hard to figure out what is helping. The realistic response that one might expect to receive in any work place? The heavy valuing of work? And there's no real dividing line between mental illness and a person's other needs and limitations. Not wanting to work might have nothing or everything to do with mental illness, but we are encountering a whole person. These things get played out in practical working settings, not therapy circles. So work is valued, and it is hard to be valued here by people without working as you can." [fieldwork journal, July 21, 2003]

What I didn't mention in this entry is that the consideration of guests' work ability also gets played out in various staff forums. Because the work program is so central to the program at Gould Farm, staff are regularly assessing guests on their work. The amount or quality of work that guests do is not assessed for its own sake, but as a measure of whether a particular guest is using the work program as staff think they are able. These staff assessments are subjective, as it is of course impossible to judge the extent of someone's inner difficulties, or potential, but they do have very real consequences. Guests might be pushed to work more, or in a more active way, if staff think they are able. There are a couple of commonly held staff opinions on why it is important to put pressure on guests to work: first, that some guests need that form of feedback and expectation to grow, and second, that the work program is fundamentally beneficial, and even more importantly—what Gould Farm offers. It is often beneficial. One guest, Simon, spoke of how being at the Farm opened him up to being more "receptive to the knowledge and wisdom of others" and even allowing him to see the benefit of "[being] pushed in a direction I might initially feel I don't need to be pushed, like to absolutely work on a day when work and the presence of people is painful." [interview, December 3, 2003]

This practice of pushing people to more fully participate in the work program certainly doesn't always work as intended, and at times it is very painful for guests. Simply from the assessment of some guests, it would seem that there are times when the centrality of the work program overshadows the best interest of guests. Greg, a guest, described a situation in which a physical injury that made it difficult for him to work was not, in his view, taken seriously. He explained:

"It was very hard for Gould Farm to understand that there was a certain situation where someone needs to just do nothing for three weeks and rest, because so much of the mission here is the ideology that work heals, but in my case, work doesn't heal; it promotes more injuries." [interview, December 13, 2003]

In Greg's words, the "inflexible dogma [of the work program] was causing me a lot of personal problems within the community, and I would have left the community a long time ago, had I the resources." [interview, December 13, 2003]

Notes and Permissions

1. McKee, William J. *Gould Farm: A Life of Sharing*. Monterey: The William J. Gould Associates, Inc., 1994. 172.

2. Steere, Douglas V. *Work and Contemplation*. From a section titled: "Gould Farm: A Case Study of the Role of Work in a Therapeutic Community." New York: Harper and Brothers, 1957. 96-103. Every effort has been made to trace copyright for this piece. Proper credit will be included in any future printings upon receipt of written notice.

3. Trelawny-Ross, Tamsin. "The Experience of Mental Illness and the Meaning of Work: 'If I'm just sitting, I don't feel I'm living.'" Thesis for M.Sc. in Applied Social Studies. Oxford University, 1999. 36-43. Used with author's permission.

4. Duhon, Anna Melinda. "Liminality in Paradise: A Dialogue with the Gould Farm Community." In partial fulfillment of the requirements for the degree with honors of Bachelor of Arts. Harvard University, 2004. 125-139. Used with author's permission.

Chapter Five

Social Service

Will Gould's only recorded comment about earlier communal experiments, specifically Brook Farm, was a note of warning: that many failed due to their intense inner absorption.[1] Gould Farm, to its credit, has resisted inner institutional absorption, and has not confined itself solely to assisting those with mental health and situational difficulties. As noted earlier, the Farm throughout its history has assisted those in need, from refugees to neighbors in situational distress.

The Farm hosted several distinguished émigrés during World War II. Karin Roon, who had been a prosperous industrial executive in Germany, spent summers at the Farm and was a singer and teacher of relaxation techniques. Her book, "New Ways to Relax," was published in 1949 and again in 1961. Agnes Gould wrote that she was "fairly educating us with her interpretation of Bach and Shubert."[2]

A concentration camp survivor who arrived at the Farm was reported to be "stick-thin" and "distrusting herself and others." She wrote to the Farm 10 years later: "A Sunday morning service in the main house is something one will remember forever; it gives consolation and contentment and a feeling of peace and hope."[3] German-Jewish refugee and actor, Franz Roehn, wrote in 1940: "To concentrate is very hard. If we succeed in doing so, in Mrs. Gould's meditations, we experience a growing faith and confidence in the sanctifying values of life."[4] Roehn appeared in uncredited roles in many movies, including "The Fly" (1958), "The Blue Angel" (1959), and in television series "Father Knows Best" (1960) and "The Adventures of Rin Tin Tin" (1956).[5]

Hugo Heimann was a founder of the Weimar Republic and member of the German Reichstag. He and his wife, Caecilie Levy, arrived in the United States in 1939 and spent time at Gould Farm in 1946. Gould Farmer Samuel Spaulding While wrote a two-page document about Heimann's life. It noted that Heimann and his wife left Germany in 1939 with only $4.00 each to live with their two sons already in the United States. According to Spaulding, he was born in 1859 in Konitz and studied publishing. Heimann returned to Germany in 1884 and bought the Berlin-based publishing firm T. Guttenttag. Heimann sold the firm in 1889, the same year he founded what may have been the first public library in Germany. Heimann was one of the first social democratic members of the Berlin City Council, and was later one of the first social democratic members of the Prussian diet. From 1918 to the end of 1932 he was a member of the Reichstag.[6] His obituary, which appeared in *The New York Times* on February 24, 1951, reported that his daughter had died at Auschwitz.

Gould Farm's assistance with those in need has continued since the 1940s. Between 1960 and 1961 Gould Farm's first executive director, John Snow, an Episcopalian minister, held conferences at the Farm hosting black and white spokesmen. In the mid-1970s the Farm hosted three Vietnamese refugees and, in 1981, it invited inner-city African-American children from Atlanta for respite during the Atlanta Child Murders (1979-1981). Most recently, the Farm hosted a family which lost a loved-one in Iraq.

Perhaps it has been the Farm's historically-rooted, non-sectarian compassion for others that has contributed to the Farm assisting those in need, promoting an atmosphere which Agnes Gould described, writing in 1956, as "quietly religious and broadly humanitarian."[7]

The following selections reflect the Farm's social service orientation, both to its guests and those facing immediate need due to situational and other difficulties. Included are letters from Harry L. Hopkins and Lillian Wald, and Abby A. Rockefeller, the wife of John D. Rockefeller, Jr.

Twenty years before becoming Franklin Delano Roosevelt's director of the Works Progress Administration, Harry L. Hopkins (1890-1946) was supervisor of the Bureau of Family Rehabilitation and Relief of the Department of Family Welfare. From March through October 1915, Gould and Hopkins corresponded about their mutual clients. How Hopkins learned of the Farm is unknown. It is possible, however, that Gould's sister-in-law, Caroline Goodyear, who directed the Chelsea District of the Charity Organization Society of New York City, and would later join Gould Farm in 1916, knew Hopkins. Hopkins speaks of seeing a "Miss Goodyear" in a letter to Gould dated July 26, 1915.

All of Hopkins' referrals apparently lived in New York City. They included a man recovering from an "attack" of pneumonia and "badly in need of the country air," and a woman "very rundown just now and badly in need of rest." Another letter apologized to Gould for a man, whom Hopkins described as having a "pretty wild spirit who is not entirely amenable to civilized treatment." Hopkins, advocating for one prospective guest, wrote that he would be "perfectly willing to do anything that is possible around the house."

The chapter concludes with a story about an exchange, in 1961 at Williams College, between Gould Farm's first Executive Director, The Reverend John Snow, a Farm guest, and Dr. Martin Luther King Jr.

The Selections

The following two letters from Hopkins to Gould, written in 1915, are representative of this correspondence.[8]

THE NEW YORK ASSOCIATION FOR IMPROVING
THE CONDITION OF THE POOR

Bureau of Fresh Air
James H. Hutchens, Superintendent
United Charities Building
105 East 22nd Street
Telephone 7040 Gramercy NEW YORK

NEW YORK, Feb. 1, 1915

Mr. W. J. Gould,
Great Barrington, Mass.

My dear Mr. Gould:

Complications have arisen which will prevent the family which I wrote you about from coming to you, at least in the immediate future. We may send the man himself in perhaps a month.

Our facilities for caring for our convalescent cases have not been as satisfactory as they might be, and I was hoping that next summer we might confine our work entirely to two or three different farms. If you could take all of our men and boys, or whatever other group you feel you could care for the best, it would be a great satisfaction to me. The results were so highly satisfactory last summer, that I wish the Association might use your farm more. I would suggest that you raise the price of your board to at least $5., as $4. does not seem hardly a fair return. In case you feel that you can take any extensive number this summer, I should very much like to come up some week end and talk the matter over with you, or perhaps you are going to be in the city soon, which would be just as satisfactory. I am, however, very anxious to see your place. If you would let me know as soon as possible about this, so that we may complete out arrangements as soon as possible, it would be greatly appreciated.

With very kind regards to Mrs. Gould, I am

Very sincerely yours,
S/Harry L. Hopkins

THE NEW YORK ASSOCIATION FOR IMPROVING
THE CONDITION OF THE POOR

Bureau of Family Rehabilitation and Relief
of the Department of Family Welfare
105 East 22nd St., New York

March 3, 1915

Mr. W. J. Gould
Great Barrington, Mass.

Dear Mr. Gould:

For some unknown reason another letter which I wrote to you several days ago has returned. It was addressed to W. J. Gould, Great Barrington, Massachusetts, but was returned as "not found."

We have a young boy here whom we are anxious to send to the country. He is about sixteen, of Algerian parentage, and was picked up on the streets of New York a few weeks ago sleeping under fruit stands and the like. He has been with us now for some time and shows an inclination to work. He has a tendency, however, to be untruthful, and seems hard to manage though not at all vicious. A woman has become interested in him and has agreed to pay his wages on a farm if a satisfactory place could be secured. She would be willing to pay $10.00 a month salary if you would care to take him for a time. He would of course be expected to work like any other farm hand and he is strong and well able to do that kind of work. He is of course entirely untrained. If things were not satisfactory he could be sent back at any time. We would advance his transportation. It will be appreciated if you will let me know about this as soon as possible.

Very cordially yours,
S/ Harry L. Hopkins
Supervisor

Lillian D. Wald (1867-1940) was an early 20th century social reformer who pioneered public health nursing. A suffragist and founder of the National Association for the Advancement of Colored Persons, Wald is perhaps best known for founding the Henry Street Settlement in 1893, which addressed the social and health needs of the Lower East Side's immigrant population.

Below is a 1920 letter from Wald to Agnes Gould.[9]

HENRY STREET SETTLEMENT
New York

Main House   May twenty-fourth
265 Henry Street   Nineteen Twenty

Dear Mrs. Gould,

I have your letter of May twenty-first and I am very bewildered because I do not know where wisdom lies in regard to Herbert. I have seen Mr. Fincke of the Katona School, but that school is not open during the summer. Meanwhile, I would like to ask you if possible to give me some concrete illustrations of Herbert's "mischief" and his "uncanny tendencies to trouble making." It would help me greatly and when I quoted your letter I was asked to be more definite. Miss Farrell is deeply interested, but also believes that we could work better if we knew just what the demonstrations of these traits were.

Will you be good enough to tell me how far Herbert has gone in school? I had one letter from Miss Blake during the winter and a report of his standing at the time, but I do not know the grade. Is there any disadvantage to Herbert in quitting before the school term ends? That may make a difference in getting him into schools that demand a minimum high school admission training. I am sorry to trouble you because I know that you must be very anxious about Mr. Gould and if, in your judgment, Herbert will not lose by leaving before the school closes, I shall ask you to send him to South Norwalk on Saturday morning, the twenty-ninth. If you will let Miss Knight know by letter or telephone (Telephone Number, Westport 15, Ring 4) she or I will meet him.

I hope very much that the news from Mr. Gould is good and with much appreciation of your interest in Herbert, I am

Very sincerely yours,
S/ Lillian D. Wald

Agnes Gould's fundraising efforts were often conducted among her well-to-do friends in New York City and in Berkshire County. Agnes Gould would later write that Will Gould showed "gratitude for their interest and gracious enthusiasm in telling them about his plans." Gould, however, never made special efforts to solicit their funds.[10]

Below is correspondence between Mrs. Gould and Abby A. Rockefeller (1874-1948), wife of John D. Rockefeller, Jr. (1874-1960). Will Gould reportedly told several at Gould Farm, after a lunch with Rockefeller Jr.: "What he and I are doing is not so different after all. He is trying to spiritualize the material in life; I am trying to materialize the spiritual."[11] Relations between Rockefeller and Will Gould, however, would strain, and Agnes Gould found it difficult to communicate with John D. Rockefeller, Jr.; it was also difficult for her to "recognize the merits of their advice."[12]

William J. McKee writes that Rockefeller, Jr. believed money would "spoil" the Farm and would provide funds only for specific constructive projects, never for meeting current expenses. Later, in 1941, in a letter in which was enclosed a check, Rockefeller let Mrs. Gould know he did not want to hear from her again.

May 20, 1925[13]
Ten West Fifty-Fourth St.

Dear Mrs. Gould:

The news of your dear husband's death came as a great surprise and shock to us Rockefellers and…(illegible).

His was such a very rare spirit and the world so needs men like him that his loss can hardly be measured.

Our son John felt greatly drawn to him and would have liked to be with him this summer, but since learning the sad news, he has made other plans for the trip that he would have been as Gould Farm.

I want to tell you how much I admired your wonderful courage and faith. I know that you will be able, with the inspiration of your husband's life, to carry on his wonderful work.

> Sincerely,
> S/ Abby A. Rockefeller

Abby Rockefeller's son John—John D. Rockefeller, III (1906-1978)—was the recipient of this letter from Mrs. Gould, written January 1933.[14]

GOULD FARM
Great Barrington
Massachusetts

January 23, 1933

Mr. John D. Rockefeller, 3rd
26 Broadway
New York, NY

Dear Mr. Rockefeller:

I wish first of all to assure you that we have fully accepted your father's decision against helping at present towards the expense of erecting a new building for us, and I feel the necessity of special emphasis on this for the very reason that the establishment of a practical working plant is so essential to any balancing of our budget that it is impossible in any comprehensive statement to avoid stressing its importance, and I must be free of the embarrassment of fearing that you may misunderstand my motive in so stressing it, or I can hardly write at all.

From his early boyhood he (William J. Gould) had a vision, gained from the life and teachings of Jesus, of a universal brotherhood among men, and this became in all simplicity the active inspiration of his entire life and work. He held this inspiration with the vision of a statesman and a prophet, as to its application to the needs of society, but he faithfully and consistently worked it out in his own life first. He helped men and women who had broken down in the competitive struggle by getting them to help him, on lines that should bring help to others—thus developing or restoring in them the inspiration and incentive for lack of which their lives had been failures. At the same time, in the very process of reclaiming these depleted lives, he succeeded (by utilizing to the best advantage such powers as they still possessed) in establishing on essentially economic lines a refuge and sanctuary which is, *potentially*, a demonstration of the Kingdom of Heaven on earth.

The unlimited application, the universality of this principle of brotherhood, trite and platitudinous though it may be, must somehow be revivified before Will's work can be comprehended...What saves William Gould from the charge of fanaticism is not any limitation of his vision or of his enthusiasm, but the fact that he "delivered the goods"—that, firm as his convictions were, he still put them to the acid test of practice and experience, and demonstrated their truth and their value in the concrete...

We have no desire for an income that would remove the necessity for our best endeavors in the direction of economy and thrift, and indeed, we recognize the fact that such necessity actually adds immeasurably to the unselfish incentive and therefore to the *therapeutic value* of the tasks in which our guests share, both indoors and out, but we do need a margin for the expense of self-respecting guests for whom no funds are available, and to establish the cure of those whose funds are exhausted before they have had time enough for complete recovery. We believe that a distinction may well be drawn between deficits due to extravagance or bad management, and those due to the heavy pressure of our legitimate work itself—provided we are doing it as well and as economically as it can be done anywhere.

Complete self-support is not our claim, though we keep it hopefully in view as a goal to strive for. We are giving our services primarily to those who cannot afford to pay for the care they need. To claim that such can be cared for on a wholly self-supporting basis would be a contradiction in terms—but we do claim that they are a carefully selected group of worth while human beings, and that the utilization and development which takes place at Gould Farm of the abilities and personality assets, that they all possess in varying directions and degrees, not only contributes markedly towards their own recovery, but is an important economic factor in the work itself. Our own staff has been largely recruited by a process of natural selection from the list of former patients, and this process is continually going on.

Again, while we freely admit that errors of judgment and experimental failures have had some share in our present deficit, we feel justified in taking real encouragement for the future from the extent to which recent difficult and drastic reforms have lowered our per capital expense, and strengthened our hope of an approximately balanced budget...

May I take this opportunity to send you my sincere congratulations upon your new happiness. I have lately received such a charming note from your beautiful bride that this message is prompted by something much deeper than mere conventionality.

Very sincerely yours,
S/ Agnes C. Gould

The following letter apparently followed correspondence between Eleanor Roosevelt and Agnes Gould, in the late 1940s. Here, Gould again writes to Roosevelt asking permission for the Farm to use her name as a sponsor for the Silent Guest program, started by former Massachusetts Governor, Robert F. Bradford, which gave Americans an opportunity to donate to relief efforts in post-war Europe. Five days after Gould's letter, Eleanor Roosevelt wrote this to Mrs. Gould: "In reply to your letter of November 24th, I would be glad to have you use my name on the committee of sponsors for the SILENT GUEST. May I congratulate you on the very helpful work you are dong. Very sincerely yours, Mrs. Franklin D. Roosevelt."[15]

GOULD FARM
November 24, 1952

Mrs. Eleanor Roosevelt
United States Delegation
United Nations Headquarters
New York, NY

Dear Mrs. Roosevelt:

You may remember the work of the SILENT GUEST of 1947 for which you so graciously gave us your name by joining the committee of sponsors. The movement as an organization was discontinued. Now it is being taken up with redoubled force on behalf of the Korean refugees.

We all know of your universal interest and achievements in helping humanity and it is because of this that I venture to turn to you, not withstanding other tremendous demands upon your time and attention.

May we use your name again as a sponsor of the SILENT GUEST? If you can think of any way of helping us to publicize this so that we may reach the largest number possible of our population, we should be most grateful.

Should you desire more detailed information concerning this new appeal, two young friends of mine are working on this project, Mr. and Mrs. John Silard, 300 Washington Avenue, Pleasantville, New York, and would be happy to talk with you.

May I take this opportunity to thank you again for your repeated kindness to our work here at Gould Farm.

Sincerely and always gratefully yours,
S/ Agnes C. Gould

The Massachusetts State Headquarters for Selective Service, in a letter to Rev. Sidney McKee, dated September 8, 1954, confirmed that, given the work at Gould Farm, the Farm would be "eligible as an agency at which civilian work in lieu of induction into the armed services could be performed by those registrants whose claim of conscientious objections is upheld by the local draft board." The letter ended with a caveat that in the Service's experience, few conscientious objectors (CO) had background in farming but that the Service would be glad to make appropriate referrals. A Gould Farmer, who grew up on the Farm in the 1930s and 40s remembered COs during WWII who disliked the Farm's practice of slaughtering its livestock for food.

The following last piece in this chapter is from an 1966 article in the Gould Farm newsletter, titled "We Take Conscientious Objectors."[16]

That the Farm is helping the Selective Service with the knotty problem of conscientious objectors may be news to many readers. Actually, the work has been going on since late 1961 when the Farm learned to its surprise that it had been included in the Army's Civilian Conscientious Objector Work Program. Early in 1962 the first CO, an 18-year old Indiana farm lad, was referred to us. Since then we have had eight young men, among the best boys we have ever had, says director Hampton Prices.

The COs do not come directly but are referred by the United Church of the Brethren, a pacifist religious organization in the middlewestern States with headquarters in Elgin, Ill., and training center in New Windsor, Md.

The draftee who has established his objections to service on religious grounds (political grounds are not accepted) is referred by the Selective Service to the Brethren who send him for 10 weeks' training at New Windsor. After this, he may be assigned to Gould Farm, where he works the full two years of Alternative Service. He is assigned to Farm work according to his capacities, carpentry, or house maintenance, or farming, or animal husbandry. He receives room and board and $10 a month the first year, $15 the second year.

Six COs have been High School graduates and two have been college men. They have adjusted well, been popular. One brought his fiancée here and was married. Two, who have completed their terms and left, write to us as their "Farm family."

As the war in Vietnam intensifies, Gould Farm expects to take more COs.

The following is a story of an exchange, on April 16, 1961, between Gould Farm's first Executive Director, the Reverend John Snow, a Gould Farm guest, and Dr. Martin Luther King Jr. The Reverend and Mary Snow's grandson, Jeremy Lloyd Williamson, wrote this in 2002 for a third-grade project. The meeting with Dr. King occurred at Williams College's Thompson Memorial Chapel where Dr. King had just lectured. While there is no evidence that Dr. King ever visited Gould Farm, it sometimes served as a place of respite for those working in the Civil Rights Movement.

Mary Snow recalled the Farm holding retreats around this time for Civil Rights workers dealing with the emotional stress from their activities. Those who came to Gould Farm included an African American Episcopal priest, and member of the Montgomery Bus Boycott Steering Committee, whose life and that of his family were repeatedly threatened. Another visitor was a woman (whose husband was an official in FDR's New Deal) and whose family, living in Alabama, had been totally ostracized. Psychiatrist Erik Erikson, upon Snow's invitation, attended these retreats.

The Reverend Snow, born in 1928 in Washington D.C., was educated at Harvard, the US Navy medical corps, Columbia University, and the former Episcopal Theological School. After his time as Director of Gould Farm (1960-1962) he became pastor at Christ Church in Cambridge, Massachusetts. He later served as chaplain at Princeton University and then as professor of pastoral theology at the Episcopal Theological School (later to become Episcopal Divinity School) in Cambridge where he and his wife, Mary, raised their four children. He died in November of 2008.

Jeremy Lloyd Williamson based this account on phone interviews with his grandfather and with the assistance of his mother and former member of the Gould Farm staff, Lydia Snow. Jeremy was raised in Evanston, Illinois, and is now pursuing an Automotive Engineering/Technology degree at Ferris State University in Michigan.[17]

The Amazing John Snow: A Biography

My grandpa John Snow was the director of a place for people who had nervous breakdowns or other bad trouble in their live. The place was called Gould Farm. Although it may seem strange, it was through his work at this place that John met an amazing man of peace. This is the story of that important meeting and how it happened. At the same time my grandpa was working at Gould Farm, Reverend Robert Dubois (an African American Episcopal priest from Montgomery, Alabama) was staying there. He was the secretary of the Montgomery Improvement Association. The MIA was a group of people who worked to defend the rights of black people in Montgomery after Rosa Parks was arrested; Martin Luther King Jr. was the head of the MIA. Well, my grandpa and Robert Dubois became friends. When they read in the paper that Martin Luther King, Jr. was coming to preach and give a lecture at Williams College, they drove over there to hear the sermon and lecture on non-violent direct action. After the discussion was over, Bob introduced my grandpa to Martin Luther King, Jr. My grandpa, Reverend King and Bob talked for a long time afterwards. They talked about racism in America and the freedom movement. They also talked about what white people like my grandpa John could do to help this freedom movement. Lastly, they talked about what could be done at Gould Farm to help this important movement. After they were done talking, my grandpa brought a lady from Gould Farm over to talk to Dr. King. This lady never talked to anyone and she was a miserable person. For some reason, she really wanted to talk to Dr. King. He took her aside and talked to her for twenty minutes. She cheered up a lot; a very famous man giving her all of his attention was very helpful to her. It tells you about the sort of person Dr. King was. This whole experience moved my grandpa enormously at the time.

Jeremy Williamson, 3rd grade, Dawes School

Notes and Permissions

1. McKee, William J. *Gould Farm: A Life of Sharing*. Monterey: The William J. Gould Associates, Inc., 1994. 72.

2. Ibid. 119

3. Ibid. 259

4. Ibid. 262

5. See http://www.imdb.com. Accessed April 5, 2013.

6. Spaulding, Samuel. U.d. "Hugo Heimann". Used with permission: The William J. Gould Associates, Inc. Every effort has been made to trace copyright. Proper credit will be included in any future printings upon receipt of written notice.

7. McKee, William J. *op cit*. 257.

8. Used with permission from Dr. June Hopkins and from The William J. Gould Associates, Inc.

9. Used with permission from Henry Street Settlement and from The William J. Gould Associates, Inc.

10. McKee, William. J. *op cit*. 21.

11. Ibid. 68.

12. Ibid. 216.

13. Every effort has been made to trace copyright. Proper credit will be included in any future printings upon receipt of written notice.

14. Used with permission: The William J. Gould Associates, Inc.

15. Used with permission: The William J. Gould Associates, Inc.

16. Used with permission: The William J. Gould Associates, Inc.

17. Used with author's permission. I thank Reverend Snow's widow, Mary Snow, their daughter, Lydia Snow, and the Williams College Archives and Special Collections for providing information for this entry.

Chapter Six

Community

The following includes studies of the Farm's communal dimensions from religious and sociological perspectives.

Gould Farm intrigued Sociologist Henrik Infield. Unlike other communities, Gould Farm, Infield observed in 1955, was not interested in developing a large permanent membership but rather keeping permanent staff small in the service of the guests.

> (U)nlike other groups that are largely self-centered, (Gould Farm) is the only one of its kind that is essentially self-transcendent... By turning community into an instrument of therapy, it completely reversed the membership policy usual in other communitarian groups.[1]

In the end, after the sociometric tests and interviews Infield conducted at the Farm, he encouraged the Farm to attract younger people, for the survival and continuity of the community; despite finding "group solidarity" somewhat lacking, Infield attributed the Farm's "atmosphere of kindness" to the Farm's success.[2]

James Luther Adams was a renowned Harvard Divinity School professor, ethicist, activist, and long-time Gould Farm Board member. His essay, "Notes on the Study of Gould Farm," is a reflection of Infield's study. Here, Adams recognized that "(a) community of this sort cannot grow in wisdom and stature without taking inventory from time to time: Gould Farm is aware of this fact." He concludes his essay with these words:

> In the Gould Farm of the future there will be, as in the past, new treasures as well as old. Indeed, without new treasures the old ones are themselves likely to disappear. This fact calls for a risking faith. Gould Farm cherishes its past, but it also moves venturingly into the burgeoning present. Its faith is in a living God. Fellowship with Him is life—New Life.[3]

Princeton Theological Seminary Professor, Seward Hiltner, after recalling when there was suspicion in the relationship between "health" and "faith," acknowledges here that the two are not mutually exclusive and that Gould Farm acknowledged and practiced this relationship, while preserving the integrity of both. As Hiltner writes:

> As I knew Mrs. Gould, for instance, it was quite clear that she did not expect any guest at the farm to lose his troubles immediately and automatically at the drop of a Bible or the bending of a knee. Yet she was convinced that, if her own faith and that of her colleagues was genuine, then it would make each of them more personally attentive to the needs of every one, more ready to supply the community so sorely needed in countering loneliness, and thus, eventually and often indirectly, with therapeutic results.[4]

Kim Hines' thesis explores the tensions, at Gould Farm, between mutuality (the meeting and sharing of mutual needs between guests and staff) and philanthropy (the rehabilitative program for which guests arrive at the Farm). Hines, a former Gould Farm staff member, suggests that while the interplay between mutuality and philanthropy reaches a moral ideal when no distinctions between guests and staff are made, this ideal is rarely met due to the non-egalitarian "constraints" inherent to the rehabilitative setting. Her anecdotal research reports "glimmers of mutuality" experienced by various community members when such constraints are balanced by the communal aspects of Gould Farm.

Neurologist and author, Oliver Sacks, who was an honorary guest at a Gould Farm function in New York City in 2006, while cautioning against romanticizing the positive roles asylums played in the past, recognizes, in this article, the hazards of relying too much on a strict chemical model of mental illness:

> We forgot the benign aspects of asylums, or perhaps we felt we could no longer afford to pay for them: the spaciousness and sense of community, the place for work and play, and for the gradual learning of social and vocational skills—a safe haven that state hospitals were well-equipped to provide.[5]

Sacks saw in Gould Farm and CooperRiis (see Virgil Stucker's essay for more on CooperRiis) residential communities which derived historically "from the asylums and the therapeutic farm communities of the nineteenth century."

THE SELECTIONS

Sociologist Henrik F. Infield (1901-1970), who fled 1930s Vienna to Palestine, wrote numerous books on the sociology of cooperation. He was Director of the Rural Settlement Institute, New York, in the 1940s.

The following is an excerpt from an essay about Gould Farm from Infield's *The American Intentional Communities: Study on the Sociology of Cooperation* (1955).[6] Footnotes from the original have been omitted here.

GOULD FARM: A THERAPEUTIC COOPERATIVE COMMUNITY

The Setting of the Study

The therapeutic community that calls itself Gould Farm—after the name of its founder William Gould—occupies among the intentional communities of America a position unique in more than one respect. Being in existence now for more than forty years, it is the oldest among them. It derives its income neither from agriculture nor from the production of goods and commodities but from the care it disinterestedly offers to people in need of physical and mental recuperation. And, by using community as an instrument of therapy, unlike the other American communities, it serves to satisfy a need that, unfortunately, is becoming increasingly urgent in these our troubled times.

The story of Gould Farm, in its beginnings, resembles that of many of the religious Utopian colonies of the past. It owes its origin to a motive recurrent in the history of these groups, an ardent belief that "life can be lived after the pattern of the Sermon of the Mount." However, unlike the leaders of religious communities such as Bethel, Aurora, Amana, or Oneida, the man who became the founder of Gould Farm, stirred by similar ideas, did not thereupon proceed to stage his own version of the early Christian apostolic community. His approach was less pretentious and more humble. Described by one who knew him well as "extremely kind and outgoing," a man "always full of fun" who "put everyone at his ease," he appears to have steered clear of all doctrinarianism. To profess the teachings of Christ to him apparently meant to practice them in one's daily relations of man to man. He had, it would seem, not much use for big words like 'sacrifice' and 'love', and cared more for what might be called their "operational" equivalents, service and kindness. Though deeply inspired, a pragmatic attitude of this kind is not likely to produce a sect, a creed, an ideology, of any preconceived notions of community. Gould Farm originated not from a blueprint, nor even from a clear-cut intention as to its form. It grew "by itself," shaped only by the will of its founder to serve those who were in need of help.

At the time William Gould moved to the present site of the Farm, in the Berkshires, near Great Barrington, Massachusetts, he had accumulated a good deal of experience with boys' camps, and had come to believe that life in healthy and friendly surroundings, away from the city, could do wonders for people of all ages. A friend lent him the eleven hundred dollars he needed to purchase the property, an abandoned farm. Together with his wife and some relatives, he went to work, tidying up the place and readying it for his "guests."

What held the little group together, we are told, was William Gould's extraordinary ability to create an atmosphere "of harmony and unity and understanding and oneness of a true family." If he had in mind any specific form for his group, it was exactly this, that it shape itself in the image of a large loving family. He emphasized, we learn, "the sacredness of the family, and put its profound, intrinsic holiness above anything else, even the church."

Some of the people who found their way to Gould Farm stayed on and in turn learned to help others. This development was not preconceived. It grew naturally out of the reigning spirit of mutual aid. In welcoming it, William Gould intuitively anticipated a technique advocated decades later by one of the pioneers of group-psychotherapy, Harry Stack Sullivan, who, as pointed out in a recent study, "found that a sympathetic interpersonal environment went far toward achieving personality reorganization. By 'sympathetic environment' he meant a group of persons, some psychotic, some relatively sane, in the latter of whom there is conscious formulation of community with the more disordered ones...the situation is one of education not by verbal teaching but by communal experience."

It is necessary to stress, however, that the basic motives of William Gould were not scientific. His intent and extraordinary therapeutic capacity were oriented rather by a deeply religious "feeling and being." He was guided, we are told, by the two commandments of "service to God and love thy neighbor as thyself," and by the ardent conviction that the mental climate created by a group of people who worked and lived together in the spirit of kindness was a powerful curative agent.

Gould Farm was founded in 1913. By 1925 it had already acquired a unique reputation. Referring to it, the head of a State Hospital felt compelled to attest: "We don't know of any other place where patients are so effectively and so quickly rehabilitated." The "family" was growing and expanding, attracting a widening circle of friends and supporters, when the group found itself cruelly deprived of its leader. William Gould died suddenly, at the age of 58, while fighting a forest fire. Under the leadership of his widow the group summoned the strength to continue and, a few years later, formed the association that, under the name of The William J. Gould Associates, Inc., to this day carries on the work in his spirit.

By the time of the study, in 1954, the physical plant of the community had grown to a considerable size. In addition to a two-story Main House—with office space, thirty bedrooms, eight bathrooms, a large hall serving as a central room, a smaller one for religious services, concerts, lectures and group meetings—the property includes at present twenty smaller or larger cottages, some of them equipped with heating systems for year-round occupancy, a dairy barn with a pasteurizing plant, chicken coops, a one-room bungalow for shop-work, and several utility sheds. The group owns 550 acres of land, mostly densely wooded hills, only partly suited for cultivation. Farming is practiced rather for the sake of work therapy than gain, but manages to supply the kitchen with eggs and poultry, milk, cream and vegetables.

The number of people that can be accommodated at one time varies with the seasons, from more than a hundred in the summer to fifty or, at the most, sixty, in the winter. Some of the guests, especially those who come in the summer, need only a rest, a change of environment. They may be overtired mothers in need of a breathing spell away from their families; newly arrived, bewildered refugees with little or no funds, at a loss in the new surroundings; or, as in one instance, a group of musicians unable to afford a more expensive vacation. There are also children or young people who, for one reason or another, cannot live up to the standards of their own age, who feel unhappy and misunderstood, and who would be out of place in a confining institution. The majority, however, are people in more serious difficulties. They come from mental hospitals, on the recommendation of their physician, a welfare agency, a church group, or by way of personal contact. In each case application must be made by letter, containing a personal reference, a medical history, and a certificate attesting that the applicant is free from communicable disease. Persons who need special treatment or close supervision or who are incapacitated to the point of not being able to take care of their room and to appear at meals in the dining room, generally are not admitted.

When an applicant is accepted, preparations are made for his reception that take into consideration the probable needs of the new arrival, whether he will need guidance or better be left alone for a time, what kind of work and how much he should be induced to take up, and so on. Usually, one of the staff or, occasionally, another guest is assigned to meet him or her at the train. The task of the host is to reassure the new arrival, to alleviate as far as possible his more or less natural apprehensions, to familiarize him with the daily routines he is to follow, and to acquaint him with such taboos as smoking in the bedrooms, or alcohol in any place. Above all, the host tries to communicate to the newcomers a sense of Gould Farm's family spirit and to make him feel at home.

After a day or two, or whenever he feels ready, the guest begins to take part in the different activities. Since hired help is kept at a minimum, there is a great deal of opportunity for real work, be it in the kitchen and around the house, in the barn, the dairy, the chicken house, in the fields or in the gardens. The guest may join one of the study groups on current events, creative writing, music, or languages; he may participate in social activities, in picnicking, hiking, or visiting nearby art-centers in the summer, or in skiing and ice-skating in the winter; or take part in such other entertainment as community singing, a private movie show, or square dancing.

All activities are essentially optional, including work as well as attendance at the regular Sunday morning service, consisting of hymn-singing and a discourse by a member of the staff or by a visitor. The only regularity that, for obvious reasons, must be insisted upon is attendance at meals. These are all taken in common, with the exception of breakfast which some of those who live in the cottages may arrange to have at home. The seating of the guests is not left to chance, but is planned with some care, especially in cases that need such attention.

In addition to a strong sense of mutuality, it is probably this spirit of kind-natured but by no means careless informality, so distinct from that of any mental hospital or sanatorium, that makes the stay at Gould Farm salutary for so many. In the words of one visitor: "Whatever you are like when you come, a strange magic soon catches hold of you and makes you over. You may yourself be in sore need, of body or mind or soul…yet you find you can help others, and while you do so you find you are helping yourself." There are no fixed rules about the length of stay, the decisive criterion being the need of the guest. However, after two weeks each case is re-examined in the light of this "probation" period. If it is felt that the guest has no chance of profiting from a further stay, the recommending agency is notified and asked to recall him. Those who may stay on, do so on the average for a period of four to six weeks. Some come only for a few days, others keep returning from time to time, and a few may join the staff or become permanent residents. Some of the latter, mostly at or of retiring age, have built cottages of their own which, when not occupied, are at the disposal of the community and become its property at the death of the owner.

True to the nature of its origin, Gould Farm conducts its affairs not in the interest of economic gain or profit, but in the spirit of service. This makes rules and regulations a matter of secondary concern. The preamble of the by-laws defines the community as a cooperative, which it certainly is in fact, but not in the legal sense of adherence to the Rochdale Principles. Again, in practice rather than by formal stipulation, cooperation is quite comprehensive, though there is no common purse. In the spirit of the classical formula, everybody contributes according to his best abilities and receives his share according to his needs. Salaries, if paid, are just sufficient for maintenance, while many of the staff who have sources of income, a pension, social security, or annuities, virtually volunteer their services. There being no medical staff besides nurses, administrative and managing expenses can be kept low. In spite of the fact that the maximum fee asked is $35 a week and that no one is denied care because of financial considerations, the community is able to cover three-fourths of its budget from fees paid by the guests. The rest is supplied by occasional donations, bequests, and the more regular contributions, from one dollar up, of the more than a thousand members of the loose organization known as The Friends of Gould Farm. Thus, in its own humble but to all appearances highly effective way, the group is able not only to continue but to expand its activities from year to year, and to offer its services to a steadily increasing number of people in need of a "half-way house" between outright hospitalization and full recovery. According to the latest published report, a total of five hundred and ninety-four people, the largest number on record so far, visited Gould Farm in 1953. Of these, three hundred and forty-six were people in need of therapeutic attention, or "guests."

The Central Issue

Unlike the studies of other experimental groups, the Zionist Training Farms, the French communities of work, or the two other intentional communities, Campanella and Macedonia, that of Gould Farm was not made upon the request of the group itself. The spiritual climate created by William Gould's genius for kindness and, after his death, devoutly sustained by his associates and successors, as well as the therapeutic intent of the community seems to leave little occasion for such requests. Like all devoted healers, the associates tend to disregard troubles of their own and, when perplexities become too great, to look for guidance in the spirit that had animated William Gould himself.

A study of Gould Farm appeared desirable, however, for several reasons. As it presented itself on our first visit, in October 1953, it was a community of a unique kind, unlike any other encountered in all our studies. By turning community into an instrument of therapy it completely reversed the membership policy usual in other communitarian groups. Instead of trying to build up a large body of permanent members and admitting new ones after careful scrutiny and probation, Gould Farm keeps the permanent part of the community relatively small as compared to the part of the "family" that is transient. In other words, unlike other groups that are largely self-centered, it is the only one of its kind that is essentially self-transcendent. Although steeped in faith, Gould Farm at the same time is non-sectarian, welcoming as it does people of all creeds, including those with no creed at all; and it is modern in the sense that, like the Kibbutzim or the French communities of work, it came into existence in response to an urgent need that could not be satisfied at all, or at least not as well, by individual action. In this way, and by sheer intuition, it would seem, it has developed a design that suggests significant solutions to some of the basic problems besetting psychotherapy on the one side, and the intentional communities in America, on the other. Last but not least, the fact that it has already outlasted all but the strictly sectarian communities and still is far from showing any signs of decline could be accepted as sufficient proof that the course it has taken is sound and viable and that the type of community it has created is capable of survival and perpetuation.

The idea of serving as an object of scientific exploration did not seem to be particularly inviting to the people of Gould Farm. Letting themselves, like their founder, be motivated chiefly by religious "feeling and being," they could not see much use or feel any particular need for the kind of rational group self-examination provided by sociological testing. However, once they realized that the important example they were setting could be better understood and more widely emulated on the strength of a more objective interpretation, they changed their minds and readily consented to the study...

It became possible to do so thanks largely to the assistance of Dr. Haigh and a group of graduate students of his seminar for psychology at Springfield College. With the help of Dr. Haigh, who, having been in contact with Gould Farm prior to the study, enjoyed its confidence, it was possible to induce the group to form a committee, consisting of four of its staff members, that shared with the researchers the responsibility for preparing the group for the tests. A number of meetings were held with this committee, as well as with other staff-members, between the time the project was first broached to the group, towards the end of December 1953, and the actual application of the tests, early in April 1954.

Once the group, through their spokesmen, the committee which kept the associates and the guests fully informed about the progress of the discussions, had caught on to the value of the 'reexamination,' it began to view itself more critically. Issues that had been glossed over before were no longer evaded. A question of principal importance, concerning the actual mutuality between the associates and the guests, came into focus. Since community was the chief therapeutic implement of the group, the degree of mutuality between the associates and the guests could clearly be seen as an index of its effectiveness. It turned out that the group was, by far, less certain of itself in this respect than its self-definition as 'one large family' meant to imply. As a matter of fact, those responsible for the conduct of affairs admitted that for some time already they had felt apprehension on this account. They welcomed, therefore, the light the tests promised to throw on this matter. This focusing of the study on an issue crucial to the group itself made the study more meaningful for all concerned. Instead of confining itself to cold fact-finding, it assumed its proper character of self-exploratory group-action.

At the time of the study the total population of Gould Farm consisted of altogether seventy-two people. According to their status they were listed as follows: fifteen associates, of whom virtually all had some function in the group; six members the staff; five permanent residents; and forty-six guests. Sociologically, the population of Gould Farm may be divided into two distinct parts: the permanent members of the community, a sector that remains relatively constant and includes all the associates, the staff, and the permanent residents, on the one hand; and the more fluctuating body of the guests, on the other.

Given the mental and, in quite a few instances, the physical state of the guests, the participation of the two different sectors, as could have been expected, was quite uneven. While the members took an active interest in the study and made every effort to participate, only less than half of the guests were capable or willing to do so. Nevertheless, the results proved to be quite adequate for the purposes of the study. They yielded sufficient insight into the social configuration of the community and lent themselves to a relevant exploration of the central issue at stake, the objective assessment of the mutuality existing between the constant sector of the community on the one side, and its beneficiaries on the other. It might be well, in the interest of such exploration, to consider separately the findings of the two sectors. This procedure should facilitate a comparison between the two sub-groups, the members and the guests, and lead to a more pertinent interpretation of the results.

Interpretation

As the tabulation of the results shows, in and by themselves, the findings of the sociometric test seem to reveal substantial weaknesses in Gould Farm's group structure. As far as it can be traced in measurable terms, the mutuality between the guests and the members appears to be too tenuous to justify the claim that Gould Farm achieves its therapeutic effect by including all in the intimacy of a "large family." The guests, though they are in the community, seem to be only to a negligible degree of it.

That the fault, if one has to be assumed, does not lie with the guests is indicated by the findings of two other devices of the battery, the personal questionnaire and the cooperative potential test. As the comparison of personal data shows, though there are some differences between the members and the guests, both are essentially similar in outlook and background. There is, similarly, little difference between the members and the guests with regard to their group score on the cooperative potential test. In the light of these findings there is little in the personal background or the potential capacity for cooperation of the guests to justify the scantiness of visible ties between them and the members. It would seem then that by sheer reduction it is the latter who must accept the blame for failing to develop and to cultivate such ties.

However, the results of the obstacles test tend to complicate the issue. There are, first, the ratings on happiness that indicate that, on the whole, the guests are just as happy at Gould Farm as are the members. There is also, and even more to the point, the relatively large number of guests who, in response to the last question of this test, volunteer statements that in glowing terms testify to the therapeutic effect of Gould Farm. A few excerpts should demonstrate this: "My adjustment to Gould Farm was not immediate," says GB, "but I had the feeling of belonging right away. The feeling of kindness and happiness and warmth so evident from the first day." Or, as GR puts it:

"Gould Farm has given me kindliness and understanding which have made me grateful and happy…" Similar statements, briefer or longer, can be quoted in addition, such as "I have been very happy here" (GC); "We work as a community and that's fine" (GL); or, even more succinctly "Now I live here it's a dream come true" (GB). Perhaps most revealing is the one by GD: "For myself I want increased capacity for understanding people. I am working toward this end by talking with the wise ones here and by reading, as well as by trying to be friendly to those who need understanding… I am deeply grateful to Gould Farm friends and *atmosphere* for help in achieving this desire."

We have underlined "atmosphere" because the term might help us to resolve the seeming contradiction between these statements, which unmistakably attest to the community's effect on the guests, and the findings of the sociometric test, which tend to disparage it. If, as we believe, the statements are as spontaneous and sincere as the findings are correct, we seem to be faced with something of a dilemma. We may, on the one hand, try to escape it by recalling the large number of guests who kept shy of the tests and by assuming that many of them were also among the least happy at Gould Farm. It might be argued, however, that those who failed to take part in the study were also those whose condition makes their opinions least relevant. We may try, on the other hand, to find a way out by questioning the pertinence of our sociometric evaluation. In the light of similar findings in other groups, we may argue, the number of mutual choices between the members and the guests is not at all as insignificant as it appears to be. Compared with the findings at Clermont, where only one mutual choice could be discovered between the "productifs" on the one side, and the "familiers" on the other, Gould Farm's three such choices look far from poor. However, it must be remembered that the members of Clermont live dispersed throughout a city and that those who, like the "familiers" do not work in the factory see the companions only from time to time; while at Gould Farm, the members and the guests live and do things together all the time. It is true that if we take into consideration the condition of the guests, particularly as it expresses itself in their present preoccupation with self-oriented wants, Gould Farm's ability to stimulate them at all into participation becomes remarkable. Still, it cannot be denied that it falls short of the professed goal of integrating all who join the community into "one large family."

It is the concept of "atmosphere" that offers rescue from the dilemma by helping to reconcile the apparent opposites. There is no necessity to deny that, as far as they go, the findings of the tests are correct and useful, even if one has to admit that they are useful and correct only as far as they go. No living organism, whether individual or social, can be fully comprehended in quantitative terms alone. The imponderables of "feeling and living" suggest the necessary, and possibly desirable, limitations of measurement. In the case of Gould Farm, those imponderables help explain the apparent contradiction between the sociometric findings, on the one side, and the evidence of therapeutic effect, on the other. The living faith of Gould Farm is based on what might be called an "operational" interpretation of the Christian teachings. In this interpretation, "love thy neighbor as thyself" assumes a direct and practicable meaning that might be transcribed as "be kind to your neighbor and trust that he will respond in kind;" and the rule "do unto others as you want them to do unto you" becomes "whatever you do unto another, do it with kindness." It is this atmosphere of kindness, created by its founder and effectively sustained by his associates, that helps explain why Gould Farm is capable of exerting its beneficial effect in spite of—or possibly without requiring—a degree of sociometric integration that is generally accepted as a mark of group coherence. It might be worth noting that of all the groups studied Gould Farm is the only that, on the three criteria found to be most pertinent, produces no "star." There is, perhaps, a lesson here that other communities, especially those of the "ideological" kind—and possibly all society—can learn from Gould Farm. Unlike plain and simple kindness and its concomitants, patience and consideration, love is a too ambiguous and too dangerously ambivalent, a too complex and potentially explosive an emotion to serve as a dependable binding-force for a community. The more intensive it becomes, the greater its danger of producing conflict and of ending in hatred. Even at its best, love cannot be forced; while kindliness can be willed. Whereas at Gould Farm, it reigns supreme, it removes the extremes and creates a social atmosphere conducive to making the old active, the ailing well, and the healthy better.

Effects of the Study

The results of the study were presented in a meeting attended by most of the permanent members and four of the guests, altogether twenty-seven persons. At that time, August 1954, only a rough analysis of the data could be offered, but the conclusions reached were essentially the same as those just discussed. The procedure was identical with that observed in other groups. It was based on an explanation of the mechanism of the tests and a display of the tabulated results. As in most of the other groups, the manifest consensus of those present acknowledged the validity of the interpretation by giving the discussion that followed a diagnostic turn. Among the subjects brought up in the discussion two in particular might be worth mentioning. One concerned the possible use of all or some of the tests as part of the admission procedure. Although the therapy Gould Farm offers defies by its very nature any purely statistical evaluation, the group itself felt that it could profit from a more accurate processing of relevant data. Information secured by the tests administered upon arrival and again upon departure of a guest, it was thought, could render more accurate insight into whether, to what degree, and in what specific way his stay in the community had achieved its purpose. Serious consideration, therefore, was given to this possibility.

Of more immediate urgency was the second issue. It concerned the very survival and continued existence of the community. As the findings showed, Gould Farm was doing quite well, on the whole. Failings such as suggested by the members in their frequent mention on the obstacles test of the need for improvement in the management of the community, for enlarging the physical facilities, increasing the staff and intensifying the therapeutic activities, were relatively insignificant. They gave added weight to some of the more negative findings of the study, but, like these, they appeared to be counterbalanced by the positive effects of the atmosphere of kindness. What could give cause for real concern was the difficulty the associates apparently had not so much in attracting as in holding younger people. At the very time of the study, the two youngest associates, a couple, aN and aO, had just tendered their resignation. They had, as their tests showed, played an important and beneficial role in the community. Nevertheless, after being with the community for three years, and although everybody wanted them to stay, they were leaving, creating a veritable crisis among the associates.

As the personal data indicate, the youngest associate joined the group ten years ago; next in tenure were two associates with 14 years of residence; and the average length of stay for all associates was 21.2 years. Given the average age of 67.1 for the old-time associates, this meant that the original group was in danger of seeing its ranks thinned without replacement. As the sociometric findings show, the difficulty—unlike in another group, the French community of Valdieu—could not be blamed on over-integration. There are probably several factors to which the adverse effect upon newcomers could be traced; but whatever may be the reasons, ways and means are obviously needed to attract new and younger people and to groom them for succession if the community is to continue beyond the life span of the present associates. With the founder gone, the experience of the original associates cannot be repeated. More rational, "objective" methods will have to replace the original intuitive approach. A research and training center for younger people interested in community therapy, it was suggested, would serve best to create an influx of the needed new blood and in this way insure the continuance of the group.

That the remarkable spirit of the present associates is in no way adverse to such suggestions is attested by their reaction to the study as a whole. While still in progress its "stimulating and thought provoking" effect was noted in the news-letter of the group. In the annual report for 1953, the following reference was made to the study: "While in the past articles have been written and published about the work here, we now find ourselves the subject of a careful and intensive study to determine the factors that make it possible for Gould Farm to continue its activities. The recognition of a widespread need for similar centers comes to us from doctors, ministers, social agencies, and individuals scattered throughout the country. From time to time there is someone or there is a group of persons embarking on a similar project. For their use and for that of others to come it is hoped that practical results will follow from this study." Significantly, the spirit in which the study was being conducted was seen to be in harmony with the ideas of the late founder: "For himself," it was stated in the same report by one who worked with William Gould in closest contact for many years, "the experience would have held the greatest possible delight. In the interested students now exploring Gould Farm he would have met with the kind of response for which he hungered all his life. For those in residence who are working together in the daily carrying of responsibility and the long-time formulation of future plans the challenge has been direct and stirring. The re-examination of common ideas and ideals is the best possible tonic for the individual worker and for the group."

The process of clarification thus proved to be "constructive and helpful as well as interesting" to the group. Apparently to its own surprise it began to realize things about itself of which it had not been aware before. As one of the staff members observed in one of the Farm's newsletters: "Like the man who was surprised and delighted to discover he had been speaking prose all his life, Gould Farm has only recently discovered, after forty years of service to its fellowmen, that it is an intentional community and that it has been practicing an effective form of group therapy all these years."

All in all, in the case of Gould Farm, sociological counseling, aided by the application of the battery, was able to accomplish, it would seem, its chief purpose of helping the group to know itself better and of enabling it to carry on more effectively its very significant task. With characteristic kindness, the group itself was pleased to acknowledge this. The annual report of 1954, which appeared after completion of the study, states that the "suggestions made" and "since carried out" have brought the group a good deal of improvement and "have led to a closer integration of the community as a whole."

James Luther Adams (1902-1994), professor of theology at the University of Chicago and, later, Harvard Divinity School, was the country's foremost theologian of Social Christian Ethics and voluntary association. Adams came to know Gould Farm through Dr. Sydney Snow, President of Meadville Theological School, who sent groups of Meadville students to Gould Farm each summer. Dr. Adams, who sat on both the faculty of Meadville Lombard Theological School and the University of Chicago Divinity School at the time he wrote this article, served on Gould Farm's Board of Directors from the 1960s through the 1980s.

The following is an essay by Adams, which appeared in "*Voluntary Associations: Socio-cultural Analyses and Theological Interpretation*" (1986).[7]

NOTES ON THE STUDY OF GOULD FARM (1955-1956)

"Fellowship is life; lack of fellowship is death." This is a line from a contemporary "psalm." It states the religious principle in the name of which Gould Farm has labored since the time of its founding. It expresses the insight of the founder, William Gould, who lost his life fighting a forest fire on the Farm but whose spirit still informs the way of life pursued there. For William Gould, his associates, and his successors the meaning and fullness of life are to be realized in responsiveness to the divine power that gives birth to fellowship, to fellowship in freedom. For them the substance of religion is not only communion between the individual soul and God. It is also a horizontal relation between man and man under God in a covenanted community: in principle religious commitment must issue in an appropriate pattern of social life and institution. In a world of extreme complexity where the personal element of "I and Thou" is constantly threatened, Gould Farm aims to be that pattern—a pattern of fellowship in worship, in work, in play, and in healing.

For over forty years Gould Farm has been that unique thing which today is called an "intentional community;" it is a deliberately formed community in which people live together sharing, receiving, and incarnating religious vision. In the world today there are numerous intentional communities. But Gould Farm is a unique species of this unique genus. Most intentional communities are short-lived; they are proud if they can survive for a decade. Gould Farm is now in its forty-second year. The uniqueness of the Farm is to be discerned not only in its survival power. With its extended, old New England farmhouse surrounded by numerous attractive cottages nestling in the fair Berkshire hills near Great Barrington, Massachusetts, Gould Farm, imbued by the quality of its purpose, has what is called "the spirit of a place." This spirit combines the outlook of an intentional community with the simplicity, the frugality, and the individualism of rural New England.

Gould Farm is a fellowship not only for the inner "family" of members who maintain the community. It is open to "outsiders," to people who in distress of mind or spirit wish for a time to participate in a community of affection that gives renewed meaning and depth to life. Gould Farm, in short, is a therapeutic community. It does not live merely for itself, as many intentional communities have done. It is a "self-transcending" community. To all sorts of people it offers healing, the healing that can only emerge, as William Gould believed and showed, in the atmosphere of harmony and mutual aid which characterizes the true family. The Farm has been a haven not only for those who in sickness of spirit desperately needed the fellowship that is new life but also for those who, like the many refugees from Europe of the past two decades, needed a place in which to get new bearings and a new start in a strange land. Many have come with nothing or little in hand to pay for shelter. For others the maximum weekly fee is a very modest one.

The extent of the fellowship that has been brought to birth through Gould

Farm is in part evident from the fact that in 1954…(a) daily average of 71 people lived at the Farm. A good many of these people return from time to time to the Farm for the major holidays, Thanksgiving and Christmas, or for brief vacation visits. This fact bespeaks the feeling of at-homeness they enjoy there. The continuing, more permanent community is made up of about thirty people of various gifts and of great devotion, most of whom have cast their lot entirely with the community and its labor of love.

An intentional community that achieves its purposes must have more than housing and food, more than atmosphere, more even than spontaneous kindliness and mutuality. Gould Farm, besides possessing these things, has of course a structure of organization, a division of labor, various subgroups for special interests and needs, and withal a way of life where society and solitude, responsibility and relaxation, counseling and being counseled obtain together. Thus it aims to provide something like what is now called "group therapy" is in certain ways formalized, but it is unprofessional. Underlying all of these factors is the "intention" of the community to achieve quiet, enduring fellowship in responsiveness to the love of God.

Through the years hundreds have entered into this fellowship, each in his own way—there is no "orthodox" pattern demanding conformity. Many of the people who have lived at the Farm are among the leaders in various walks of life—artists, writers, clergymen, lawyers, businessmen, scholars. Some of the workers have been theological students undertaking an informal internship. Others have come because of an initial interest in intentional communities as such. Let me speak personally here. Students as well as faculty from my own school at the University of Chicago have been coming to the Farm now for over a generation. One of my former students, the Rev. Donald Harrington, now minister of Community Church in New York City, in the summer of 1936 took a group of underprivileged boys from Chicago to the Farm in order to give them the advantages of community life. As for myself, a visitor who for almost a decade has lived at the Farm for periods up to three months at a time, I have come to know the life of the community in a measure "from the inside"— assigned as I was to dish-washing, to giving an occasional sermon, and to participating in a music-appreciation group.

At the Farm one meets people who have been hospitalized and who require a half-way station on the road to complete recovery. Or one meets the young man or woman whose doctor believes he requires the social contacts he has been avoiding, the person who has had a shattering experience of bereavement, the woman who on becoming blind must learn to read Braille, the mother who needs temporary relief from over-heavy responsibility, the person impeded by physical handicap, the taxi-driver recovering from alcoholism, the gifted young Negro musician who has been suffering from the indignities of segregation. At first blush most of these people appear to be like normal folk anywhere. Only after closer acquaintance does one become aware of the special need. Some of these people come only seeking help, and soon they find they are needed by others. And then, too, one meets the people who look upon their stay at the Farm as an unusual opportunity for service to others. Over the years I have witnessed the benison gathered from the fellowship by its permanent members as well as by those guests who have come in search of healing and have found it. Inevitably, to be sure, some have gone away without fully satisfying benefit. This brings us to an important finding gained from a recent study.

In a brief comparative study of intentional communities Dr. Henrik Infield has brought into bold relief the uniqueness of Gould Farm which has made it a veritable "second home" for many a seeker for fellowship. This is the first formal sociological study that has been made of Gould Farm.

A community of this sort cannot grow in wisdom and stature without taking inventory from time to time. Gould Farm is aware of this fact. Its acceptance of Dr. Infield's offer to make a sociological analysis of the structure and functioning of the community is evidence of that. Its agreeing to the publication of his findings is itself a sign of its desire to invite others to participate in the process of new seeking. There are few of such communities, if any, in this country. More of them should be established. As Dr. Infield says, the example of Gould Farm makes the task easier.

In his outlook at the end of his book, Dr. Infield gives some consideration to the future of Communities in America, conjecturing as to how they can hope to reach firmer ground and begin to start a stronger impact on the American scene. He sees two possible ways in which this might happen—a breakdown of the American economy or the use of community to tackle the spread of mental illness through the curative effect of the group itself as "group therapy"—not in artificial groups as now generally familiar, but in natural community groups. Dr. Infield rules out the possibility of the first, the "artificial" way, and goes on to say, "The only solution would seem to lie in a step forward to the genuine, naturally grown group, the therapeutic community, a community that, in order to be able to offer therapy as a service and not for profit, will have to be cooperative in function if not in name."

Dr. Infield's findings have done much to make the Gould Farm members and the guests alike newly aware of the unique significance and mission of Gould Farm (of which I have spoken earlier). They have revealed elements of strength in the community and, as might have been expected, also elements of weakness, symptoms of frustrated purpose. The strengths of the community which Dr. Infield discloses will not surprise and will gratify all friends of Gould Farm. The weaknesses revealed provide occasion for taking new soundings and new directions. It is apparent, for example, that some new, youthful members must be recruited for the permanent therapeutic community; new structures and dispersions of authority and cooperation must be sought. Perhaps new opportunities for group decision and for the distribution of the work must be devised.

New means for old purposes are already being tried at the Farm. To say this is to say that Gould Farm is a living community. The community recognizes that a living fellowship must be a fellowship of renewal. Gould Farm, unlike those intentional communities that have not survived, is relearning this law of life. Dr. Infield's studies and proposals have already become an important part of this relearning venture. Indeed, since the study was made, some new people with qualities of leadership have become working members of the community.

The old friends of Gould Farm and the new ones (now increasing in number) will take heart. In the Gould Farm of the future there will be, as in the past, new treasures as well as old. Indeed, without new treasures the old ones are themselves likely to disappear. This fact calls for a risking faith. Gould Farm cherishes its past, but it also moves venturingly into the burgeoning present. Its faith is in a *living* God. Fellowship with Him is life—New Life.

Seward Hiltner (1910–1984) was a Presbyterian minister, professor of Theology and Personality at Princeton Theological Seminary, and leader in the field of pastoral theology. Hiltner had earlier chaired the Department of Religion and Personality at the University of Chicago.

Here is Hiltner's 1964 essay titled "Faith and Health at Gould Farm," which appeared in *Pastoral Psychology*.

FAITH AND HEALTH AT GOULD FARM

I was honored in being invited to give the article that follows as the principal address at the recent fiftieth anniversary celebration of Gould Farm, in Great Barrington, Massachusetts. As Professor James Luther Adams, of the Harvard Divinity School, said on the same program, Gould Farm was our first modern experiment in rehabilitation through group therapy with premises explicitly Christian and pastoral.

Not a medical or psychiatric institution, Gould Farm takes, for limited periods, persons "who need a sympathetic and supportive social environment in crises of life, such as grief, broken home, divorce, emotional shock, change of life, recovery of strength after an operation or illness," and sometimes also persons "who need respite from situations causing extreme emotional and physical tension and fatigue, or who need time to make a crucial decision or to experience socialization." Applicants must attest, through certificates from physicians and otherwise, that they are not in need of close supervision or constant medical care. General medical and nursing care is of course provided.

This remarkable institution was founded by an imaginative and dedicated social worker named Will Gould and his wife, who came from the well-known Goodyear family. Although the Goulds are now dead, the enterprise they began is flourishing, but with numbers still strictly limited so that the purposes of a true small community may still be carried out. The director is now Hampton E. Price, an American Baptist minister, from whom further information may be secured.

When I first visited Gould Farm a little more than a quarter-century ago, the general understanding of the relation of faith and health was quite different from what it has since become.

In medicine, the groundwork had been laid in studies of psychological factors both in the production of illness and as aids to healing. But most physicians and medical students knew little or nothing of those developments, and tended to be suspicious of them as being, somehow, unscientific.

In the ministry, we had begun then to have clinical education of a few theological students, to get them acquainted with the sufferings and problems of real people in their formative educational years, but only a handful of students was able to get this training.

At that time there was only a handful—perhaps a hundred or two Protestant ministers—giving responsible full-time service as chaplains in hospitals and other kinds of health and welfare institutions. True, patients were seldom neglected entirely; but most of them received pastoral service only on the run. Not more than a dozen or two of the chaplains at that time had had special education for their work.

Good literature in the field had then just begun to appear, especially the two classic works: The Art of Ministering to the Sick, by Richard C. Cabot and Russell L. Dicks; and The Exploration of the Inner World, by Anton T. Boisen. Other literature was small in quantity; and while much of it was well intentioned, it tended to be not well informed theologically, medically, or psychologically.

The general public at that time, including the majority of church members, tended to be either skeptical or gullible about the relation of faith to health. Some thought this whole realm of interest was a throwback to an age we should have outgrown, or else they tended to fall for extreme and sectarian positions.

Without adding to this catalogue of the situation nearly thirty years ago (for it could be greatly extended), it was clear that you could not then be quite respectable and believe faith had an intimate relation to health, without at the same time running the risk of becoming some kind of muddle-headed fanatic.

Throughout this period, I am glad to confirm by my personal investigation, Gould Farm steadfastly and wisely refused to be either skeptical or gullible. The leaders then—many of them with us still today—had a solid conviction that Christian faith, when in-teriorized (sic) and made real both in individual lives and in a community, had important implications for health. They did not profess expertness on the technical aspects of the subject. But they showed what it could mean in practice. No magic and no nonsense! But no retreat either from their basic conviction.

In the intervening years, the situation has altered greatly. Not only can a physician direct his attention to this subject and remain respectable. The American Medical Association has established a department of religion and health. Several medical schools offer imaginative non-sectarian instruction about religious matters to their students. I myself teach part-time in the nation's largest postgraduate school of psychiatry.

The number of our ministers who give responsible full-time service to patients in all kinds of healing institutions has increased at least tenfold, and the great majority of them have now had some special education for their work.

Virtually every theological school now offers its students at least some good introduction to their pastoral work with real people; and the number of students who get supervised clinical training increases slowly and steadily from year to year.

Both the amount and the quality of literature in the area have greatly increased. Three journals in this country devote their entire attention to this area, and many others give it some coverage. Unfortunately, a really solid magazine for lay readers about faith and health is not available. Despite noble attempts by Russell L. Dicks to keep such a journal going, this was not possible. This is, currently, the big gap; and it tends to be filled, for many lay readers who should know better, by peripheral literature that is unsound either medically, theologically, or both. But the literature for professional readers is good, and getting better.

What are the reasons for this happy change? Certainly there are many. Certainly the individual leadership of persons like Boisen, Cabot, and Dicks has been important. So is the responsible re-examination of the nature of medical education by good medical educators, eager not to turn out a product with good technical knowledge and no competence in human relations. The movement for clinical education of ministers has been important. Under its guidance, literally hundreds and even thousands of doctors, nurses, psychologists, and social workers each year see eager young theologians who want to learn how to get down to cases in order to help their people. Often a real human encounter like this is worth a hundred theories.

But theory has helped also. Theologically, we have gone back to study the New Testament view of the relationship of faith to health. We are re-impressed with Jesus' interpretation of health as in accord with God's will, with his interest in and concern for any who lacked health in any dimension of life, and with his intuition that the relationship between faith and health is close. But at the same time, we see that he rejected any notion of faith that would guarantee health; many of his own healings were accomplished in people who obviously had no faith, and some of the most faithful, like Paul, continued with thorns in their sides. Thus, the New Testament is clear that there is a relationship and that this requires attention and work. But it is very far from being simpleminded. Declarations that any one who has enough faith can be healed of anything are as mistaken theologically as they are medically.

On the medical side, many of the theoretical contributions have come initially from the negative side. A man who develops a certain kind of basic outlook on life—which may include his religion or his lack of it—may very well be predisposed to become ill, or may be impeded in his recovery from illness. Here in your own state, important studies have shown that recovery from the deep pain of bereavement can be impeded by illusory, bitter, or escapist kinds of attitude and outlook. In recent years the doctors have also begun to turn attention to the positive aspects of these same phenomena. If one kind of attitude can help a man to get sick, another kind may help him to get well. There is even a beginning at studies on creativity. For instance, my colleague at the Menninger Foundation, world famous Doctor Gardner Murphy, is currently studying the possible relationship between human creativity and capacity for extrasensory perception. Directly or indirectly, these studies slowly build up year by year a body of data interpreting the complex relationships between faith and health.

I cannot, you see, be honest to what I know about this—and to what I don't know—and say that everything is simple. But what is clearly true, and also simple, is precisely the kind of convictions that have guided the leaders of Gould Farm from its beginning. As I knew Mrs. Gould, for instance, it was quite clear that she did not expect any guest at the farm to lose his troubles immediately and automatically at the drop of a Bible or the bending of a knee. Yet she was convinced that, if her own faith and that of her colleagues was genuine, then it would make each of them more personally attentive to the needs of every one, more ready to supply the community so sorely needed in countering loneliness, and thus, eventually and often indirectly, with therapeutic results. Such a conviction has always been true. We can now support it with a bit more evidence.

I like to think that Gould Farm itself has played a real part in this fortunate change during these last years. To the joy of us all, the nation is finally beginning to look with more realism and at the same time with more hope at the masses of mental sufferers that exist, that can be helped, and that are worth helping. Not only mental illness but also mental retardation, much delinquency and some crime, dissatisfaction in jobs or in leisure, and much else—these are being attacked with new vigor. Here in your own neighborhood you have a great leader in such thought and work, in the Austen Riggs Foundation and

Doctor Robert P. Knight.

But more and more of what the most imaginative leaders see to be needed cannot be provided by "big places." Some apparently big places are not big at all in the negative sense; for they have been made into small units where every one may know every one face to face. I foresee no day when what Gould Farm offers will be needed any less. Indeed, it is likely to be more needed, and more appreciated, in the future.

As a visitor then, as a well wisher, and as one who can be critical if he thinks it necessary, I bring the warmest possible appreciation for what has been done in these fifty years that are past. It is equally gratifying to have here so many who have helped guide Gould Farm in its formative years, and so many others, of younger years but of equal imagination, ready to chart the course toward the century mark. I have done unofficial public relations for Gould Farm for more than twenty-five years, and I intend to continue.

"MAN is the only animal that laughs and weeps; for he is the only animal that is struck with the difference between what things are, and what they ought to be. We weep at what thwarts or exceeds our expectations in trifles. We shed tears from sympathy with real and necessary distress; and we burst into laughter from want of sympathy with what is unreasonable and unnecessary, the absurdity of which provokes our spleen or mirth, rather than any serious reflections on it."—William Hazlitt

Kim Hines and her husband, Chris, raised their three young children, Mason, Graham and Madigan, at Gould Farm from 1990 to 2000. Kim finished her ten-year stint at the Farm as Director of Community Relations during which time she also completed her graduate studies, focused on the unique, mutual-benefit philanthropy of Gould Farm. Kim is the Director of Augusta Locally Grown, a nonprofit organization that promotes local, sustainable foods education in Augusta, Georgia. She is also the founder of Camp Kokua, a service-centered youth camp model that started in Hawaii. Chris is the Chief of Inpatient Psychiatry at Fort Gordon Army Medical Center.

We continue with excerpts from two sections from Part One of Kim Hines' 2003 Masters thesis (Indiana University) titled "Glimmers of Mutuality: Achieving Solidarity within the Social Relations of Philanthropy."[8]

Seeking the Benefits of Empowerment and Personal Freedom
"If you're sweeping floors and it seems like nobody cares, then it's not meaningful work. But if you're sweeping floors and you feel that it makes a difference in other people's lives, then you feel part of something bigger than sweeping floors."—a volunteer at Gould Farm

At Gould Farm, every guest and every staff member is expected to work. New guests—some arriving directly from a stay at a psychiatric hospital—will be assigned to work within several hours of their arrival. New staff find that work is their orientation to work, sometimes to their dismay. Visitors are pulled into daily tasks plus extra chores: weekend kitchen duty, breakfast dishes and gathering hay bales in the evening hours while the sun goes down. A former guest noted: "I never expected to sweat my way through depression in a cow barn. But I think it might have worked."

Perhaps the most celebrated feature of Gould Farm is the shared work efforts of guests and staff to keep the Farm and its programs running. A do-it-ourselves mentality is a source of pride as well as a matter of financial sustainability at the Farm. As described by a staff member: "Work is the focus of our culture. It's what we do. If you don't work, you can't stay."

Work provides the central structure for therapy, empowerment, rehabilitation and community. Most of the Farm's staff and physical resources are dedicated to the work program. Work leaders attend clinical meetings and counseling sessions. New work opportunities and time-off-work are used as incentives in behavior modification. Friendships and mentorships, conflict resolution, coping skills, symptom management—all are fostered in the work place. For some, work becomes the safety net, the one place where roles and expectations are clear in this otherwise untraditional mental health setting. One guest described it this way: "I knew I was getting better when I didn't dread weekends anymore."

Work is considered a method of healing; good work, a sign of health. It is in reference to work that most guests, staff, volunteers and visitors describe their most memorable accomplishments while at the Farm. Community members might build a chicken coop; lead the preparation of a community meal; chop firewood; or help take care of young children, an experience unheard of for many people who are in treatment for psychiatric illness. At Gould Farm, the day is defined by work accomplished—or not accomplished. Relationships are often described in terms of work responsibilities, tasks done or not done to the benefit or detriment of others. Work provides a vehicle of mediation between individuals, a way to know each other. Many comment that, in a community of 120, it is easy to see one's personal efforts reflected in the well-being of others. Noted one guest, "If I don't mop that floor, it'll get mopped by someone else, but I'll have to look that person in the eye the next day and know that he did it."

Work both defines and sustains the individual within community. Farm work provides ample niches into which individuals may fit themselves (or be fit), perhaps awkwardly at first, perhaps always awkwardly for those for whom work presents a great mental or emotional or physical challenge, for whatever reason. Awkwardness acknowledged, work remains the expectation.

At Gould Farm, quality of work becomes less a matter of accounting, more a matter of relationship to self and others. The individual's relationship to the community seems to grow—or fizzle—in accordance with his or her willingness to give, to care, to work. Work quality is often described as "good" when it is perceived as better than it was "before." But this perception is not usually reached by precise measurement of how many lawns one can mow in an afternoon. Rather, it seems to be gleaned by constant assessment of the spirit in which the lawn mowing is approached. It is this spirit, this attitude toward work (and toward community) that is nurtured at Gould Farm, both because it is tangibly necessary that the work get done and because it is believed that the individual gets "better" as the self is realized and sustained in relationship with others.

Work also sustains the community itself, though perhaps not in as straightforward a fashion as bottom-line-only mathematics would assume. To cover the costs of its programs, and to continue to serve people of all income levels, Gould Farm makes use of fees, private donations, voluntarism, commercial enterprise and investments. But the most visible, most lauded form of financial stability is the work contribution of community members.

While the actual financial benefit of the work program is difficult to calculate, (and perhaps impossible to measure using standard methods of accounting) the endorsement of the belief that every member's work contribution is financially vital to the whole community becomes, itself, a form of sustainability. It requires faith in the notion that every member's work contribution is vital, despite mental or emotional limitations, despite personality conflicts, despite the tendency toward more efficient work methods which risk excluding those who currently approach their work with awkwardness, fear, lack of personal awareness, or even hateful resent. Ultimately it is this faith, in self and others, that is described as healing and sustaining. "It's like pretending you're not sick!" exclaimed one guest. This interdependent process of sustainability provides a groundwork for the possibility of mutuality.

The work design at Gould Farm can be linked to the organization's defiant adherence to a rather unfashionable agrarian lifestyle. In fact, people familiar with the history of mental health care in America are shocked to discover that a place like Gould Farm still exists. That a small family farm remains a viable treatment option after a century of precipitous change in medicine, psychology, religion, social work, charity care and family farming is surprising. Gould Farm confidently promotes the claim that living closely to the land—and experiencing oneself as part of the land—is very good therapy. Thus, the possibility of mutuality extends beyond the human relationship into the world of creatures, plants and earth.

In running the Farm, together, community members ideally confront each other and themselves as both the nurturers and the nurtured. This duality implies the potential of a more rounded relationship than Aristotle's "friendship of utility." Drawn toward such idealism, Gould Farm community members find themselves in unexpected roles—as care provider, or as care recipient...and then as both. This experience requires suspending, to a degree, one's sole identification with one institutional role or another. It is letting go a bit of one's identity as a mental patient, or releasing a bit of one's personal distinction as a care-providing professional, or more closely examining one's motives as a volunteer ready to serve others—and just getting the food on the dinner table by 6pm.

Farm work is a key ingredient to the goal of mutuality at Gould Farm. It is the nature of the work—farm work—and not just work itself that provides opportunities for dualism and, thus, for mutuality. For example, farm work demands that the focus of the day be on getting the new-cut hay in the barn before it rains. Ideally—(and it is important to say "ideally" often, for Gould Farm is a place where ideals are embraced, but less-than-ideal circumstances abound)— ideally the focus of the day is not on this patient's psychosis or that patient's urgent desire to use drugs. Unlike settings in which a health care provider's primary job focus is on the patients, a large percentage of Gould Farm's staff members and volunteers are charged with the daily operation of a portion of the Farm: harvesting, cooking, cleaning, fixing, etc. Their responsibility is to assure the accomplishment of these operational tasks by including guests in the work. Likewise, the intended focus of the guests' work day is not on themselves—although that element is certainly inherent to their stay—but on the same responsibilities that consume staff time: harvesting, cooking, cleaning, fixing, etc. Community members experience themselves in a multitude of roles as they arise in common day circumstances, not in artificial workshops or isolated activities.

Sustaining the Farm as a farm—and not as an institution that looks like a farm but acts more like a country inn or a picturesque halfway house—requires more attention be paid to nature's processes than is necessary in institutions where clients are served but not provided ample opportunities to be of service to others. Nature mediates the dual experiences of care giver and care recipient, and provides opportunities for knowing oneself, and others, in both roles.

Practicing health at Gould Farm means that community members grow their own meats and vegetables, feed themselves and each other, keep a watchful eye on the children (especially around the frog pond!), spend time with a teary-eyed newcomer, sweep manure from the cow stalls, and clean up after someone's been sick in the toilet. Inclement weather requires that someone— anyone with a shovel—carve a path through the snow for less physically-able others. Neither natural disaster nor death shuts down the place; rather, community members unite forces and provide emotional support to one another through tragedy and grief—even more so, it seems, than during times of relative tranquility.

By relinquishing much of its control to the seasons, to the whim of the land, and to the will of its eclectic work force, Gould Farm chooses a more risky, more capricious path than many mental health agencies and nonprofit organizations are willing to follow—particularly when funding and credibility rely so heavily on measurable, quantifiable results. While one can point to the success rate of the Boston Area Programs (a transitional setting for graduating guests of the Farm) with confidence, it is much more difficult to explain that "Annette" now has control over her severe eating and anxiety disorders and is doing well in her own apartment in a Boston suburb, in part, because she had developed a mutually gratifying, neighborly relationship with the head farmer, his wife and their dog, and that that dog needed to be fed and walked when the farmer and his wife were away on vacation.

Gould Farm is a pretentious approach to psychiatric rehabilitation and charitable care. Its model infers that—in failing to see all people (including those with mental illness) as potentially productive citizens—modern society is flawed. By contrast, Gould Farm provides an experience in feeling productive that might benefit any population of people. Indeed, this experience is described as an essential attribute of Gould Farm, one which is constantly rediscovered by community members and visitors alike.

Work, Empowerment, and Expressions of Self

"Mark" came to Gould Farm as a guest in 1991. He arrived from a psychiatric ward where he was diagnosed with severe depression and suicidal ideation. He stayed at the Farm for little more than a year before returning home to the suburbs of New York. Mark is well spoken and well dressed, a patron of the arts. He describes himself as "chronically mentally ill." Mark proudly recalls his time as "the Pig Man" when he worked with the farm department as a guest at Gould Farm. He visits the Farm, on average, once a year, and always brings a big bag of apples "for the piggies." He usually volunteers a day of work at the barns, and then visits with individual staff members whom he knew as a guest. While his ambivalence toward the Gould Farm program on a whole is evident in his conversation, his speaks fondly of many relationships he formed with community members. He also states that he considers the farm-based work program an excellent format for rehabilitation.

In an interview conducted eight years after his departure, Mark is deliberate and thoughtful in describing his opinions about Gould Farm and the nature of the relationships he experienced while there. Remembering his year on campus, he acknowledges the power of mutuality in the Gould Farm setting, but sees limitations to that experience as a guest. He says:

"(The work program) requires and expects that the first thing you do is work every day. It forces you to make a commitment to the community. And if you start to care about that commitment to the community, you conversely start making a commitment to yourself... And that's the beginning of the healing process. That's when the treatment starts to take effect."

This commitment to oneself through commitment to the community creates the gray area that provides guests and staff with room to explore and shape their lives together.

While Mark says he understands the strength and purpose of the community arrangement he says he resents a lack of recognition of individualism at Gould Farm. Conversely, he also says he believes that the Farm "couldn't do what it does" if it focused on the individual as a priority. "The Gould Farm community ignores the power of the individual and recognizes the collective powers of individuals instead. I resent this kind of community."

But Mark says he knows that he benefited from being at the Farm, particularly from the experience of the work program. He describes a kind of ebb and flow between guests and staff, staff picking up the work slack where guests need to withdraw at times, or staff stepping back to let guests take on more work when they are up to the challenge. And he describes this relationship as creating an atmosphere of low-stress and personal freedom. "(Gould Farm) allows you to withdraw and engage depending on how you feel. The one absolute requirement of the program is that you work from the day you arrive, but the degree to which you withdraw or engage within the work and within the community is left up to your own desire and need."

He notes: "When I was my most productive during my stay at Gould Farm and in the work program, I naturally made more of a commitment to my own personal needs. I actually became more self-centered." He acknowledged that he believed that other community members—and the community as a whole— also benefited from his personal gain. But, as a guest, he says he experienced a "limitation to mutuality" while in the Gould Farm program:

"Gould Farm is a measured exchange between community members, and there is a limit to the depth of that exchange. Once you've reached that limit, that becomes one of the indicators to staff that a guest has reached his highest level of commitment possible and it's time to move on."

Mark's careful reflection illustrates the developmental stages of mutuality, a spiral sort of build-up in relationship between oneself and others. At first he describes his activities of receiving services and helping others as completely separate, unrelated functions. He says that any early contributions he may have made to the community were purely "coincidental" as he began to grow stronger in mind and spirit. Later in his stay, his self identification as "the Pig Man" suggests an acceptance of more responsibility and a more mature attitude of caring. But even that initiative is rejected by Mark as a gesture of caring on his part; he describes his role in the pig pen as one of purely personal gain. "Animals give and don't expect anything back," he maintains, (even though he remembers to bring apples each visit. Finally, he describes the experience of mutual exchange between self and community as a sign of health, but also as a sign that the original relationship between oneself (as recipient) and the community (as provider) is coming to an end. He states that guests can only allow themselves to be "so unselfish" within the treatment program. After a certain point, he notes, the inclination to do things for the community, rather than for oneself, is a sign that rehabilitation has been achieved and that the relationship of the guest to the community needs to change.

Mark's perspective captures the grace of mutuality as a goal of Gould Farm's work program and in the philanthropic relationship in general. At mutuality, the philanthropic relationship seems to reach peak as a new form emerges. His observations suggest that the path toward mutuality is vague and choppy. Mutuality seems to appear as sporadic wisps of friendship or citizenship, and seems to increase in frequency as the relationship between provider and recipient draws closer to its intended goal.

In the interview, Mark displays a desire to measure, to compare and contrast the benefits of guests and staff. He goes back and forth to describe what Gould Farm did for staff, and then what it did for him, and then what it did for staff again. For Mark, the idea that "we help ourselves by helping others" is muddled by the fact that he was a client, that his father paid a significant sum of money for client services, and that he believed he was entitled to a set of such services. He is adamant in his view that the central priority of Gould Farm should be the guests. At the same time, he firmly states his view that staff—not guests—benefit most from Gould Farm. "I think staff most certainly benefit from Gould Farm, almost beyond explanation."

Mark's statements illustrate the mystery that surrounds the notion that giving to others brings unexpected benefits to the giver. For Mark, it is a somewhat dubious exchange. As he reflects upon the benefits he sees experienced by Gould Farm staff members (both paid and volunteer), he begins to question the virtue of their work motives as they relate to guests. He seems put off by a disconnect between Gould Farm as a place that benefits guests and Gould Farm as a place that benefits staff because, he says, it is unclear where the "real power" lies. There is an air of doubt hanging at the end of the interview.

"Mandy," a volunteer staff member, spoke of a similar disconnect. As a newcomer, Mandy notes that her motivation to work as a volunteer sometimes confuses others, as well as herself. When she is asked to consider her motives for volunteering, she says she has a difficult time justifying her decision in the language of service to others, preferring a language of mutuality:

"I think that some of the guests kind of wonder sometimes what we're (volunteers) doing here. We're this group of people who aren't getting paid much at all, and kind of came all the way out here to the middle of nowhere to do something. And people kind of wonder 'why would you do that?' Not necessarily in a really admirable kind of way, but in more of a distrusting kind of way. It's not that great of a feeling. Sometimes when I'm doing an overnight (shift) I get this feeling from some guests like, 'I don't get it. I don't get why you're here.' And I don't feel like I can explain it. It's sort of mushy, sort of weird, like 'oh, I'm here to serve.' It makes me feel funny because I can't explain it. I feel like I can't explain it without making it into some sort of an 'I have something you need and I'm going to give it to you' kind of thing. I don't want to come across that way."

She continued:

"Striving for mutual benefit just seems more genuine to me. When I hear people talk about just wanting to serve other people, and wanting to just do good things for other people, I kind of wonder who they are and what's driving that. I think I kind of don't trust it. I think a lot of times it's connected to (a lack of self) without people wanting to say it is. If you want to serve someone, it can't be quite as fulfilling unless you're receiving from the experience too."

Like Mark, Mandy says she experiences mutuality only on rare occasions. "I see only glimmers of mutual benefit here. Maybe that's because it's hard to say—when you're interacting with someone else—that they're benefiting. It's hard to feel it concretely." She went on: "I feel like I'm benefiting from being here, and I feel like I'm doing service by being here, but the connection between the two experiences is not as clear, not as strong."

Mark and Mandy both describe the disconnect between staff benefits and guest benefits as a disappointment in their experience at Gould Farm. Their reports of "glimmers" of mutuality suggest that more connection between their own benefits and others' would be welcome. Both seem to imagine that the discovery of more connection is possible. However, this perceived connection-through-mutuality holds slightly different meanings for each. Mandy describes it as "more genuine," whereas Mark describes it as an indication that "it's time to move on." Both descriptions suggest that mutuality is the point at which the philanthropic relationship hits the ceiling of its potential. Bumping up against that ceiling is a triumph for one, an ending point for the other.

While their Gould Farm experiences are quite different—and divided by nearly a decade—both Mark and Mandy seem to perceive themselves as caring individuals whose care-giving potential was enhanced at the Farm. Mandy says she came to the Farm to serve others; Mark said he came to the Farm strictly to help himself but, along the way, the community also benefited from his work contributions as his emotional health grew stronger.

We conclude this chapter with an excerpt from Oliver Sacks' 2009 article, "The Lost Virtues of the Asylum," which appeared in *The New York Review of Books*. Footnotes in the original have been excluded from this excerpt.[9]

What is the situation now? The state hospitals that still exist are almost empty and contain only a tiny fraction of the numbers they once had. The remaining inmates consist for the most part of chronically ill patients who do not respond to medication, or incorrigibly violent patients who cannot be safely allowed outside. The vast majority of mentally ill people therefore live outside mental hospitals. Some live alone or with their families and visit outpatient clinics, and some stay in "halfway houses," residencies that provide a room, one or more meals, and the medications that have been prescribed.

Such residences vary greatly in quality but even in the best of them (as brought out by Tim Parks in his review of Jay Neugeboren's book about his schizophrenic brother, Imagining Robert, and by Neugeboren himself, in his recent review of The Center Cannot Hold, Elyn Saks's autobiographical account of her own schizophrenia), patients may feel isolated and, worst of all, scarcely able to get the psychiatric advice and counseling they may need. The last fifteen years or so have seen a new generation of antipsychotic drugs, with better therapeutic effects and fewer side effects, but the too exclusive an emphasis on "chemical" models of schizophrenia, and on purely pharmacological approaches to treatment, may leave the central human and social experience of being mentally ill untouched.

Particularly important in New York City, especially since deinstitutionalization, is Fountain House, which was established sixty years ago, and provides a clubhouse on West 47th Street for mentally ill people from all over the city. Here they can come and go freely, meet others, eat communally, and, most importantly, be helped to secure jobs and fill out tax forms and tricky paperwork of one sort or another. Similar clubhouses have now been established in many cities. There are dedicated staff members and volunteers at these clubhouses, but they are crucially dependent on private funds, and these have been less forthcoming during the current recession.

There are also, intriguingly, certain residential communities that derive, historically, both from the asylums and the therapeutic farm communities of the nineteenth century, and these provide, for the fortunate few who can go to them, comprehensive programs for the mentally ill. I have visited some of these, *Gould Farm* in Massachusetts, CooperRiis in North Carolina, and seen in them much of what was admirable in the life of the old state hospitals: community, companionship, opportunities for work and creativity, and respect for the individuality of everyone there, now coupled with the best of psychotherapy and whatever medication is needed.

Often it is rather modest medication in these ideal circumstances. Many of the patients in such places (though schizophrenia and manic depression remain lifelong conditions) may "graduate" after several months or perhaps a year or two, moving into independent living, and perhaps going back to work or school, with a modest degree of ongoing support and counseling. For many of them, a full and satisfying life with fewer or even no relapses is within reach.

Although the cost of such residential facilities is considerable, more than $100,000 a year (some of which is funded by family contributions, the rest by private donors), this is far less than the cost of a year in hospital, to say nothing of the human costs involved. But there are only a handful of comparable facilities in the US; they can accommodate no more than a few hundred patients out of the millions that exist.

The remainder the 99 percent of the mentally ill who have insufficient resources of their own must face inadequate treatment and lives that cannot reach their potential. The National Alliance for the Mentally Ill does what it can, but the millions of mentally ill remain the least supported, the most disenfranchised, and the most excluded people in our society today. And yet it is clear from the experiences of places like CooperRiis and *Gould Farm*, and of individuals like Elyn Saks that schizophrenia is not necessarily a relentlessly deteriorating illness (although it can be); and that, in ideal circumstances, and when resources are available, even the most deeply ill people who have been relegated to a "hopeless" prognosis may be enabled to live satisfying and productive lives.

Notes and Permissions

1. Infield, Henrik. *The American Intentional Communities: Study on the Sociology of Cooperation.* New Jersey: Glen Gardner Community Press, 1955. 82. Every effort has been made to trace copyright. Proper credit will be included in any future printings upon receipt of written notice.

2. Ibid. 104-105.

3. Adams, James Luther. "Notes on the Study of Gould Farm" (1955-56). From *Voluntary Associations: Socio-cultural Analyses and Theological Interpretation.* Ed. J. Ronald Engel. Chicago: Exploration Press, 1986. 258. We also thank Stephen Mott, Ph.D., President of the James Luther Adams Foundation, for permission to reprint this essay.

4. With kind permission from Springer Science+Media: *Journal of Pastoral Psychology,* "Faith and Health at Gould Farm, Vol. 15, No. 8, June 20, 2005 (license content date), Seward Hiltner. Originally appeared in *Journal of Pastoral Psychology,* Vol. 1, November 15, 1964, 27-30. Springer Science + Business Media makes no representation or warranties with respect to the licensed material.

5. Sacks, Oliver. "The Lost Virtues of the Asylum." Vol. 56, No. 14. September 24, 2009.

6. Every effort has been made to trace copyright. Proper credit will be included in any future printings upon receipt of written notice.

7. Adams, James Luther. Op cit.

8. Hines, Kim. "Glimmers of Mutuality: Achieving Solidarity within the Social Relations of Philanthropy." Submitted to the faculty of the University Graduate School in partial fulfillment of the requirements for the degree of Master of Arts in the Department of Philanthropic Studies, Indiana University, April 2003. 27-39. Used with author's permission.

9. Excerpt from "The Lost Virtues of the Asylum" by Oliver Sacks, originally published in *The New York Review of Books.* Copyright © 2009 by Oliver Sacks. Used by permission of The Wylie Agency LLC.

Chapter Seven

Associates and Guests

Included here are ten selections written by guests, acquaintances, friends of Gould Farm. They reflect various therapeutic and programmatic understandings about the Farm. This chapter opens with a letter from someone who most likely was a WWI veteran; the last is a poem written in the 1990s by a former guest. Novelist Mary Antin's letters from the 1920s poignantly express the emotional anguish she felt and which drew her to the Farm, particularly its founder.

The letters by Rabbi Stephen Wise and Amos P. Wilder (the father of the playwright) are examples of the many distinguished individuals who corresponded with Agnes Gould. The selection from the Farm Yarn, an in-house, mimeographed weekly, provides a humorous glance of a guest's first day at the Farm. The reflections of a guest from the 1980s was commissioned for the Reader.

Also included is an excerpt from former *New Yorker* Journalist Pulitzer Prize winning *Is There No Place On Earth for Me?(1983)* which chronicles the life of "Sylvia Frumkin" (a pseudonym used at the time for former Gould Farm guest, Maxine Mason), a piece first serialized in the *New Yorker* in 1981. The excerpted selection from *Rickie* (1990) intersperses letters from a former guest, Rickie, and provides a touching account of a father's investment in his daughter's health and treatment.

THE SELECTIONS

Below is an excerpt of a letter written by a 25-year-old man (whose signature is illegible), from Brooklyn, New York, seeking Gould Farm's services. It is unknown whether this man ever visited the Farm. Will Gould, in a letter dated March 28, 1919, wrote to his sister: "We have several soldiers, nice young fellows, and the Red Cross wants me to keep taking them all summer..."[1]

107

Brooklyn, N.Y.
April 5, 1920

...I am a young man of 25, and have been in over-sea service for 12 months and received an injury that has affected my nerves. Doctors of the War Risk* have advised that some light farm work would greatly help to remedy my condition. Hence, my writing to you.

I have never worked on a farm before but am willing to do my best on your farm, or what I am able to do. Can furnish you best references as to my character.

Hoping to be favored with a reply by return mail, I am,

Yours respectfully,
S/

*Probably the Bureau of War Risk Insurance, Department of the Treasury (1914-1920).—Editors

The following is an excerpt from a letter that Mary Antin wrote to industrialist Thomas A. Watson (the same "Mr. Watson" who collaborated with Alexander Graham Bell), written from Gould Farm.[2]

October 2, 1924

Dear Mr. Watson:

I have thought of you a great deal recently during my readings. I have just reread Carpenter's Drama of Life [Love] and Death, and I am astonished to realize how much more I am able to get from this writer than a few years ago. I thought this would interest you as evidence that my education in mysticism has advanced very rapidly since I began this new life at Gould Farm. The bulk of my reading is in the general field of religions, mainly of the mystical order. I am learning a new language. My tendency, as you know, was always in this direction, but whereas formerly I nibbled feebly at this particular form of the bread of life, at this period I find myself able to derive from it most of my material for growth.

Let me tell you more about this when I come. Also, you will be amazed and pleased to learn what a tremendous increase of power, both physical and mental, I have received...

I study the subject of the Geulah (Hebrew word meaning redemption) in the new light, and still find it a profound and precious instruction. I pray heartily for a conviction of sin in this respect—that, if there was indeed, sin, I might have the benefit of repentance. But I have had no answer to that prayer so far. I suspect I shall not be allowed any light on this question until I confess that whole chapter to some one with whom it might make a difference—the Goulds, perhaps?...

The following is an excerpt from Antin, then living in Chappaqua, New York, to Caroline Goodyear at Gould Farm, dated July 23, 1928.[3]

Dear Caroline:

...Returning from my walk, all in the dark last Friday night, I was drawn to the (Gould Farm) living room where I sat for a time, listening to the clock—Agnes's clock—as I have done so many times during the years of my residence with you all, after all the house was still. The fireplace was black but some unquenched life in the buried embers whispered an accompaniment to the clock. Long, long thoughts—thoughts that failed to rise to prayer, but that did count, afterwards... Then the clock struck the hour for me. Surely for me, for no one else was listening. Midnight, by Agnes's clock; and the hidden fire still murmured. How I have treasured every little thing that Agnes has shared with me of her wifely experience, even such a public fact as that the beloved clock was Brother Will's first wedding anniversary gift to her!... And then I went to bed—and squirmed at the thought of Priscilla! The sublime and ridiculous very close indeed in the linked moments of that farewell evening.

I had no intention of using that word, *farewell*. A true word that spoke itself. For I shall never come to the Farm again after the same fashion as my comings up to this last one. I shall come—to visit briefly, to live, if God will permit it; but it will be after a new fashion. I may have been on the train, when I woke up after a more or less uncomfortable nap, or it may have been later—Saturday, Sunday: I don't really know when, when I realized that my last visit has had a quite unexpected effect. It has driven me more deeply in on myself. On God, that means. That is good. I *have* been a lame duck, clinging, clinging, though not in the fashion our superficial critics think. I have complained of the desert-loneliness of my life. A sojourn in the desert is what I need. I take up my solitary life willingly now, and when I come to you again it will be after the new fashion.

Amos Parker Wilder (1863-1936)—the father of Playwright Thornton Wilder—was a newspaper owner and later United States Consul General to Hong Kong and Shanghai.[4] Below is a letter he wrote to Agnes Gould.[5]

Clifton Springs, NY
December 2, 1929

Dear Mrs. Gould,

I feel a bit guilty in telling I have been here for ten days but another week should see me back in New Haven. I sought some examinations. The progress I think I am making in nerves I attribute mainly to Gould Farm; rest periods, judicious exercise, wholesome mental activities. Good cheer, faith—the cure for the increasing thousands who need nerve and mental up-building lies along these lines. Gould Farm has long sensed the need, knows the cure and reports results. Perhaps to the formula I should add drinking water on every side; I firmly believe that your management must uncover conspicuous supplies and magnify them—making the place a water cure in addition to all else. I am sure your associates have got over to you something of the appreciation I feel for your help to me—may I say that radiant women are among the chosen of humanity. This is a hasty note dictated by a friend. I have only to add that when the time comes the Gould Farm management should have some honorable scout get all the ideas that this place and Battle Creek can furnish. We can do as well and better in many ways at Gould Farm and of course your ideas have a unique mission. Pardon this hasty line; with leisure I shall not only write but come and see you. I am not boastful but time which is a factor in all such cases as mine registers progress. Tell Miss Minnie she is one of the best of women and give greetings to my Topside and all associates.

Rabbi Stephen S. Wise (1875-1949), an American Reform Rabbi, established the Free Synagogue in New York in 1907, and later served in leadership of the American Jewish Congress in 1930s and 1940s.[6] There is no evidence that Rabbi Wise ever visited Gould Farm, but he was in communication with Agnes Gould, at least once, below, in a letter dated June 9, 1933.[7]

Free Synagogue   Synagogue House
New York   40 West 68th St.
                                                  Near Central Park

Mrs. William J. Gould
Gould Farm
Great Barrington, Mass.

Dear Mrs. Gould:

How good of you to remember your own gracious invitation to us to come to Gould Farm. There is nothing we would rather do than give ourselves the pleasure of paying a visit to Gould Farm, but we can hardly hope to do that any more this year. Incredible as it may seem to you, I have not had a day off since the beginning of the Hitler war upon my people in Germany and, what is more, I shall have to stay in New York until the day we sail for Europe.

With appreciation of your kind invitation, and cordial greetings in which Mrs. Wise joins, believe me

                                                  Faithfully yours,
                                                  S/ Stephen Wise

The *Farm Yarn* was Gould Farm's weekly, in-house published newsletter from 1972 until 1990, then more sporadically until printing stopped in 2004. Funny, feisty, and at times irreverent, the Yarn ran poems, a list of comings and goings, events, community issues, and essays. Its artwork was usually of high quality and had a realist folk-art feel. The covers depicted portraits of Gould Farmers, Farm scenes, country and farm objects like flowers and animals.

The printing equipment during the Yarn's early years was primitive. A guest wrote this in an August 1974 issue of the Farm Yarn:

I usually type pm Wednesday and Thursday. As I type I try to arrange the material in an interesting layout. The material is typed on mimeograph stencils. In the meantime someone draws the cover, and traces it onto silk screen stencil...(Someone) then runs it off on the silk screen. (There are times when it must be traced on two stencils and run off twice, for two color effects.)

Below are the impressions of a Gould Farm guest who arrived in 1974, which appeared in the May 23, 1974, edition of the "Farm Yarn."[8]

MY FIRST IMPRESSION

I arrived at the farm at about 8:30 PM after a 2½ hour drive from Keene, N.H., and after making a wrong turn which slowed us down somewhat. At about 9:00 p.m. my sister and her roommate deserted me and left me stranded in a strange place of which I knew no one. I was greeted by a guy named Bill who showed me the place but I had to practically run to keep up with him. We went upstairs, downstairs, upstairs, up this hall, down this hall. I was already confused and I had only been here 45 minutes.

I was very tired and nervous and I didn't dare to unpack for fear of rousing someone. So, to bed, in clothes and all. I slept very soundly.

I was awakened by a loud ringing bell and felt it was either a fire drill or the real thing. Suddenly I remembered it was the "out of the sack" call. So, I crawled out of bed thinking what an unearthly hour to be up. I gathered up my early morning care articles to take into the bathroom which was occupied. So back to my room to wait. The toilet flushed so, assuming the person was through, I gathered up all my belongings once again and was ready to turn the doorknob when I heard the bathtub water running. So, I decided to venture down the 2nd floor. Well, what do ya know, it was empty. So was the toilet paper holder. I eventually got down to the first floor bathroom and it was waiting just for me.

Breakfast was very good but as I was taking my last bites of oatmeal I looked down and my bowl was gone. I was full anyway and thought "you sure have enough to eat" when they brought out eggs and toast. Gosh! Who in the world could ever eat that too. They all did.

My first chore, Vicki assigned me to vacuum the offices and hall and clean the first floor bathrooms. How do you write home and explain your very first farm chore was to vacuum? My mom would say it's about time she learned that.

At lunch time I had a chance to look at all the people who were soon to be my temporary family. I thought, "what a bunch of farmers." Dungarees, old shirts, work boots, dirty fingernails etc. And, you know what, I just described myself. Hey, I'm a farmer!

In the afternoon, I helped to plant asparagus and peas and lettuce. A real nice lady taught me named Mrs. McIntosh.

At supper time I felt like a kid playing go around and round the table, go around and round the table till you can find your name. But now that I think of it, it's kind of nice to be able to sit with different ones because you can get to them better and feel a little closer to each individual. During the meal I wondered what on earth is that lady handing to people in a little manila envelope until I got one too. It was Rachel handing out medications.

In the evening, it was off to Friendly's. It seems to be a pretty popular place around here. The ride to get there is an experience in itself. Try riding in the back of a van on these roads, that have practically no springs, it seems. You had better wear a helmet if you want a flat head. But, I think of it in this way. It's good exercise for the rump.

It was finally time to turn in. I was thinking over my whole day and it was all worth it. And thanks to Nance and Kent Smith for making me feel welcome.

As I was undressing I heard a noise like a cat's meow and scratching on the wall and as I turned around I jumped 10 feet in the air. There was a black cat lying on my bed. Out he went, until 3 a.m. when I suddenly awoke to a black cat being thrown at me. Apparently this person didn't realize someone had moved in to the room and he was depositing the cat that was bothering him. Right Bob?

So, meanwhile back to bed, as I wondered what's in store tomorrow. Gould Farm is a great place to be.

Below is an excerpt from Susan Sheehan's "Is There No Place On Earth For Me?", published in 1983.[9] It first appeared in serialized form in *The New Yorker* in 1981. "Sylvia Frumkin," which was the alias used by Sheehan for Maxine Mason, was reportedly highly intelligent but deeply troubled. First diagnosed with schizophrenia at age fourteen, she had been hospitalized several times before arriving at Gould Farm in early 1974. She left the Farm in 1975. Ms. Mason died in 1992 of cardiac arrest at the Rockland Psychiatric Center, Orangeburg, New York. Susan Sheehan revealed Frumkin's true identify as Ms. Mason in *The New Yorker* in 1995.

In March of 1974, Harriet and Irving Frumkin met with the Clearview social worker to discuss Sylvia's discharge. The Frumkins had by then become active in the Long Island Schizophrenia Association. One member of LISA had given them a pamphlet about Gould Farm, a community rehabilitation center that occupied six hundred acres in the Berkshires, in western Massachusetts. Gould Farm's community was composed of about thirty full-time staff members, their spouse and children, and about forty guests—both men and women, most of them between the ages of nineteen and forty... In early April, miss Frumkin was given a week's leave from Creedmoor. The Frumkins had made an appointment at Gould Farm, and they drove Sylvia there for a required twenty-four-hour trial visit. They liked Gould Farm immediately. Sylvia was accepted there. The Frumkins drove her back to New York. She returned to Creedmoor for a few days...and was discharged. There were two residential buildings at Gould Farm, each supervised by houseparents. Guests had private rooms, and were required to take care of their rooms and their personal hygiene. They were also required to work six hours a day, helping in the dining room, in the kitchen, or on a hundred acres that were used for farming... Miss Frumkin gathered eggs, set tables, and did her share of the seasonal chores—raking leaves, shoveling snow, clearing trails, making maple syrup. The guests had the rest of the day free to go to square dances, parties, and community meetings; to take trips to movies and concerts; to engage in sports; or to spend time in the weaving studio and craft shop. At Gould Farm, Miss Frumkin learned to weave, to do needlepoint, and to crochet.

The first thing Miss Frumkin did at Gould Farm was to give up smoking—a habit with which she had always felt uneasy. The second thing she did was to start gaining weight on the ample breakfasts, lunches, and dinners, midmorning coffee breaks, afternoon teas, and bedtime snacks provided. She was also caught skimming cream off the tops of bottles of unhomongenized milk in the milk room. After several months at Gould Farm, she weighed 196 pounds. She decided to go to a Weight Watchers group in the nearby town of Great Barrington. The executive director of Gould Farm remembers her running compulsively from table to table snatching meat from other guests' plates, to be sure of having precisely the number of ounces of chicken or liver specified in the Weight Watchers diet; he came to regret having given his approval to her going to Weight Watchers. She lost some of the weight, but she did not stick with Weight Watchers long; diets lost their charm for Sylvia Frumkin as quickly as psychiatrists did...

Gould Farm had a consulting psychiatrist, Dr. Dale Greaney, who came to the farm once a week to see the guests. A few months after Sylvia's arrival, Dr. Greaney began to see her every second or third week for between half an hour and forty-five minutes. Sylvia was always lucid but circuitous. In Dr. Greaney's opinion, she was no more and no less ill than most of the other chronic-schizophrenic guests he saw at Gould Farm, but three things did set her apart from the others. The first was her physical clumsiness and lack of coordination. Like several other psychiatrists who have treated Miss Frumkin, Dr. Greaney believed that she might have a neurological problem. He sent her to a neurologist for a consultation. The neurologist gave her a thorough examination and a test to rule out the possibility that she might have Wilson's disease, a hereditary condition characterized by toxic deposits of copper in many organs and tissues, including the central nervous system; the test was negative. The neurologist also determined that she didn't have any other neurological problem that would explain her behavior... The second thing that made her different from guests at Gould Farm with whom she shared many of the symptoms of schizophrenia was her imperious behavior. Dr. Greaney knew many schizophrenics who were quiet, were neat and kept their rooms clean, and had good manners. Miss Frumkin was loud, her room was messy, and she irritated most people at Gould Farm by her social clumsiness... The third thing he believed that set Miss Frumkin apart from other schizophrenics he had seen was her unwillingness to settle for the half life of halfway houses and "sheltered workshops," as so many chronic schizophrenics did.

Some months after Miss Frumkin began to see Dr. Greaney, her legs started to move back and forth involuntarily when she was seated. He changed her medication from 80 milligrams of Stelazine to 600 milligrams of Mellaril, which was the equivalent of 600 milligrams of Thorazine—a reduction of over sixty percent in her medication... Dr. Greaney changed Miss Frumkin's medication from Stealzine to Mellaril because he believed that of all the neuroleptics Mellaril caused the least hyperactivity... He didn't notice any change in Miss Frumkin's behavior for several months after he lowered her medication. (Some patients "decompensate" twenty-four hours after a reduction or cessation of their neuroleptic medication, and some decompensate only after eighteen months, but the average time is about three months.) Dr. Geaney did notice that Miss Frumkin was suddenly talking a great deal about religion. He decided that her preoccupation with religion was nondelusional and therefore didn't do anything about it.

After Miss Frumkin had been at Gould Farm a year, the staff met with the director to discuss her future. Most guests either suffered relapses and went back to hospitals or improved sufficiently to go to a halfway house or return home. An occasional guest was allowed to stay on at Gould Farm if he or she was no trouble and fitted into the farm's therapeutic community. The staff told the director that no exception should be made for Miss Frumkin. They had hoped that they could change her behavior, and had expended a great deal of energy on her, but she was as obnoxious as she had been when she arrived. On June 1, 1975, Miss Frumkin was told that she would have to leave Gould Farm in three months. The Frumkins were distressed. "Gould Farm was such a wonderful time for us," Harriet Frumkin recalled some years later. "Sylvia was in reasonably good shape, she wasn't in a hospital, and she was *away*." The Frumkins knew from having had Sylvia living at home several times in the early 1970s that it would be better for the whole family if she did not return there. The social worker at Gould Farm tried to get her into a number of halfway houses in Massachusetts, where she had placed other Gould Farm guests. Miss Frumkin was unenthusiastic about the halfway houses, and they were unenthusiastic about her. Between June and September, as she was threatened with the sort of change that had triggered psychotic episodes in the past, and was more vulnerable because her medication had been lowered, she began to decompensate quickly. She became increasingly preoccupied with religion. Unknown to some people at Gould Farm, Miss Frumkin had met a member of the American Board of Missions to the Jews one Saturday in 1972 on her way home from the internist's office where she was then working. Members of the ABMJ are primarily Jews who believe that Jesus is the Messiah; they consider themselves spiritually reborn, and believe that their purpose in life is to bring the message of Jesus to other Jews. Miss Frumkin had not pursued the invitation to come converted to Christianity in 1972; instead, she had become a Buddhist in 1973. She had turned against the Buddhists after she was asked to leave the Hotel Martinique. At Creedmoor, after she ran away from Jewish services, she had had several counseling sessions with Creedmoor's rabbi, and had once again seemed to accept Judaism. At Gould Farm, however, a guest who was a born-again Christian had converted her to Christianity. She considered herself born again and started going to church. Although Gould Farm was nonsectarian, its director was an ordained Presbyterian minister, and a few of the staff members were evangelical Christians. As Miss Frumkin became obsessed with Christianity in the summer of 1975, two staff members at Gould Farm were counseled against proselytizing her. As the deadline for leaving approached, her room became "a disgrace," she stopped taking her medication, and she started running around without any clothes on. The director telephoned the Frumkins and told them they would have to come and get their daughter.

Dr. Greaney was on vacation on August 29, when miss Frumkin left Gould Farm; he was not surprised to learn later that her exit had been a dramatic one. He recognized that even though her ability to function had become increasingly impaired as she had grown older, her will to succeed had survived. The reason that the staff at Gould Farm felt that her prognosis was so poor was that they could not imagine an entry point into any normal life for Miss Frumkin. At staff meetings, they asked each other, "What would she do?" She couldn't even be hired as a clerk, because of the awkward way in which she presented herself, and, on top of that, she didn't really want to be a clerk. She still wanted to be a star. Dr. Greaney believed that Miss Frumkin's combination of intelligence and grandiosity not only made her prognosis poor, but also accounted for the Dionysian quality of her psychotic episodes. "If you have to be Sylvia Frumkin, maybe this is the way to be," he said not long ago. "Many schizophrenics are grandiose, but she has such a high intelligence coupled with her grandiosity. If you see yourself going from defeat to defeat, and the next awesome chasm presents itself and you can't cross it, maybe you stick with the grandiosity in your head instead of facing up to your homeliness and awkwardness and limitations. I think she's a genius at being insane."

The following is from Frederic Flach MD's *Rickie* (1990).[10]

Kent Smith, the director at Gould Farm, was a soft-spoken man who exuded a quiet gentleness tempered by years of experience.

"We don't use the word 'patient' here," he told us. "We call them residents. Rickie will work on the farm, like the others. Every youngster has an assignment. We grow much of our own food. A couple of times a week we meet in groups to talk about ourselves, to get to know each other and learn ways to cope with life. We call it social skills training. You can understand how important that is for those who, like Rickie, have been out of the mainstream of life for years. We also have an arrangement with the local public school system so youngsters who want to can finish their education. And although I hope it won't be necessary for Rickie, we have several consulting psychiatrists available; they are called on in emergencies and actually see a few of our residents on a regular basis if more active psychotherapy seems indicated."

During her first months there, Rickie described herself as being happier than she could remember since the spring of 1965. She loved working with the animals, even though it was physically arduous.

In one of her letters she wrote:

Dear Dad:

I really like it here. I have a good time. I love the animals. I don't love shoveling manure, but even that isn't too bad. Every morning we get up and do chores. The weather doesn't matter. Hot, cold, rain, whatever. A lot of the days I walk down to the barn, shovel the cow dung, feed the cows, take care of any calves that have to get their mild, and then do a general cleanup. It is hard work, especially cleaning up, but it's okay. Sometimes I get to help milk the cows, but we don't do it by hand. We attach the milking machines.

I get a big kick out of the calves. When I stick my hand in their mouths, they suck on it. Boy, their tongues feel like sandpaper! The odor in the barns leaves a lot to be desired, but I've learned to breathe through my mouth instead of my nose.

The one thing I hate is the chicken house. I had to clean it one day, and collect eggs; I got a small case of chicken lice from that experience. My friend Lindy had it all over her body. I hated the chickens so much that they haven't made me go back in there again!

I also like the weaving shop and looms. I've made a lot of gifts in that shop already.

Come see me soon.

            Love, Rickie

Rickie had her own room on the third floor of the main house, with a large window that overlooked a pasture with white birch trees standing in the far distance. She seemed to fit in well with the people at the farm.

Most of the people had been in a hospital at one time or another before coming to Gould Farm. I did like them a lot. Lindy came shortly after I did, and we became best friends quickly. A nurse, she (Lindy) suffered from diabetes, and shared my occasional urge to hurt herself. She often abused herself by eating candy or sometimes an extra piece of bread so she'd go into insulin shock. I'd be there to pour the orange juice down her throat when that happened. Lindy was an attention getter, like me, and that meant competition. I didn't like it. But it seemed that our whole lives had revolved around being ill. Now that I think about it, that was true for most of the people at the farm.

Though I had promised never to hurt myself while at Gould Farm, I wasn't quite sure if I could live up to it, and that thought gnawed at me quite often. Just as often, though, I didn't think about it at all. I enjoyed working outdoors in the summer and indoors in the winter. And the farm itself was great! There were about forty people in residence. The main house had a large, wonderful kitchen, a huge dining room, and a television room. Western Massachusetts' winters get freezing cold. I used to beg to stay inside, but we had plenty of warm clothes. Everyone had their own room, and I cherished my privacy. We were all responsible for keeping our rooms clean and tidy. They were small rooms, but they were very, very nice.

Kent Smith, the director, had a lovely wife, Nancy. I liked her a lot. Then there was "Miss Eleanor," as she was called, an eighty-two-year-old woman who had lived there from the very beginning, when Mr. Gould had opened his home to others in need. The farmer Tim and his wife Elizabeth were also good friends of mine. When they had their first child, they asked me to be the godmother. I felt truly honored.

I wanted so much to be successful there, like I had as a little girl at the convent winning my très bien. Sometimes I even thought that although I didn't want to spend the rest of my life there like Miss Eleanor, it wouldn't be all that terrible if I had to.

Hilary visited Rickie at Gould Farm faithfully once a month, either driving up with a friend or taking the train. I'd spend the weekend about every six weeks, sometimes alone, usually with Joyce and a varied assortment of children. To this day my memories of those visits—walking about the farm with Rickie as she explained her chores, watching her dive into the swimming pool at our motel, sitting together at an inn in Lenox, surrounded by our family, hearing her laugh as if nothing had ever gone wrong in her life—possess a special feeling of nostalgia.

Below are reflections from a former Gould Farm guest (1980s), written for this Reader.[11]

What I have been thinking about is the importance of schedule that Gould Farm showed me. Get up, do your task and be done with your day. Working class hero. And I had a funny memory of this guy, whose only job, every friggin' day, was to sweep out Main House. At first I thought, that's not fair, I am on my knees in the garden all day, or cleaning toilets or chopping wood and all he has to do is sweep. I don't know if an explanation was ever given to me but it soon became apparent that that was what he was good at, that that was what he could do, so that is what he did. And I understood a lot about jobs around the Farm since that insight. I was very lucky, had my hand in every part of the Farm duties. And felt good getting up and feeling accomplished when done, going for tea, and getting ready for dinner.

I also have thoughts of Roma. The napkin place setter. She knew everyone's name and did her job. What was a real trip was that she REALLY KNEW where to place you. Whether you were quarreling with someone and needed to work it out, or whether you were feeling crappy and needed a boost by sitting at the head table, Roma knew where to put you. She is a legend.

My angelic brother signed me out of the hospital, packed me up and off we went to Western Mass., where he lived. Of course, I had to be interviewed and accepted but I had been so misdiagnosed, over-medicated and messed up, that my chances weren't 100% for getting accepted to GF, even though I was packed and ready. Since Kent was out, Nancy did my interview, and I soon realized that the Farm was not accepting people who had attempted suicide, like myself. Nancy and I bonded. Big time. And I looked her square in the eye and promised I was not going to be a suicide risk. She drilled me a bit and soon she believed me and thus, I believed myself. I would never lie to this woman—I had made a promise and promises I do keep. Nancy seemed to know this and believe this and thus, I was accepted. And my life at Gould Farm began at East House.

I did not sail through GF. I was hospitalized a couple of times, even went into Boston for electro-convulsive therapy (ECT). Nancy Smith supported me throughout. (I would talk with her about certain funny issues, like the lesbian psychiatric nurse who wrote me love letters. Not knowing what the hell to do, I shared the letters with Nancy. And I think the nurse got fired. We have stories. And we had late night philosophical stories about "ants," as they relate to our human experience. Makes me want to get right on a train, RIGHT NOW, and plant a huge kiss on Nancy's cheek). Nancy was my GF. And like I said, when she left, I knew it was time for me to leave too. And I did.

And then there were the glorious trips to this fantastic used book store. I would save my allowance and those trips were heavenly to me. I think I bought every philosophy book, from Plato to Nietzsche and back again. So here I am, all weekend at the Farm, on a beach chair, in the snow, with boxer shorts on and a tee shirt and real warm socks and those Sorrell snow shoes. And I read all weekend! Every weekend! I even read the Bible out there in the snow! And Nancy was so wonderful. Talking to me about what I have been reading. And another thing, at GF, you had your own room. So fantastic! I brought all of my music from California and made tapes for various people, including Nancy. For me, give me books, music and people to love and that was all I really needed. Just call it 2 or 3 years that I was there, even though I left once and returned for a short while and departed finally when the Smiths did.

What is and always will be is the reality check that leaving Gould Farm stamped on me. Why weren't people in the "real world" honest? Why couldn't people just be honest? And simple. For me, deciphering between a clean life at the Farm and moving back to the hustle and bustle of life in Los Angeles was quite hard. Aside from being bipolar myself, I also had a relative with bipolar disorder. We had this saying, "You gotta fake it 'til you make it." So when people ask how you were, you responded, "fine, thank you. How are you?" Bullshit I had to try and get used to.

After leaving GF, I was lucky enough to return to college and complete my Bachelor's Degree in Psychology. I immediately learned never to speak of my past, my diagnosis, or, in truth, who I really was. This was, and still truly is, hard on my psyche. While there are words about mental illness more being accepted, this was not my experience. I advocated for the mentally ill throughout college, graduate school and my social work career. The one thing GF was unable to cure me of is my mental illness. And sadly, my manic-depression made my career in social work shorter than most. However, I must say that I have been a Director of a program at a very prestigious social service agency. And I also had a successful career as a private practitioner. But alas, I am bipolar and some things are out of my control.

Today I am functional, independent and volunteer to better my community. But there is still such shame about my diagnosis and shame about really the core of who I really am. Over 20 years after leaving GF, I still live with much shame. While I am proud to have hurdled life in academia and a career, there is still something, something so deep and strong within me, that I would so long to be proud of. In my defense, to be mentally ill is truly, really just another perspective that someday will be more accepted. Remember Thomas Szasz who wrote "The Myth of Mental Illness?" In Szasz's day, the biological proof for mental illness did not exist, and so he argued that mental illness did not exist, and that all perspectives should be listened to. Of course later, he was disproven (but I still love him. He was also against medication). Today, the head of the USC School of Law practices with schizophrenia. A Johns Hopkins University Professor has chronicled her struggles with bipolar disorder in "An Unquiet Mind." So things are changing. Just slowly.

We end this chapter with a poem by a former Gould Farm guest.[12]

WITHOUT WALLS
1997

Silence fills my world
In the most unlikely place of silence
I sit in my cell contemplating
The last four months I have spent
locked away from the outside world
In those months, I have turned twenty-one
seen Thanksgiving, Christmas, and a New Year
all from within these same old prison walls
I have become a number, a useless con
The only thing I have to look forward to
is a place called Gould Farm
somewhere in the corner of Massachusetts
A voice from nowhere crackles
for Jeremy Martin to get his stuff
his time has come to leave these forbidden walls
a reprieve, a crack of light I haven't seen in months
I walk down the narrow halls to the gate of my freedom

Checking to see if I am the real Jeremy
the guard walks me to the outside world

I am free
Should I run...cry...laugh...shout
I do nothing except grin from ear to ear
My parents are there to take me to the farm
saying a prayer to the god of all travel
we set out to my new home
a place without walls, a place to dream
We turn off route 23
at a sign that says Gould Farm
pulling around the big farmhouse, we are greeted
by a man with graying long hair and a beard
He says hello, my name is "David"[13]
he takes us for a tour down the main road
which has been patched through and through
We check out the barn that was raised in a day
just like the one by our old house in Pennsylvania
the newborn calf is there to greet us
Life!
all cornered in this small piece of heaven
I settle into McKee House
which will be my home for the next year

Gould Farm is known for
rehabilitating people with mental illness
and also those who say they are normal
Guests are thought to be staff and vice versa
there is no stigma on this farm
all are welcome
People come and people go but the spirit remains
I have found many different ideas and opinions
but all are backed with love for one another
I have seen progress in so many people
I've seen life and death and everything in between
I've seen winter which brings maple syrup to our table
and summer for hikes and swims
vegetables in the fall along with trees of every color
and animals coming and going in all seasons
Since I have been on the farm
I have experienced many things
and learned many different skills
I've seen many a sage, a couple of prophets
and many aspiring saints
all who flow with reverence for life and love

I have moved now to a sister house close to Boston
I've been here a week
and I've already used the skills I learned on the farm

I know a new freedom
one without prejudices and imposing walls
I hope to spend these holidays
without barred doors, with people I love
knowing that Gould calls all of us
to commune with him forever

Notes and Permissions

1. McKee, Rose L. *Brother Will and the Founding of Gould Farm*. Monterey: The William J. Gould Associates, Inc., [1963], 1975. 59.

1a. Letter reprinted with permission: The William J. Gould Associates, Inc.

2. Letter quoted in Salz. 99-100. Original held in Boston Public Library. Every effort has been made to trace copyright and obtain permission to reprint this letter. Proper credit will be included in any future printings upon receipt of written notice.

3. Used with permission from The William J. Gould Associates, Inc., which may not hold the copyright. Every effort has been made to trace copyright and obtain permission to reprint this letter. Proper credit will be included in any future printings upon receipt of written notice.

4. See http:/www.twildersociety.org. Accessed December 26, 2012.

5. Public domain. We thank the Wilder Family, LLC, for assistance with copyright matters. For more information about the Thornton Wilder Family Literary Estate, please go to: www.thorntonwilder.com.

6. *New York Times*. March 13, 1949, pg. 24. "Synagogue Is Renamed to Honor Rabbi S.S. Wise." Accessed November 24, 2013. See Also Wyman, David S. Pantheon. 1985. *The Abandonment of the European Jews: America and the Holocaust, 1941-1945*, especially Chapter 8.

7. We thank the family of Rabbi Stephen S. Wise for permission to reprint this letter.

8. Used with permission from The William J. Gould Associates, Inc., which may not hold the copyright. Every effort has been made to trace copyright and obtain permission to reprint this letter. Proper credit will be included in any future printings upon receipt of written notice.

9. Excerpt from IS THERE NO PLACE ON EARTH FOR ME? by Susan Sheehan. Copyright © 1982 by Susan Sheehan. Reprinted by permission of Houghton Mifflin Harcourt Publishing Company. All rights reserved.

10. From *Rickie*, by Frederic Flach, M.D., copyright © 1990 by Frederic Flach, M.D. Used by permission of Ballantine Books, a division of Random House, Inc. Any third party use of this material, outside of this publication, is prohibited. Interested parties must apply directly to Random House, Inc., for permission.

11. Used with author's permission.

12. Used with author's permission.

13. Name changed to maintain confidentiality.

Chapter Eight

The Future

This final chapter begins with one of the earliest pieces, by Donald McMillan, (1935) and ends with Virgil Stucker's essay, written for the reader. Both address the need for and establishment of communities based on the Gould Farm model. It was the intention of the Gould Farm founders that the Farm would inspire similar endeavors. The Farm's 1929 Charter of Incorporation reads, in part, that "It is a further purpose of the associates to foster according to their ability and opportunities other out-growing enterprises having special social value, whether eleemosynary, educational, therapeutic or industrial."[1] The Farm recognized the need in 1953 in a report, which Henrik Infield spotted, which read in part:

> (T)he recognition of a widespread need for similar centers comes to us from doctors, ministers, social agencies, and individuals scattered throughout the country. From time to time there is someone or there is a group of persons embarking on a similar project. For their use and for that of others to come it is hoped that practical results will follow from this study.[2]

Both the McMillan and Stucker essays reflect an optimism shared by the Farm's founders. McMillan envisioned a "country-wide network" of Farms (he sometimes identified them as "spas of the spirit" and "retreats") to address the needs of the "modern world," especially those plaguing the cities. To be successful, such future Gould Farms, for McMillan, would need to be founded by those filled with the "spirit of Gould Farm," those people dedicated to both social service and to community. Stucker identifies three tasks of those wanting to establish a community based on Gould Farm: 1) the necessary capital; 2) finding the right staff leadership; and 3) regulations which Stucker believes can be addressed by better public relations and policy discourse. These tasks, but especially the third, differ from those which McMillan likely anticipated.

Also included here are three short pieces about a Gould Farm-inspired venture, Crossing Creeks, a residential therapeutic community, from 2000 to 2010, in the Shenandoah Valley of Virginia. Former Gould Farm nurse, Nancy Smith,

Gould Farm Associate, John Otenasek, and others who visited the Farm, helped found Crossing Creeks.

THE SELECTIONS

Rev. Donald C. McMillan (1909-1974), who was most probably a student of Clayton Bowen McMillan, served Unitarian churches in Massachusetts and Maine. He was active in the United Nations, World Affairs Council, and the United World Federalists.

The following is from the last chapter of McMillan's 1935 dissertation, "The Story of Gould Farm."[3] Footnotes from the original have here been omitted.

THE GOULD FARMS OF TOMORROW

The crying need of the modern world for a great number of such centers of individual and social reconstruction as Gould Farm is only too apparent. There is need of them, everywhere, but especially are they needed near our large cities, to serve them as Gould Farm serves New York and Boston. To the social-minded person who lives in Chicago, for instance, the vision of a dozen Gould Farms at convenient distances from that city is a happy one. It is not too visionary; a William Gould could find quite a sufficient number of satisfactory sites—if he reconciled himself to the lack of Berkshire hills. Certainly it would be much easier to establish Gould Farms today, as far as physical equipment is concerned, than it was for "Brother Will" and his few disciples. (But perhaps it should not be easier—those disciples of Will Gould say today that in their struggle they found their strength.)

The person who is at all concerned with the needs and welfare of his fellow-men must certainly be uplifted and challenged by the vision of a country-wide network of such places as Gould Farm, where the underprivileged might find relief from city streets and noise and filth; where they might have proof that human relationships may be based on something greater than a ruthless competition in material self-seeking; where, in short, they might win back their health, their personal integrity, and their respect for humankind.

A lengthy Utopian treatise could be written upon the myriad implications and possibilities of the Gould Farm idea. Here we may but mention in passing a few of its most general aspects.

Along with their being centers of individual regeneration, the Gould Farms could serve as experiment stations in all the most important aspects of social reconstruction. They could become communities, colonies, where the most progressive methods of educational, economic and political reform could be applied upon the basis of a few great time-tested spiritual principles. This was involved in William Gould's vision—to demonstrate the practicability of carrying out all human relationships upon the basis of eternal spiritual laws, rather than allowing those relationships to degenerate through the practices of worldly expediency. The Gould Farms, being relatively free from the manipulations of vested interests and the corruptive influences of mechanized urban life, could serve as the living embodiments of the ideals to be achieved in those more complex situations. They could serve as the "mountain-tops" from whence our modern life in all its aspects could be objectively viewed with a truer perspective. An official in the present national administration, being acquainted with Gould Farm, has recently said:

"World recovery and reconstruction can only come when the world is ready to receive them. I am strong for national and international preparedness—not with arms and ammunition, but along the lines of Gould Farm, where business men, bankers, statesmen, and the like, might spend a few weeks each year— regaining their idealism and perspective."

Quoted by Mr. Spalding in "Farmers of Men," December 29, 1934.

Here clearly is indicated the value of such model communities as Gould Farms—the "retreats" which would really constitute the vanguard of human progress. Such is the really stable, the really evolutionary approach to national reconstruction—the deliberate creation of model communities where an enlightened social consciousness, which is the first principle of true democracy, could be fostered, and disseminated through the guests of the Farms who would return to their former places of residence with this vision of nobler human relationships in their hearts.

Along such seemingly impracticable and Utopian lines does the Gould Farm idea carry us. But they are impracticable only to those who have not the "long view" of human affairs or an appreciation of the basic laws of human progress, say the Gould Farmers. They hold before the impatient radical theorists the only enduringly constructive way, the liberal way, to social reform, knowing full well that, in the present order of our society, it is idealistic. But they also know that all human progress consists in the painfully slow and partial realization of ideals, and they are confident that all mankind will eventually give its allegiance to the spiritual way of life they demonstrate, if for no other reason than the discovery and the conviction, through practical experience, that it is the one true way to live, both individually and collectively. So the Gould Farmers cling to their vision of a great network of such "spas of the spirit," extending throughout this country and eventually throughout the world.

Dr. Bowen of course shared in this hope of the Gould Farmers, and in speaking of it he touched upon the primary requisite to its being successfully fulfilled.

"There is no reason why such homes should not multiply, and the country everywhere be made to minister largely to the city's distresses. Yes, there is one reason. It cannot be done as it is done at Gould Farm without such wise and gracious personalities as make Gould Farm what it is. Given such personalities, the thing can be done with ease... The really important factors are those which money does not and cannot provide."

Certainly the Gould Farms of tomorrow would need to be founded in a manner similar to the founding of the present Farm. They would have to be established in each instance by a group of people who were filled with what we have called "the spirit of Gould Farm," people who were indeed the spiritual kindred of Will Gould and his disciples; people who were completely consecrated to that type of service. They would need to establish a home, live in it together in the noblest way they could, and open the doors of that home to the needy, being governed by the same motives and principles as were the original Gould Farmers. A Gould Farm could not be established by a group of people, no matter how well trained they were in social service and therapeutic techniques, who did not come together with a profound desire to live together in the "Christian" way we have described, or who did not all possess a transforming sense of a mission to be fulfilled in this type of healing ministry. The "something more" that we recall as the genius of Gould Farm would be missing.

It is in view of the unique character of the present Farm that we recognize the necessity of modeling the proposed Farms (Hospital Social Service article) after it. For its uniqueness is the secret of its distinctive contribution to modern social service, and is the chief instigation for creating the Farms of Tomorrow.

"Aunt Agnes" and her helpers would correct the writer by saying that it is the Farm of tomorrow which they hope will be the pattern for the Farms of Tomorrow. That is to say, they feel that the present Gould Farm is not yet sufficiently perfected to serve as such a model. They wish to bring the life and the work of the Farm nearer to their ideals before they offer it as a definite example. But this is more in regard to the details of organization and equipment than with reference to the principles upon which they operate. They but wish to make those principles more apparent and effective. They wish to grow more before they assume that larger responsibility.

Those principles, however, are really the only important preparation for the Farms of Tomorrow. The home Farm of course could not be precisely duplicated anywhere else, as far as its tangible aspects are concerned. Each new Farm would have its own outward characteristics, in accord with its location and the other conditions which would shape its formation. But the essential principles and characteristics—the peculiar combination of them which would make a Gould Farm—would be universally applicable, and they could be flexibly applied to particular circumstances. It is those few essential features that we are here concerned with, and the Farm of today can well serve as an exemplar of them.

The first of those principles we have noted as the character of the persons which would establish the Farms of Tomorrow. The second, obviously, is that each new Farm must be a settlement definitely apart from the environs and atmosphere of city life; it must have nature as its environment, and be primarily a farm economy, in which all the residents might share equally in the processes of production and consumption, meeting their simple economic necessities as autonomously as possible.

Above all, each new Farm must be based upon religious family life, for that would be its genius. Each must be a home in the highest sense of the term, where a "dear togetherness" forms a spiritual bond of kinship and mutual helpfulness. The life of each Farm would have to be a discriminative, shared quest of the true values of human life—the "spiritual values" we enlarged upon in an earlier chapter. Thus would the cultural excellence and the healing ministry of each Farm be assured.

Included in these few fundamental principles would be that implied by Brother Will's' saying, "This is a growth, not a scheme,"—a growth in the spiritual approach to, and increasing solution of, all their problems and relationships. Thus would institutionalism and an over-hurried development be avoided through a gradual and stable evolution from a small, simple beginning. The writer takes the liberty of quoting from a letter from "Aunt Agnes" to him, in order to illustrate the philosophy of the Gould Farmers as to this principle of spiritual growth. It is in reference to the new main building on the Farm, but its comprehensive quality is apparent:

"It is difficult to put such things in writing and it would be more exciting if I could tell you that we had the building fund complete, but I am inclined to think very seriously that we are better off for growing at the roots and that to get the spiritual matters more firmly in hand is much better than to have got the building while we wait for the more vital and important things. I know that we are coming to a deeper realization that the Farm must stand by the truths that are so vitally important for the souls of men... We have had some remarkable instances that prove this and I am happier than ever in believing that Gould Farm is to carry a message of supreme truth, that the welfare of mankind depends upon its allegiance in all things great and small to the laws of God."

What nobler modern expression of faith in the spiritual law, "Seek ye first the kingdom of heaven..." would be found! It is this very faith that will initiate the creation of the Farms of Tomorrow, and insure their success.

Where among us are those who will follow the example of the Gould Farmers? Who among us are who wish to make our religion count for something in the redemption of our society are willing to express it in this most practical and effective way? Here is a challenge for our liberal churches especially to ponder over. So few of them do anything significant in the way of definite measures toward social reconstruction. Do they not have here the opportunity of sponsoring the creation of Gould Farms? Would not any church, and the individuals in it, feel that their function as members of a universal "democratic theocracy" were being much better fulfilled if they became "Gould Farmers," if they made possible the healing ministry of such farm-homes of Christian living for the needy ones of their community?

May we be courageous enough, religious enough, to make the ultimate ideal of the Gould Farmers a living reality, through the Gould Farms of Tomorrow!

From about 2000 through 2010, Crossing Creeks provided support and residency to those with persistent mental illness from Virginia's Shenandoah Valley. A grass-roots effort, it established a residential therapeutic community on a 150-acre farm. Its founders had ties to Gould Farm. The organization, struggling financially, later sold the property to Our Community Place, Inc., based in Harrisonburg, Virginia, which is now using the property as a residential facility which assists those with drug addiction and other disorders.

The following is from an article titled "Field of Dreams: Group Crusades to Build Local Community for the Mentally Ill." It appeared in the August 5, 2000, "Skyline" section of the *Daily News-Record*, published in Harrisonburg, Virginia.[4]

Earl and Pat Martin's lives changed five years ago when they got close to a mentally ill family member.

They know the trauma of seeing the person suffer.

"You go through all the stages of grief—denial, the anger, the bargaining." Earl Martin, a Harrisonburg carpenter, says. "Here is your beloved who is struggling, struggling, struggling and in anguish."

The Martins visited Gould Farm in Monterey, Mass, where mentally ill residents live and work with staff, volunteers and family members without mental illness.

The experience showed them "a decent, fruitful life was possible" for the mentally ill, Martin says.

The couple is in a Harrisonburg-based group, Crossing Creeks Association, that plans to develop a community for the mentally ill in Rockingham County.

The private, nonprofit group wants to buy a farm of about 125 acres and "create a community where each person would be seen and understood as having unique and valuable gifts to contribute for the mutual enhancement of all," Martin says.

The mentally ill would live, do farm chores and other work with volunteers and staff including mental health professionals, gardeners, artists and others without mental illness. Woodworking, ceramics and other shops might be offered.

That arrangement would be unique in Virginia, Martin notes.

Such a supportive environment could boost confidence and self-esteem of the mentally ill by their being with people "who understand that for some folks even to get up in the morning is a fairly heroic act," Martin says.

The goal is to integrate the mentally ill into society with jobs and a way to live independently or in a community apart from their family...

We continue with a selection from Crossing Creeks Newsletter, in a section called "From Earl's Files," written by Crossing Creeks founder, Earl Martin. Earl Martin works as a renovation carpenter in people's homes in the Shenandoah Valley. His family has first-hand experience with mental health issues, and he helped found Crossing Creeks, a therapeutic farm for folks with mental health struggles.[5]

We've all hoped that Crossing Creeks might get up and running more quickly than it has. But good gestation can be quite valuable and it seems traction is picking up again. For inspiration, I sometimes look back over the notes of the meeting we had with Liz and Virgil Stucker of Gould Farm fame. (Gould Farm, you remember, is that inspired community in the Berkshire Hills of Massachusetts where folks with mental illness live and work together with other folks for mutual enrichment and healing.)

When Virgil asked us why we wanted to establish a place like Crossing Creeks, these were some of our responses:

"I hope my son might be a member of this 'farm' as a guest or volunteer."

"Yearning for whole, meaningful, joyful lives for all of us as broken, incomplete persons."

"I have personal experience with mental illness, and see that it can enrich our lives."

"I want to see a more productive and respectful residential community be developed because my commitment to those with mental illness is great and this area has been woefully underserved."

I believe that vision remains strong and that community we dream of is a-birthing!—Earl Martin

The last of the three pieces included here about Crossing Creeks is by a Virginia-based writer, Melodie Davis, from her 2005 article titled "New Farm in the Valley for Persons with Mental Illness." It appeared in a quarterly called *Valley Living for the Whole Family* based in Harrisonburg, Virginia.

"There's not a big fat lock on the door!" says Jayme, an artist and one of the first resident renters at Crossing Creeks farm not far from Endless Caverns just inside Rockingham County. She was comparing its innovative program to traditional mental hospitals or programs where she has lived while seeking treatment for mental illness. "We have rights, everything is voluntary, and it's like a family."

Crossing Creeks is a one-year-old (closed on the property last June) planned residential community for persons living with long-term mental illness. Its statement of purpose says it "seeks to be a supportive therapeutic community where persons with persistent mental illness can live and work with others for the mutual benefit of all."

Traditional hospitals isolate acutely ill patients from their natural environments and support systems, remove them from their homes and communities, and place them in restrictive institutional settings. This often has the unintended result of making feelings of paranoia, alienation and depression worse...

There is no other "working farm" program for the mentally ill in Virginia. Crossing Creeks is patterned after the nearly-century-old Gould Farm in Massachusetts, but there are only five additional such programs in the U.S....

Nancy Smith, a psychiatric nurse at Gould Farm for 10 years and now retired in Harrisonburg, served as co-president for Crossing Creeks for the past four years. She said that her sister, who had a son who experienced mental illness, and a group of parents in the Shenandoah Valley whose adult children had lived at the farm in Massachusetts, planted the seed for a program here because there was none...

This chapter concludes with the following essay by Virgil Stucker, founding Chairman and President of the Foundation for Excellence in Mental Health Care and current and founding Executive Director and President of CooperRiis Healing Community. He has integrated his life with therapeutic communities since 1975 when he first started at Gould Farm, America's oldest therapeutic community for individuals recovering from mental illness. Gould Farm is one of the models CooperRiis has followed.

Virgil felt destined to help create therapeutic communities; after 14 years at Gould Farm, he was the founding Executive Director of Rose Hill in Michigan which opened in 1992 and of Gateway Homes of Richmond, Virginia, which opened in 1986. In 1978 he was the founding Program Director of Gould Farm's Boston Program.

Virgil also took some "sabbaticals" (as he puts it) from the life of therapeutic community, each of which further explored his interest in community and the power of relationships. In Massachusetts, he is past founding president of the REACH Community Health Foundation, Vice President of Planning and Development for Northern Berkshire Health Systems, President of the Berkshire Taconic Community Foundation, Senior Vice President of Legacy Banks, a community banking system, and Adjunct Professor of Philanthropy for the Visionaries Institute of Suffolk University. His degrees include an MBA with a focus on non-profit creation and management and a BA in philosophy.

In addition to their personal involvement with therapeutic communities, Virgil and his wife Lis share their lives with their four children, two daughters-in-law, one son-in-law, and seven grandchildren.

Stucker's essay, which follows, was written specifically for this Reader.

GOULD FARM: ONE HUNDRED YEARS AND STILL "CONNECTING THE DOTS"[6]

If Will and Agnes Gould were alive today, I believe they would be managing many Gould Farms and inspiring others to do the same. Will and Agnes were operating Gould Farm on three separate sites in Monterey when Brother Will (as he was called by those at Gould Farm) died; the current one, one on Wellman Road in Monterey, and one in New Marlboro. Will had also been planning on opening a City Home in New York City. A likely heart attack, while fighting a fire threatening the Main House, took him from Gould Farm in 1925. Agnes incorporated Gould Farm as a nonprofit in 1929 and infused a spirit of replication in its official mission. The discussion about replication was also articulated years later by Rev. Sydney McKee, one of Gould Farm's early leaders, pastor, and visionary. His wife, Rose McKee, also held social work and leadership positions at the Farm. The Corporate Minute Books of The William J. Gould Associates contain a quote from Rev. McKee, in the 1940s, wherein he envisions "Gould Farms dotting the landscape."

It would be many years before active expansion efforts would be launched. After Brother Will's death the broader replication vision became inactive and some of the properties were sold, shrinking the Farm to its current 600 acres from 1200 to 1400 accumulated acres. The healing community of Gould Farm flourished on its current site for decades. Although Will and Agnes' hopes and dreams were never intended to be contained within this Monterey property, the vision of Gould Farms dotting the landscape would need to wait for another day to be re-ignited.

In the 1950s and 60s the long-serving Executive Director, Rev. Hampton Price, helped to move Gould Farm from being a family-run endeavor to an organization which still operated within an atmosphere of kindness and generosity. During this time, academics like University of Chicago Sociologist Henrik Infield studied the workings of Gould Farm with his students and found that its "atmosphere of kindness" was one of its primary criteria for healing.

Kent Smith, ordained Presbyterian minister and long-serving Executive Director, replaced Hampton Price. During Kent's tenure as Executive Director from the mid-70s to early 90s, confidence in the broader Gould Farm vision grew and the words of "expansion" and "replication" once again emerged. Religious leaders like Theologian James Luther Adams of the University of Chicago and Harvard Divinity Schools studied the work of Gould Farm and also had a summer home there. A proponent of the social power of "voluntary associations," Dr. Adams would dialogue into the night with frequent Farm visitor, author, and psychiatrist, Eric Fromm, about the healing power of the "communal process" at the Farm. (As reported in the Summer 2010 Newsletter from the University of Chicago Divinity School.) I remember fondly getting to know Dr.

Adams. Our first encounter was when he, Kent, and I travelled to the Bruderhof (Society of Brothers) in Norfolk, CT. Encouraged by Gould Farm's communal success, our shared purpose was to foster a dialogue with this religious community about expanding their spiritual work into social service. It worked. They subsequently launched a line of wooden toys for handicapped children, a move which seems to have been prompted by Dr. Adams' encouragement.

Kent and I, as a Gould Farm staff colleague, next planned a vertical expansion of Gould Farm's work. We desired to expand its community support into more urban settings where housing and work could be available for recovering residents. We planned to do this in Pittsfield, MA. Former staff member Rev. Henry Stewart diverted our attention with a potential offer to use the 80 acres of Farrington Memorial in Lincoln, MA. On September 21, 1978, we travelled to see this property, a former TB sanatorium. By Christmas of 1978, my wife Lis, our son, Dominic, and I moved to the 40-room house on the grounds of Farrington Memorial, and Gould Farm's Farrington House and, ultimately, today's 'Boston Program', was born.

A few years later Gould Farm pondered what to do with a testamentary gift of a 250-acre estate from the Beineke Family of S&H Green Stamp fame in Great Barrington. This property was held by the Farm for quite some time and produced new thoughts of expansion. Kent and I discussed the possibility that this property could be a site for a specialized Gould Farm for long-term care. We were attracted instead to expand Gould Farm's growing presence in the Boston area and the property was sold. The cash was invested in apartment buildings which became part of Gould Farm's extended community.

Kent Smith's attention was next drawn to a suggestion that Gould Farm should consider a full replication on the grounds of the Koinonia Community, a Maryland-based missionary community (not to be confused with the one in Georgia) which operates as a foundation today. He, Lis, and I visited, pondered this possibility, and backed away. The challenge of fully replicating Gould Farm seemed too daunting at that time.

During this time, I was growing through most of the positions at the Farm and had been asked by Kent to consider one day becoming the Executive Director after his term. I had joined the Farm in 1975, thinking I would stay only for three months. Enamored of the restored lives I saw unfolding before me, I stayed for 14 years. In 1976, Lis Otter, a beautiful, 24-year old, red-headed German came to Gould Farm as a peace volunteer through Action Reconciliation Service for Peace. She thought she would stay for only a year. Within six weeks I had asked her to marry me as we sat on a riverside rock near the Gould Farm sauna. Married a few months later on Topside Knoll overlooking the Farm's garden, we stayed and stayed...by 1983, four children had joined us: Dominic, Christoph, Heidi and Stephanie.

By 1986, a call from Virginia for a 'dot on the landscape' (a new community) arrived. Lis and I responded and we joined the Moore Family in Chesterfield, just south of Richmond, Virginia. The newly incorporated, nonprofit Gateway Homes, Inc., was envisioned as a Gould Farm replication. We settled into the plantation home on the James River. Unfortunately, progress stalled for reasons beyond our control. Instead of a farm community, we began Gateway's operation as a 'city home,' sort of like Gould Farm's Boston Program. This was my first 'executive director' experience. Seeing that the timing was not right for a full replication, my family and I returned after a short while to Gould

Farm, pleased at least with having established Gateway's city home. Years later, Gateway's full rural and urban program has unfolded and its work fits well
with the Gould Farm mission.

Upon returning to Gould Farm in 1987, new career challenges were posed
and I continued to grow through all of the various positions at Gould Farm, except for the role of Executive Director. In 1989, another 'dot' arrived on the
horizon. Daniel and Rosemary Kelly of Detroit, whose family member had
been helped by Gould Farm, envisioned a full replication of Gould Farm in
Michigan. They were to be the Chairman and Vice Chair of the Board of Rose
Hill Center, Inc., in Holly, Michigan. Lis and I were to lead the staff with me as
Executive Director. We built Rose Hill from the ground-up, stone-by-stone, so
to speak. From 1989 until 1992, we toiled daily to design, develop, and open
Rose Hill. We boot-strapped the fundraising and eventually helped to raise well
over the $5M needed for success. In May of 1992, we opened Rose Hill. Rose
Hill and Gateway are both doing well today, as separate nonprofit organizations
imbued with the principles of Gould Farm.

While working in other areas of philanthropy—building the Berkshire Taconic Community Foundation and the REACH Community Health Foundation
(both in the Berkshires a few miles from Gould Farm)—occasional 'dots'
would call. I worked as a consultant for Clara Rankin whose Board subsequently opened the Gould Farm-oriented Hopewell Inn in Mesopotamia, Ohio. The
Menninger Clinic also hired me as a consultant, with the hope of building a
Gould Farm-like place on their 700 acres in Kansas. (Later, the Menninger
Clinic was sold to the Baylor Health Care System in Houston, Texas, and these
acres were sold.)

In 1999, Lis and I met Don and Lisbeth Riis Cooper and their daughter as
they reviewed existing programs with the hope of finding a 'best model' for a
program for the Southeast. Kim Hines of Gould Farm connected us. The Coop-
ers wanted a special program that would help other families not go through the
personal hell they had experienced as they sought proper care for their daughter. Spring Lake Ranch in Vermont (started in 1933) had been helpful to their
daughter and they wondered if a similar program would be helpful in the
Southeast. Lis and I gave them some documentation and written plans we had
developed through our experience and wished them well.

Time passed and they came back to us. In October 2002, Don reached out
to us and we learned that they had begun to accomplish some magnificent
things. They had raised the needed donations and construction of a new healing
community was well underway. They wanted a Gould Farm- and Spring Lake
Ranch-type of facility and they wanted us to lead the staff to do it. We joined
them and opened CooperRiis in June 2003. CooperRiis will be ten years old on
the 15th of June, 2013, and has grown to 100 residents in its multiple settings
and has 180 staff.

The essence of Gould Farm is replicable. Perhaps you are a Gould Farmer
who already knows this to be true. Or you may be working on other versions of
recovery programs and may have also captured the essence of healing community in your own work. Step back a moment and ponder both the concepts that
underlie the modernized Gould Farm and the historic paradigm shift that is underway in the United States and abroad, a shift that is making good on the hope
of Gould Farms "dotting the landscape," in the words of Rev. McKee. Theologian James Luther Adams also encouraged replication 58 years ago in his book

entitled *Voluntary Associations*. He wrote of Gould Farm, "There are few of such communities, if any, in this country. More of them should be established. As Dr. Infield says, the example of Gould Farm makes this task easier." (Page 257)

Approaches to 'mental health care' cycle through the millennia between reductionist thinking (seeking a single solution for all) and broader thinking that tends more to rely upon comprehensive, collaborative, compassionate, and community-based approaches, which can be individualized. In the 1700s scientists thought that psychosis was caused by excess blood in the brain, so we bled the afflicted. Ice-pick lobotomies were also once the conclusion of reductionist thinking. We appear today to be at the end of an era that relied too much on trying to find the perfect pills. We found that some medications help some individuals for short or longer time periods, but we see now that our over-use of them as singular-solutions-for-all is raising more doubts than hopes. Internationally known science writer, Robert Whitaker, in the *Anatomy of an Epidemic*, even argues that our over-use of medications has contributed to excessively high levels of chronicity, indeed a tripling of the number of chronically mentally ill in the last 25 years.

As we broaden our focus, we are now recognizing that chronicity can be replaced with the modern concepts of recovery. The goals, as traditionally defined and practiced, of "housing" and "maintenance" are no longer acceptable. These have turned into warehousing and social shame with over 600,000 of our modern day mentally ill in the United States languishing in jails and prisons. My personal mission has been to maximize recovery outcomes by infusing the power of healing community into today's recovery programming, which I shall describe below as the New Mainstream.

In my own work at CooperRiis, we have also added a strong practice of psychotherapy, optimized medications mixed with nutraceuticals, holistic nutrition, and exercise programming along with other complementary modalities. The framework for these myriad modalities is still the healing community concepts drawn from my experience at Gould Farm and the development of its Boston program and my earlier efforts of replication at Gateway Homes and Rose Hill Center. In addition to these communities, we acknowledge the contributions of members of the American Residential Treatment Association (www.ARTAusa.org), especially those who are nonprofit healing communities in their own right, such as Spring Lake Ranch and Hopewell.

Honest, mission-driven research is needed to help promote and develop the New Mainstream of mental health care that is represented by these organizations, which believe that Recovery should be expected as the norm. This is also one of the objectives of the new Foundation for Excellence in Mental Health Care, Inc. (www.FEMHC.org), the nation's first community foundation for mental health care, for which I am the volunteer Chairman of the Board. The Foundation is a group of scientists, psychiatrists, researchers, public policy analysts, users and providers of mental health services, philanthropists, and community members that formed the Foundation to find and promote the best ways to achieve long-term recovery and help people with mental health challenges to thrive. It represents the "New Mainstream" which endorses comprehensive approaches in the middle and eschews radical reductionism that on one bank says, "Medications are a Must," or on the other bank says "Medications are Never an Option."

Both CooperRiis' and Gould Farm's outcome data also already show that their broader, more comprehensive, yet individualized approaches are indeed helping the afflicted achieve 'recovery' from their mental health challenges. The time has come for us to ramp up our activities and increase our investment of philanthropic and creative resources into strengthened efforts to help Gould Farm-type organizations to 'dot the landscape.' These types of healing communities need to become our nation's new paradigm of mental health care.

Concepts Underpinning the Healing Community: Change requires a unifying vision and sound conceptual principles. The field is struggling. Debates continue to draw some into factions, with some seeing mental health challenges as interior, even as biological entities, and with others seeing them as only exterior experiences caused by trauma and/or one's environment. Historically, the Freudian approach overly focuses on the interior and even sub-consciousness-oriented therapies. On the other hand, B.F. Skinner's behaviorist approach did the opposite and assumes that focusing on exterior forces alone could achieve the desired 'recovery' results.

As I look for the middle ground, I have found balance between these seeming polar opposites in the conceptual understanding of psychiatrist Harry Stack Sullivan (a colleague of Eric Fromm's and contemporary of James Luther Adams). Dr. Sullivan believed that a healthy personality is the result of healthy relationships beginning in earliest infancy and that understanding of what he called "problems in living" arises form an understanding of interpersonal relationships. This was the cornerstone of Sullivan's theory of interpersonal relations. Sullivan spent his life working with patients, psychiatrists, and social psychologists to prove that people are influenced mostly by their relationships with others. For example, his special ward for individuals living with schizophrenia at Sheppard Pratt Hospital in Maryland demonstrated the power of a healing community's ability to treat residents previously thought to be untreatable.

Thanks to my colleague Kent Smith and to the writings of Barton Evans, Sullivan scholar and psychologist, my understanding of the more balanced approach to psychology and psychiatry of Harry Stack Sullivan has helped me to value more fully the power of the dynamic between both the exterior and the interior. Dr. Sullivan's interpersonal psychotherapy resonates with the relationship-centered care found in healing communities. He envisioned "Schools of Personality Development" to help mentally health-challenged individuals to reintegrate with community and with life. Gould Farm, which began in 1913, naturally used Dr. Sullivan's approach as one of his 'Schools' even before knowing it. Kent Smith, influenced by Dr. Sullivan's ideas, infused his own and Sullivan's ideas into the daily life of Gould Farm in a way that resonates with my understanding of human nature.

Steve Smith, son of Kent and Nancy Smith (long-serving nurse at Gould Farm), also connected me with the works of Sullivan scholar Dorothy Blitsten of Hunter College, who wrote:

"He [Sullivan] has given us some insight into the function of group contexts in the development and maintenance of personal integration itself in all human beings, which is, in the final analysis, the basis for enduring human life. By demonstrating in practice that the personal reorganization of people who were severely disintegrated can be achieved—or prevented—by reorganizing the group contexts in which they live, Sullivan supplied proof of the functional relationship between group integrations with their regulating prescriptions and the personal integration of their members." (Page 11: *Harry Stack Sullivan's Suggestions Concerning the Place of Small Groups in Personality Development.*)

Dorothy Blitsten also wrote that "Sullivan came to feel that what he referred to as the 'apparent tendency of personalities to enter into group relationship' is a universal human phenomenon..." (Page 7). My philosophical study of metaphysics and basic understanding of quantum physics also leads me to believe that humankind is indeed meant to live naturally in community and in relationship. Furthermore, the 'logos' or unifying principle of community is 'philanthropy,' translated as the love of humankind. Community life can, however, be disturbed. For some, the resulting mental health challenges can be disengaging and cause one to become 'stuck.' How can one resolve this state of 'disease?' Consider how relationship-centered care (a.k.a. Sullivan's Interpersonal Psychotherapy) can be offered in healing communities like Gould Farm and CooperRiis that dynamically relate external and internal factors to help the afflicted person to recover their engagement in life.

Pragmatic idealists and academic researchers devoted to building and validating mental health recovery programs should turn to these principles of therapeutic and healing community embodied at Gould Farm and its sister organizations. Dr. Sullivan's prescriptive concepts for interpersonal support have given us some of the basis for planning; Gould Farm has given us an example of successful practical application for many decades. Building on this awareness, we now have an opportunity to merge modern 'recovery principles' into balanced approaches that will help to move us toward the paradigm shift that is needed.

Gould Farm, the Historic Leader: As demonstrated above, the journey toward this vision actually began at Gould Farm 100 years ago. In the coming 100 years, Gould Farm and its sister organizations can be the motivating forces for re-humanizing mental health care and for bringing into public discourse needed dialogue about the healing power of community. A few years ago, recognizing and supporting this emergence, Oliver Sacks, MD, wrote in the *New York Review of Books* (September 24, 2009) that CooperRiis and Gould Farm are indeed attempting to "restore the lost virtues of the asylum," namely those virtues that infuse the compassionate, community-based, comprehensive care that is offered by their programs.

Gould Farm is the historic leader of this movement and can now be seen as an awakening giant, taking its place in the pantheon of healing communities. Within the giant's bones rests the full vision for the movement it is destined to help lead. The time is right for Gould Farm to realize that it was never meant to be contained on its idyllic acres in Monterey. As the giant stands erect and casts its vision toward the horizon, it will attract and energize its current and future community of staff, guests, and Board members with a sense of mission that will make possible its original calling to help Gould Farms to "dot the landscape." It is my belief that this energy will also strengthen, rather than weaken, the home base of Gould Farm.

Today is a better time than ever to capture the stars and toss them onto the horizon with each being a seed for a new community. Today, we have more promise for philanthropy than ever before with the potential for millions to be raised each year in donations from aging baby boomers who are still looking for their destiny. The Foundation for Excellence in Mental Health Care could be a platform and matchmaker for this philanthropy. Whether through the Foundation or not, the time is right for Gould Farm leadership to help light the way for replication, even though the vision is daunting and may feel impossible. There are three main tasks that stand before each new 'impossible' start-up that can be overcome: a) raising the philanthropic capital (it can be done); b) finding the right staff leadership (it will be done through a Leadership Institute that would be developed); and c) traversing the myriad regulations that can extinguish energy and efforts (improved public relations and policy discourse will accomplish this).

Fortitude and foresight will help the practical idealists to prevail. Consider the essence of "Gould Farm" and "CooperRiis" which spans many decades and years, 100 and 10 respectively. Each points in profound ways toward a better future for mental health care. F. Barton Evans III, recent CooperRiis visitor and author of *Harry Stack Sullivan, Interpersonal Theory and Psychotherapy*, said, "I really sensed the connection between your work at CooperRiis and Sullivan's ideas... What you are doing on the CooperRiis Farm and at your Asheville center are in many ways the fruition of what Harry Stack Sullivan started at Sheppard Pratt, only you are doing it far better than even he could have imagined." I believe Dr. Evans would say the same of Gould Farm were he to see it.

Even though Dr. Sullivan died in 1949, three years before my birth, his concepts seem fresh and unifying during these fractious days. There are thousands and thousands of individuals who seek recovery from their mental health challenges and they could benefit by having access to Gould Farm and CooperRiis models of care, which resonate with Dr. Sullivan's progressive concepts. The path to excellence in mental health care is clear; courageous and practical idealists along with visionary philanthropists are called into the journey. The grander vision of "dotting the landscape" is yet to be fulfilled!

The words of Rev. Dr. James Luther Adams call us to action. He wrote in *Voluntary Associations*, "In the Gould Farm of the future there will be, as in the past, new treasures as well as old. Indeed, without new treasures the old ones are themselves likely to disappear. This fact calls for a risking faith. Gould Farm cherishes its past, but it also moves venturingly into the burgeoning present." (Page 258) Risks, courage, and adventure; this is the stuff of recovery. Let us be bold.—Virgil Stucker, December 11, 2012

Notes and Permissions

1. See chapter 2 for the entire text of the charter.

2. Infield, Henrik F. "Gould Farm: A Therapeutic Cooperative Community." *The American Intentional Communities: Study on the Sociology of Cooperation*. New Jersey: Glen Gardner Community Press, 1955. 108.

3. McMillan, Donald. A Dissertation, submitted to the Graduate Faculty in Candidacy for the Degree of Bachelor of Divinity. The Meadville Theological School, Department of Practical Theology, 1935. Used with permission from Meadville Lombard Theological School.

4. Used with permission from the *Daily News Record*.

5. Used with author's permission.

6. Used with author's permission.

The Content and Context of Justice

Should more Gould Farms exist? The following will attempt to address this question by further examining the perspective of the Gould Farm process itself and the Gould Farm process in relation to broader perspectives, scholarship, and movements concerning the treatment of mental illness.

This *Gould Farm Reader* directs attention away from individualist accounts of deficiency and exclusion, and redirects attention towards social accounts of inclusion, participation, and productivity. Gould Farm, now celebrating 100 years of service, in many ways is 150 years ahead of its time! Finding one word to define Gould Farm is inadequate because the Farm, as you have read, means different things to different people: reciprocity, dignity, mutuality, respect, caring, inclusive community, democracy, and so on. People are served and serve in different ways according to their own abilities and needs and in relation to others who also serve and are served in the life of the community. This flexibility is part of the success of Gould Farm. This moves the process of achieving justice toward an open-ended collective endeavor rather than judgment.[1]

An urgent question, relating directly to this *Reader* and also to justice and social organization in general is: Who is responsible to do what for whom? The following will address this in terms of the historical and social context of Gould Farm and in relation to justice. The indirect answers provided by Gould Farm are rich and insightful. Part of the answer lies in justice and participation, discussed below. Another crucial component of the answer is not found in a formal proclamation or creed but in the unique context of coping with the (often ambiguous) daily process of meaningful interaction, found above in the life story of Will and Agnes Gould, in the history of the Farm itself, and especially in the life stories of many of the accounts of Gould Farm guests. In terms of meaning, research confirms that "people leading meaningful lives get a lot of joy from giving to others."[2]

This *Reader* is a tribute to the multiple ways in which those who have been served and serve at Gould Farm. That it may not be immediately apparent who is a guest and who is staff is one of the achievements of the Gould Farm approach. Stereotypes around mental illness are difficult to dissolve and assumptions about those with mental illness diagnosis are difficult to shift. However, a number of those who use mental health services are articulating their own recovery narratives away from pathology, creating alternative communities, and even engaging in political activism demanding greater rights for the mental health community.[3] At the same time, many diagnosed with mental illness are actively helping each other.

In terms of justice, this shift in emphasis is slowly transforming a mental health system that once was oriented around control to a system increasingly articulating and demanding procedural issues of due process and participating actively in their own recovery. A former guest of Gould Farm once referred to the transformation of wide-spread mental health services as the civil rights movement of the 21st century. It is here that we discover the full meaning of "inclusive community" at the Farm. What happens at Gould Farm also reaffirms due process concerns in democracy. Justice in democracy requires, on the one hand, individuals to share in "communities that control their own destinies" and individuals "who identify sufficiently with those communities to think and act with a view to the common good," and, on the other hand, communities that serve and nurture the capacities and freedoms of individuals.[4] The virtues of civic participation, a large component of justice, are developed and nurtured in this complex process of mutual participation and reciprocity at Gould Farm.

A former guest of Gould Farm, John Otenasek, shows insight into the dynamics of the Gould Farm approach. John was institutionalized for mental illness at the age of 18. He is now a highly-functioning professional mental health service provider, a former Johns Hopkins University researcher, and a current Gould Farm board member. John remarked that when he is feeling at his lowest he does something counter-intuitive to much mainstream therapeutic guidance: rather than seek immediate help for himself, he looks for someone else to help. Serving another human being somehow has a reciprocity effect that helps him in return. This former guest is taking more control of his own treatment at the same time that he is helping another, perhaps more troubled, person. Perhaps this is best explained in his own words:

Thirty years ago I was facing a life of disability and told to not hope for school, marriage, kids, a good job. My job was symptom management and, oh yeah, there is no cure. I became dependent as I struggled to accept this burden—a yoke—I felt like I was just an experiment. What came to me in a rush was this: maybe if something I am going through now helps another patient somewhere else, well then, that would serve some purpose to my suffering. This thought sustained me through the dark nights of the soul. I was detached and resistant to treatment—uninvolved in my own life. My art therapist used to complain: "John, can you use another color now besides black?"

After three hospital stays totaling 20 months and two halfway houses the power of Gould Farm came into my life. It has been an alternative to traditional treatment for almost 100 years and has been a part of my life for 26 of those years. I came seeking health and life and received expectations I could achieve;

these were work and community. I was going to find what I could uniquely contribute to the farm, be it scrubbing a bath, milking a cow, or making lunch for 75 people. I also played a role only I could fulfill in that community. This was my chance to self-actualize and rise above my diagnosis to become the person I was meant to become. Realizing along the way that in ministering to others we ourselves are ministered to...thus beginning a 20-year career in service to the mentally ill. I am uniquely qualified to work as a peer-provider—a role informed by the sum of my experiences and revelations since my childhood of my own mental illness.[5]

John Otenasek raises several important points. At the Farm, John was able to move from a sense of hopelessness and a life centered on *managing* his mental illness to a life contributing to a community and *overcoming* perceived limitations that his diagnosis placed on him. He highlighted the contrast between being "dependent" on others and "fulfilling a role only I could fulfill in a community."

John's positive experience at the Farm is centered in actively participating in the life of a community. Communities, as he recognized, can serve one's own needs through the process of serving the needs of others. Farm guests, he continues, are active:

They aren't waiting for a doctor or pill to cure them; they are taking care of themselves and those around them. This I thought is the future of mental health care in our country. Never doubt that a small band of concerned people can change the world—indeed it is the only thing that ever has...

John makes a radical proposal: for many diagnosed with mental illness it may be better to take mental health care out of the institutions and "put it into the community and into the hands of those who need it and deliver it to them on their own terms." It seems impossible to overstate the importance of participating in life in a meaningful way. Gould Farm is a space in which community is created and where serving one's own needs are woven into meeting the needs of others in the community.[6] At the very least, the insights of John, a service-user and service-provider, give points to ponder. Work, community, participation, meaning, and service provide insights into the "magic" that can occur at the very mundane day-to-day life of an intentional community.

To understand the selections from this *Reader* and the contribution made by Gould Farm it is important to locate the 100 years of Gould Farm within the broader context of perspectives on mental health and the attempts at mental health reform. Placing the Gould Farm approach within this larger context is not done to disparage mental health care professionals and institutions designed to serve those with mental illness. Gould Farm incorporates best practices from mental health care. However, Will Gould's "experiment" does deserve a closer look from mental health care professionals and from those suffering mental illness.

PERSPECTIVES ON MENTAL HEALTH

The concept of mental health and mental illness is highly contested. Different theoretical perspectives provide different evaluations of normality and abnormality. Much of the literature discusses the individual characteristics of the mental abnormality. Anne Rogers and David Pilgrim outline four distinct individual approaches to mental illness: psychiatry, psychoanalysis, psychology, and the legal framework.[7] *Psychiatry* is the dominant discourse on mental illness and alternative discourses compete for recognition and authority within this dominant medical model. In particular, biological diagnosis and biological treatment are favored. Mental abnormality is viewed as an illness embedded in neurological conditions.[8] *Psychoanalysis* emphasizes personal history and the interaction between the unconscious and conscious. When maladjusted, this dynamic gives rise to psychopathology. Social aspects of life history are interpreted as personal. *Psychology* focuses on "normal" and "deviant" experience and conduct through statistical frequency, maladaptive behavior, and/or cognitive distortions. Finally, the *legal framework* defines two conditions of mental illness. First, the conditions are defined under which mental health professionals can and cannot constrain or compulsorily treat patients when no criminal law has been broken. Second, it defines criteria by which someone who has violated the law is deemed mentally accountable and subject to sentencing accordingly. Judgments about mental health and categories of illness or disorder are subject to a myriad interpretations. None of these above descriptions captures adequately what happens at Gould Farm. Finally, another perspective, both implied and made explicit throughout this *Reader* and as described in more detail below, the *sociological* perspectives on mental illness are gaining in relevance and do provide better insight into the Gould Farm approach.[9] To be clear, Gould Farm does not attempt to replace or ignore the benefits of psycho-pharmaceutical interventions or the contributions made by staff and visiting psychiatrists and mental health specialists. However, the success of Gould Farm is better explained by utilizing the sociological perspective, discussed in more detail in a later section.

BRIEF HISTORY OF MENTAL HEALTH REFORM

To better understand and appreciate the Gould Farm contribution, it is important to compare what happens at the Farm and how this differs from other professional mental health treatments and perspectives. Gould Farm "guests" (the Farm's term for those seeking help) are in a very different social environment than are "patients" of mental health services, inpatient or outpatient. The broader history of the treatment of mental illness in the United States is essentially a history of different reform movements to correct perceived deficiencies in the framework and systems for serving those with mental illnesses. Gould Farm, anticipated, in a way, each of these reform movements, which now it beckons back to the "lost virtues of the Asylum"[10] (see the above excerpt by Oliver Sacks).

Over the past three centuries in the United States, mental health services have been described as a "patchwork...determined by many heterogeneous factors rather than by a single set of organizing principles" sometimes overlapping and never fully disappearing.[11] Gerald Grob provides an extensive historical survey and overview.[12] Briefly, during the colonial period in America individuals with mental illness were cared for at home until urbanization induced state governments to build institutions (asylums and hospitals). *Moral treatment*,[13] the first reform movement, was introduced to remove the person from family and society and place these individuals in asylums in order to restore the rational (moral) reasoning of the individual. The first reformers, including Dorothea Dix and Horace Mann, were concerned to cure people from becoming chronically ill. The second reform movement, *mental hygiene*, combined the emerging orientation of public health and scientific medicine. The third reform movement, *community mental health*, argued that long-term institutional care for mental illness had been ineffective and many times harmful. With the optimism in new drug and therapeutic treatments, a period of deinstitutionalization led to a dramatic increase in outpatient services and emergence of community care centers. None of these movements fully succeeded. The latest reform movement, *community-support,* favored a voluntary support social network facilitated with both mental health professionals and service-users. Notably, service-users/survivors of mental health services are now taking active roles in their own recovery and in helping others. By forming community social networks, not only have service-users/survivors helped themselves, they have helped each other and have established sources of advocacy.

This "patchwork" mental health system is a complex that has been changing over time from a wide array of factors, not least of which is the evolving and sometimes competing understanding of mental illness itself. Integrating these various treatment orientations is difficult. Importantly, the voluntary support network component of the most recent community-support movement provides more room for optimism and more closely approximates the Gould Farm approach.

EXPERIMENTS WITH COMMUNITY, THE SOCIAL APPROACH

The above discussion of mental health is located primarily within *intra*personal phenomena, with phenomena that manifest in the biology or in the mind of an individual. While acknowledging to some degree the social context, the causal or treatment features are isolated within the individual. In fact, those diagnosed with severe and potentially harmful mental illness are institutionalized in facilities that resemble modern prisons (see Foucault, *Discipline and Punish*, 1995). On the other hand, though marginalized by the predominantly *individualist* mainstream professional understanding of mental illness and treatment, the discipline of sociology has a long history of studying *contextual* factors that affect care and the development of mental health problems.[14]

One pioneering reaction to these "impersonalized isolated institutions," developed in the United Kingdom, was to introduce a more personally engaged approach to care.[15] Following World War II and the return of large numbers of emotionally scarred soldiers, therapeutic communities (TCs) were introduced, largely out of pragmatic necessity, by psychiatrists. Scarce resources (too many patients per specialist) and TCs transformed the individual model of treatment. Encouraged to experiment with group methods, the goals of TCs were twofold: to re-socialize patients who had become dependent on individual care practices, and the use of the hospital environment as a therapeutic agent by establishing greater social engagement.[16] A resonating underlying theme of Therapeutic Communities is the further democratization of mental health care:

> Central to these objectives was the need for rapid change in the organization of the hospital in order to make it more flexible and egalitarian. Attempts were made to break down the traditionally rigid and hierarchical role divisions between staff and patients, and decisions on the running of the TC were to be decided through group discussion.[17]

However, TCs became marginalized after the 1960s and their success at changing psychiatric practice has been rather modest. The failure of many TCs seems to be directly related to the inability to further democratize the custodial practices and of bureaucratic and administrative structures of those providing mental health services in the asylum and mental hospital.[18] However, the pharmacological revolution,[19] issues of "fiscal efficiency,"[20] and the rise of "community care"[21] over the past several decades has generally replaced the old model of separating and housing all but the most severe mentally ill in the asylum. As described by John Otenasek above, peer support groups are forming with the purpose of service-users helping other service-users as a first-step support system. As noted in many of the contributions to this *Reader,* support groups were an integral, if sometimes informal, part of Gould Farm. This is a crucial development in providing adequate mental health care and, as John noted earlier, mutually help provide meaning for peers in the process. Could it be true that those with mental illness diagnosis are, to paraphrase John, indeed "uniquely qualified" to work at least in some capacities as service-providers since this is "a role informed by the sum of my experiences and revelations since my childhood of my own mental illness?"

Critical Theory—social analysis oriented toward critiquing and changing institutions and society as a whole, in contrast to traditional theory oriented only to understanding or explaining it—posits that resistance to the democratization of mental health care in the United States, by and large, comes indirectly and sometimes directly from the mental health care profession itself.[22] With varying degrees, this process of democratization is in tension with the professional separation of the specialist. While professions tend to give rather flattering self-descriptions, the sociological study of professions proceeds with varying degrees of criticisms.[23] For example, in the tradition associated with Emil Durkheim, professions are stable social stratums that regulate their own practitioners and enhance stability and social cohesion for the wider society they serve. In contrast, in the tradition inspired by Max Weber, professions develop strategies to advance their own social status, monopolize the market, and convince potential clients to utilize their services. A third perspective, Symbolic Interactionism, found in Irving Goffman's (1961) now classic study of life in the asylum, examines the "microsociology" of the meanings which are negotiated by various actors in the ritual of changing the individual's identity to that of mentally ill patient.

In order to begin to understand and manage mental illness, it is not enough to see someone with mental illness simply as someone with "delusional beliefs" and "treatment-resistant." Most mental health workers begin by defining symptoms, deficits, and dysfunctions, and then direct efforts and base evaluations to the extent to which these symptoms are managed or removed. However, this severely shapes the attitude of mental health service providers to look for negative signs and a continual focus on negative phenomena often has destructive impact on the person who experiences mental health problems:

> Deficit-obsessed research can only produce theories and attitudes which are disrespectful of clients and are also likely to induce behavior in clinicians such that service users are not properly listened to, not believed, not fairly assessed, are likely treated as inadequate and are also not expected to be able to become independent and competent individuals in managing life's tasks.[24]

For example, nearly half of those treated for mental illness who were successful in gaining employment were told by a mental health worker that they would never find work again.[25] A troubling cycle of blame is too easily asserted. However, there is no necessary correlation between reduction of symptoms and a person's sense of control or engagement.[26] One problem is that it may be difficult for mental health professionals to see people with mental health illnesses living meaningful, productive, fulfilling lives—because they only see people when their problems are at their worst. When problems subside, people tend to move away from services. In fact, most professionals do not know what life with mental illness is like. An increasing number of service-users are recognizing the possible limitations of professional expertise:

> Ex-patients are beginning to turn to each other rather than to mental health professionals for emotional and instrumental support. They are finding that people with experiential knowledge (i.e. having learned through personal experience) are more able to understand their needs than are professionals who have learned through education and training. Moreover, they are finding the support and help they can give each other to be as valuable—or sometimes more valuable—than the interventions of trained professionals.[27]

Relationships of any kind are complex and dynamic and fraught with possible problems, but people in a similar position are often well placed to help each other. It is noteworthy that mental health users did not report removal of symptoms from a list of common desires; rather, the list is comprised of themes such as acceptance, emotional support, a reason for living, taking control and having choices, and being in the company of others who shared similar experiences.[28] For Julie Repper and Rachel Perkins: "restoring dignity and self-respect [is]...at least as important as treating symptomology."[29] Numerous famous artists, scientists, writers, and leaders have experienced mental health problems.[30] Arguably some greatness is in fact the *result* of mental illness (such as manic depression).[31] Deficit and dysfunction are part of the story, but only part of it. How different might mental health services look if their primary focus was to enable the use and development of skills? We see hints and examples of these dynamics in the story of John Otenasek and others at Gould Farm above.

From a communitarian perspective in democratic theory we can perhaps better understand the insight of Will Gould and Gould Farm and the impact these have. Contrasting with the classical liberal emphasis on the isolated and autonomous individual,[32] Robert Bellah describes four core values of democratic communitarianism.[33] First, the individual is of primary importance and that morally vigorous communities are prerequisites for healthy virtuous individuals. Second, reciprocity and shared commitment to others in the community are defining features of human life. Third, belonging to a community brings complementarity in reciprocity. And, finally, participating in communal life is both a right and a duty. Within that right and duty is the responsibility of caring for and being accountable to others. It is difficult to overemphasize the importance of life in community from this perspective.

The communitarian insight appears in the work of scholar-researcher Harry Stack Sullivan (mentioned earlier by Stucker). Similar to the more recent humanistic psychoanalysis of Eric Fromm and others,[34] Sullivan understood the past as a window into the present and future. However, investigation is not limited to what happened in the past; the crucial component is how individuals integrate relationships with others. Sullivan's pioneering clinical work in psychiatry led him to argue that the most important distinguishing feature of psychological pathologies (especially schizophrenia) lies in the disconnection from ordinary life and relationships with other people. To understand mental illness, Sullivan increasingly believed the individual is simply not the proper, or sole, unit of analysis. The personality or the "self" is not simply something that resides "inside" the individual. Rather, "Personality is made manifest in interpersonal situations and not otherwise."[35] The individual is involved in continual interactions with other people. The self is, accordingly, "the relatively enduring pattern of recurrent interpersonal situations and not otherwise."[36] The social environment, *not the lone individual* as the most meaningful unit of study has profound implications for thinking about mental health and pathology. The primary focus is enabling service users to maintain, rebuild, or transform their lives to be more valuable and satisfying. It is crucial to move beyond symptoms and deficits to an understanding of people in their daily life routines. Appreciating abilities and possibilities of service-users is one way to enhance social inclusion. In this perspective:

focusing on the individual without considering past and present relationships, wrenches the object of study from the context that makes it understandable, like studying animal behavior by observing an animal in a cage rather than in its natural environment.[37]

A preoccupation of the past or an exclusive focus on the individual ignores key components of what it means to be human. While early childhood and neurological conditions of the brain surely impact human beings and deserve serious attention, adolescents and adults continue to have social experiences. Sullivan considered that all people have *integrating tendencies* which can draw people together in mutually satisfying ways. Children *and adults* both have negative and positive experiences at generating social reciprocity. The "self-system" is actively steering behavior and understandings. The crucial insights are that all people engage the human social environment and both individual behavior and understanding can change, just as the social environment can be changed. The past need not determine the present and future.

How are we to better understand the recipients of mental health care? For one, an ongoing shift is occurring over the past 30 years:

Notions of patients, service-users, and survivors have entered the discursive canon and they are actively utilized by consumers to socially construct their perspectives on mental health.[38]

Recipients of mental health services are more commonly and openly participating in their own treatment. This alternative way of conceptualizing mentally ill patients—service users—is to view recipients of mental health services not as objects of clinical investigation but as users of services. No longer passive recipients of treatments, the new movement is engaging service-users not only in the type of treatment but in desirable outcomes as well. According to comparative research, service-users place more importance on relational aspects of treatment plans and in particular challenges faced in their daily lives.[39] Research supports that in the past 10 years a shift is occurring that is "patient-centered" and "recovery-oriented"[40] As noted earlier, service-user priorities (often) differ from the priorities of service professionals.

Service-user preference is for more exploration in social alternatives and complementary social therapies. The research on the self-reported needs of the service users tends to emphasize the material and social aspects of daily life. For example, the need for a job is a high priority for those recently discharged from a hospital as well as having a decision in their own living arrangement.[41] Another survey of recently discharged patients found that the benefits of quality of life in community and the support from others was highly important (Sheldon 1997). The history of the treatment of mental illness includes the recent shift from viewing mental illness treatment as isolated within the individual's biology or mind to acknowledging the importance of communal social life. A number have noted the growth in increased participation and collective activities of mental health service-users over the last three decades.[42] Since 1970, service users, or "survivors," formed multiple organizations which argue for reform of the more typically practiced isolated medical model.[43]

JUSTICE AND MENTAL HEALTH

Turning to the broader context of justice and mental health raises a number of issues. Who do we exclude in a democracy and what are the criteria for exclusion? The often tragic consequence of those suffering from severe mental illness is that they may not be able or allowed to participate as full citizens in a democracy. However, the history of mental health care in the United States is a history of the transition from exclusion to greater inclusion. The selections in the *Reader* above give numerous examples of Gould Farm as a community of inclusion; see, for example, the account of Kent Smith. Recall John's earlier statement when he went to the Farm: "They aren't waiting for a doctor or pill to cure them, they were taking care of themselves and those around them. This I thought is the future of mental health care in our country." This is a profoundly different orientation than that presented by many mental health care professionals. Mental health service providers are placed in the center of a tension.[44] The Department of Health's protocol is that services be arranged according to the needs and wishes of those who use them. However, at the same time, mental health professionals are required to protect and make decisions for those who are assumed not to be able to make competent decisions and to protect society from dangers the service-users are presumed to present.

Suppose that we are committed to utilizing fair procedures and to furthering just outcomes, why might we fail to bring about the results intended with the procedures chosen? One reason is fallibility. Any number of assumptions, procedures, and desired outcomes could be flawed.[45] The accounts of Will Gould show his deep commitment to procedural justice. When he was first envisioning the Farm he did not have a fixed vision for the outcomes; rather, he was committed to allowing the Farm to develop and grow in the process of serving others. This is true also in the reflection above of former director Kent Smith when he described the Farm. Formulating procedures and establishing outcomes requires making judgments about the people with whom we are dealing and about our own competency. When we commit social actions we are impacting others. When we define, label, and allocate resources we are establishing institutions. When we have power, we should critique our own use of that power. When we are dealing with issues of justice, what are we to do? We first should acknowledge uncertainty and therefore make *accuracy* a priority. Second, we should act according to the *dignity* of those affected by our actions, and "we can best understand this distinct quality...as involving a respect for people who are subject to them."[46] Social justice scholar, David Miller, claims that procedural justice trumps just outcomes when outcomes may interfere with healthy processes. The logic rests on the possibility of fallibility and the dignity of all people: if we are wrong-headed and determined in our belief of best outcomes, then we can do much harm. If justice is central in our process, we maintain dignity while we can still make adjustments to the final goal or outcome.

For the service-user, a diagnosis of mental illness carries with it the negative impacts of prejudice and discrimination often resulting in social exclusion and isolation. Stated bluntly, this means that many "people with mental illness are denied the rights and opportunities that are available to non-disabled citizens."[47] The nature of stigma compounds an already challenging situation: while dealing with mental health problems, service-users face greater social difficulties of discrimination and prejudice. The terms and concepts we use lead to different understandings of where responsibility lies for the "problem" and lead to different prescriptions for action. Individualist accounts, the most common form, focus attention to individual deficits. Speaking of oppression and discrimination (similar to the discussion of racism) draws attention to the group and individual of perpetrators practicing institutional stigmatization of a population.[48]

Issues of systemic discrimination and oppression of the mentally ill are seldom or never mentioned in accounts that deal with human rights. Speaking to my university class (Justice and the American Experience), John would commonly begin his story with "you are not guaranteed justice..." John is referring, I believe, to the idea that justice is not something that we are given, nor simply a legal development,[49] but rather something that we must make and re-create every day. His experience is that of transitioning from being constrained within the mental hospital to the liberty and responsibility of sharing life with others in the Gould Farm community. John reflected on his own experience and the point when he began to participate more in his own recovery.

The mental health service-user/survivor movement is the modern expression of a 150-year-old social justice, human rights movement devoted to securing the rights and just treatment of persons identified as mentally ill.[50] Persons diagnosed with mental illness, many committed to psychiatric hospitals and treated against their will, are increasingly engaged in an ongoing and growing social movement. Often termed service-users/users/survivors, those with mental illness diagnosis are increasingly objecting to oppressive forms of involuntary social control.[51] When viewed from a perspective of justice, issues of due process are at the center of concern:

> The restriction of human rights had its stark expression in differences of power between the committed and those who had committed them—power defined by differences in gender, race, nationality, wealth, ideology, mental health status, and status in the family. Thus the mental health movement has been embedded from the start in deeper social and political struggles.[52]

Though heterogeneous and complex, the mental health movement has consistently sought more responsive, humane, and socially just inclusion in treatment options and decision-making for those receiving the treatment. Change, especially since the 1970s, in both mental health and legal systems impacts directly those under their power. Perhaps the most significant transformation is found in service-user/survivor/users themselves. The unthinkable willingness of most care professionals to collaborate with service-user/survivor/users 30 years ago is now being normalized and routine.

Justice as a standard for the distribution of goods or justice as an equation between guilt and punishment does not capture the full spirit of Gould Farm. Justice here goes beyond forgiveness and charitable altruism. Paternalistic aid and forgiveness are inherently condescending and "assaults the self-respect of the person it attempts to help."[53] Not all communities foster healthy individuals. Though imperfect, why have so many spoken so admirably of Gould Farm? I believe it is because the emphasis here shifts from retributive and distributive forms of justice to procedural forms of justice and empathy towards others.

Another way of expressing this is to stress that life in the community at Gould Farm is voluntary service seeking, in Biblical terms, to "bear one another's burdens" (Galatians 6:2). Though this may not be the explicit purpose of living in an intentional community, Carl Rogers emphasizes the importance of reciprocity and empathy for relieving suffering because it dissolves alienation.[54] For Rogers, empathy is not simply a condition of healing; it is the healing agent itself: "This in-tune-ness is in itself healing, growth-promoting."[55] In this process empathy is both the means used to relieve suffering and the actual healing agent itself.[56] This reciprocity response is located in the creation of new values that follow in the wake of empathy. This interpersonal ethic holds equally for the friend and the most hated enemy and to the lowest social status. This radical idea in the intentional community, according to Erik Erickson, that occurs in "the elemental sayings [of Jesus]…is the universal *We*." Without requiring theological language, life at Gould Farm is an intentional, voluntary and healing community because those at the Farm actively participate with concern for others. Every act need not be designed with such therapeutic ends in mind; however, the effect of sharing life in a caring community can be positive since, as Heinz Kohut acknowledges, the mere presence of empathy has a curative, therapeutic effect.[57] Recall the statement from John above: when he is feeling at his lowest he does something counter-intuitive to much mainstream therapeutic guidance: rather than seek immediate help for himself, he looks for someone else to help. Serving another human being somehow has a reciprocity effect that helps him in return. In theological terms, briefly, Gould Farm is a site where a serving and healing *Agape* community is continually re-created (however imperfectly) by recognizing the dignity of the guests. *Agape* justice is bestowing worth in the very act of creating a person and a community.[58]

Gould Farm has been described using a number of terms—reciprocity, dignity, mutuality, respect, caring, inclusive, democratic, and so on—which leads to less analytic clarity. However, these descriptions all lead to the pragmatic flexibility of Gould Farm and to those who come in contact with the Farm. Gould's vision is less about a predetermined set of outcomes and more about being open to the fullness and richness of human possibility. As the above account of John Otenasek and this *Reader* attest, many diagnosed with mental illness have been making profound contributions to their own lives, to the lives of others, and in the communities in which they live. Rather than being the object of fear, derision or pity, scholars Julie Repper and Rachel Perkins prefer envisioning living meaningful lives with mental illness. Drawing on the inspiration of civil-rights leader, Martin Luther King, they:

> *Have a vision...*
> ...that those of us with mental health problems can be better known for our contributions that we make to communities in which we live,
> ...to end the national disgrace demonstrated by 82% unemployment among people who experience mental problems, and
> ...to enjoy all the rights and opportunities that nondisabled people enjoy.[59]

These are examples of attempts of greater inclusion and participation in a community and further enhance dignity and self-respect by gaining greater citizenship and civil rights. Who is responsible to do what for whom? We learn from this *Reader* that we all have unique skills and abilities to serve others in a community. We each have unique needs. We all have responsibilities to ourselves and to others in the unique social context in which we live and relate to others. Gould Farm is one way to make this vision a reality.

Terry Beitzel

Notes and Permissions

1. Shapiro, Michael. *Studies in Trans-Disciplinary Method: After the Aesthetic Turn.* London: Routledge, 2013. 81-85.

2. Vohs, Kathleen, quoted in Emily Smith, "There's More to Life than Happiness" in *The Atlantic*. Available at http://www.theatlantic.com/health/archive/2013/01/theres-more-to-life-than-being-happy/266805/, viewed January 21, 2013. See also, Frankl, Viktor. *Man's Search for Meaning.* Boston: Beacon Press, 2006 [1946]. Also, Gould Farm staff member, Amy Dillingham, deserves special mention.

3. Adame, A. L., and Knudson, R. M. "Recovery and the Good Life: How Psychiatric Survivors are Revisioning the Healing Process." *Journal of Humanistic Psychology* 48, 2 (2008). 142-64.

4. Sandel, Michael. *Democracy's Discontent: American in Search of a Public Philosophy.* Cambridge: Harvard University Press, 1996. 116, 274. This is an ongoing and complex debate beyond the space available here. The debate is commonly discussed in terms of "liberals" and "communitarians."

5. Personal correspondence, July 2012. John is currently the sole Peer Support Specialist for Sheppard and Enoch Pratt Hospital in Maryland. Prior to this John was director of VOCAL (Voice of Mental Health Recovery) in Virginia.

6. For the importance of living in community, see the writings of Michael Walzer and Charles Taylor.

7. Rogers, Anne, and Pilgrim, David. *A Sociology of Mental Health and Illness.* Berkshire, UK: Open University Press, 2010.

8. Of course, some psychiatrists challenge this framework. See Szasz 1961, and Pilgrim and Rogers 2009. Some are moving toward a "biopsychosocial" model which takes into account biographical data and social context (Engel, 1980; Pilgrim et al. 2008).

9. For a comprehensive collection of the social origins of mental illness, the social construction of mental health, and the treatment of mental illness, see Jane McLead and Eric Wright, editors, *The Sociology of Mental Illness: A Comprehensive Reader* (Oxford: Oxford University Press, 2009). See also, Carol Aneshensel and Jo Phelan, *Handbook of the Sociology of Mental Health* (New York: Springer, 2006), and Jessica Rosenburg, *Community Mental Health: Challenges for the 21st Century* (New York: Routledge, 2012).

10. See Oliver Sach's discussion above of the "recovery" movements: they are too often narrowly and intensely individualistic.

11. The following is a brief summary of the 1999 Surgeon General's report on mental illness, *Mental Health: A Report of the Surgeon General*, available at http://www.drjohncervantes.com/PDF/Mental_Health_-_A_Report_Of_The_Surgeon_General.pdf. 77.

12. See *Mental Illness and American Society, 1875–1940* (Princeton: Princeton University Press, 1983); *From Asylum to Community: Mental Health Policy in Modern America* (Princeton: Princeton University Press, 1991); and, *The Mad among Us: A History of the Care of America's Mentally Ill* (New York: Free Press, 1994).

13. According to the Surgeon General's Report, citing Gerald Grob 1994, "The term 'moral' had a connotation different from that of today. It meant the return of the individual to reason by the application of psychologically oriented therapy." 78.

14. See Avison, William; McLeod, Jane; and Pescosolido, Bernice, editors. *Mental Health, Social Mirror*. New York: Springer, 2007.

15. Rogers, Anne, and Pilgrim, David. *A Sociology of Mental Health and Illness*. Berkshire, UK: Open University Press, 2010. 195.

16. Main, T. F. "The Hospital as Therapeutic Institution." *Bulletin of the Menninger Clinic* (1946). 10:66-70.

17. Rogers and Pilgrim, *op cit.* 195.

18. See Perrow, C., *Handbook of Organizations* (Chicago: Rand McNally, 1965) and Ingleby, David, "Mental Health and Social Order." *Social Control and the State* (Oxford: Blackwell, 1985).

19. Gelder, Michael; Harrison, Paul; and Cowen, Philip. *Shorter Oxford Textbook of Psychiatry*. Vol. 4. Oxford: Oxford University Press, 2006.

20. Schull, Andrew. "Madness and Segregative Control: The Rise of the Insane Asylum." *Social Problems*. 24 (1976). 337.

21. Pilgrim, David, and Rogers, Anne. "The Contribution of Lay Knowledge to the Understanding and Promotion of Mental Health." *Journal of Mental Health* 6, no. 1 (1997): 23-36.

22. Horwitz, Allan. *Creating Mental Illness*. Chicago: University of Chicago Press, 2002.

23. For an overview of early influential writings, see Adams, Hazard, and Searle, Leroy, editors. *Critical Theory Since 1965*. Tallahassee, FL: Florida State University Press, 1986.

24. Chadwick, P. K. *Schizophrenia: The Positive Perspective*. London: Routledge, 1997. 22.

25. Rinaldi, M. *Insufficient Concern*. London: Merton Mind, 2000.

26. Strauss, J. S. "Negative Symptoms: Future Developments of the Concept." *Schizophrenia Bulletin* 11 (1985): 3.

27. Besio, Wilson, quoted in Repper and Perkins, *Social Inclusion and Recovery*, 14.

28. Faulkner, A. and Layzell, S. *Strategies for living: A summary report of user-led research into people's strategies for living with mental distress*. London: The Mental

Health Foundation, 2000.

29. Repper and Perkins, *Social Inclusion and Recovery,* 4.

30. Post, F. "Creativity and psychopathology: a study of 291 world-famous men." *British Journal of Psychiatry* (1994) 165: 22-34.

31. Lawrence, P. N. *Impressive Depressives: 75 Historical Cases of Manic Depression from Seven Centuries.* London: The Manic Depression Fellowship, 1988. Included in this list are Bach, Churchill, Einstein, Handel, Keats, Roosevelt, Tolstoy, Van Gogh, and Wittgenstein.

32. For a contemporary reading of liberalism, see Rawls, John. *A Theory of Justice.* Cambridge: Harvard University Press, 1970.

33. Bellah, Robert. A Defense of "Democratic Communitarianism." *The Responsive Community,* Volume 6, Issue 1, Winter 1995/96. Available at http://www.gwu.edu/~icps/bellah.html.

34. For a more thorough discussion, see Detrick, D. and Detrick, S., editors. *Self-Psychology.* Hillsdale, NJ: Analytic Press, 1989.

35. Sullivan, H. S. *The Fusion of Psychiatry and Social Science.* New York: Norton, 1964. 32.

36. Sullivan, H. S. *The Interpersonal Theory of Psychiatry.* New York: Norton, 1956. xi.

37. Mitchell, Stephen, and Black, Margaret. *Freud and Beyond: A History of Modern Psychoanalytic Thought.* New York: Basic Books, 1995. 63.

38. Speed, Ewen. "Patients, consumers and survivors: A case study of mental health service user discourses." *Social Science & Medicine,* Volume 62, Issue 1, (2006). 28-38, 28.

39. Ibid

40. Rose, Diana; Fleischman, Pete; and Wykes, Til. "What are mental health service users' priorities for research in the UK?" *Journal of Mental Health* 17, no. 5 (2008). 520-530.

41. Hatfield, Barbara; Huxley, Peter; and Mohamad, Hadi. "Accommodation and employment: a survey into the circumstances and expressed needs of users of mental health services in a northern town." *British Journal of Social Work* 22, no. 1 (1992). 61-73.

42. See, Chamberlin, Judi, and Rogers, Joseph. "Planning a community-based mental health system: Perspective of service recipients." *American Psychologist* 45, no. 11 (1990). 1241. See also, Crossley, Michele, and Crossley, Nick. "'Patient' voices, social movements and the habitus; how psychiatric survivors 'speak out.'" *Social Science & Medicine* 52, no. 10 (2001). 1477-1489.

43. For more details, see Polgar, Michael. "Mental Health Care in Organizations and Systems." *A Handbook for the Study of Mental Health: Social Contexts, Theories, and Systems.* Edited by Teresa Scheid and Tony Brown. Cambridge: Cambridge University Press, 2010. 499-509.

44. Perkins, R. "Danger and Incompetence: Mental Health and New Labour." *Critical Social Policy* (2001) 21: 536-539.

45. See, for example, Elster, Jon. *Local Justice: How Institutions Allocate Scarce Resources and Necessary Burdens.* Cambridge: Cambridge University Press, 1992. 62.

46. Miller, David, in *Principles of Social Justice.* Cambridge: Harvard University Press, 1999. 102.

47. Repper and Perkins, *Social Inclusion and Recovery,* 2003. 203.

48. For a more thorough discussion, see Sayce, L., *From Psychiatric Patient to Citizen: Overcoming Discrimination and Social Exclusion* (London: Macmillan, 2000), and

Chamberlain, J., "Equal Rights, not Public Relations," *World Psychiatric Association Conference, Together against Stigma* (Leipzig, 2001).

49. Several important legal developments have taken place in the US. The passage of the State Comprehensive Mental Health Plan Act of 1986 (P. L. 99-660, Title 5) directed attention to consumer/survivor/users because states were mandated to provide mental health plans that supported consumer self-determination and involvement in policy planning. Since 1999, three significant legal developments have aided the consumer/survivor/users movement. First, the U.S. Supreme Court in Olmstead v. L.C., 527 U. S. 581, ruled that unnecessary institutionalization dramatically reduces a person's quality of life and therefore policies that promote integration within the community need to be encouraged. Second, the Surgeon General's Report on Mental Illness (USDHHS, 1999) challenged reductionist biomedical models of mental illness by arguing that mental conditions vary immensely in etiology and that external factors are increasingly important. Finally, the President's New Freedom Commission on Mental Health (NFCR 2003: 86) recommended "fundamentally transforming" from a system that "simply manages symptoms" to a system that is "consumer-centered [and]... recovery oriented." Changes in laws and mandates that improve care should not be underestimated. However, this is not the only way to conceptualize justice.

50. McLean, Athena. "The Mental Health Consumers/Survivors Movement in the United States." *A Handbook for the Study of Mental Health: Social Contexts, Theories, and Systems.* Edited by Teresa Scheid and Tony Brown. Cambridge: Cambridge University Press, 2010. 461-477, 461.

51. Hubert 2002.

52. McLean, Athena. "The Mental Health Consumers/Survivors Movement in the United States." 461.

53. For a broader theological discussion, see Kraus, C. Norman. *The Community of the Spirit.* Scottdale, PA: Herald Press, 1993. 158.

54. Rogers, Carl. *A Way of Being.* Boston: Houghton Mifflin, 1980. 151.

55. Rogers, Carl. "Rogers, Kohut, and Erickson: A Personal Perspective on Some Similarities and Differences." *Person-Centered Review,* I (1986) [pp 125-40]: 130.

56. Goodman, Geoff ."Feeling Our way into Empathy: Carl Rogers, Heinz Kohut, and Jesus." *Journal of Religion and Health.* 30, 3 (1991): [191-206]: 200.

57. Kohut, Heinz. *The Search for the Self: Selected Writings of Heinz Kohut: 1950-1978.* Edited by P. Ornstein. New York: International Universities Press, 1978.

58. See also, Redekop, Calvin, *The free church and seductive culture* (Scottdale, PA: Herald Press, 1970); and, Burkholder, J. R., and Redekop, Calvin, editors, *Kingdom, cross and community* (Scottdale, PA: Herald Press, 1976).

59. Repper and Perkins, *Social Inclusion and Recovery,* 221-22.

APPENDIX A

OFFICERS AND DIRECTORS
1936
(From Gould Farm Brochure op cit)

Below will be found lists of the Officers and Directors, and of those who, among others, have kindly consented to the use of their names as references.

Officers: President, Mrs. William J. Gould; Vice-President and Secretary, Miss Caroline Goodyear; Treasurer, Rev. Sidney McKee.

Directors: The Officers and:

Illinois: Rev. Sydney B. Snow, D.D., President, Meadville Theological School, Chicago.

Massachusetts: Dr. Richard C. Cabot, Cambridge; Mrs. Howard F. Colt, Miss J. Eleanor Goodyear, and Miss Florence E. Scovill, Gould Farm; Dr. John B. Beebe, Great Barrington.

New York City: Francis H. McLean, Family Welfare Association of America; Mrs. Robert E. Speer, 24 Gramercy Park (Chairman, Gould Farm Co-operating Committee).

REFERENCES

The Directors and:

Connecticut: Mrs. John Sherman Hoyt, Darien.

Massachusetts: Prof. Edward Ballantine, 51 Brattle St., Cambridge; Lawrence K. Lunt, M.D., Concord; Frank J. Pope, Great Barrington; Rev. C. Thurston Chase, Monterey; Horace E. Allen and Rev. William G. Ballantine, D.D., Springfield; Austen Fox Riggs, M.D., Stockbridge.

New York City: Emilie M. Bullowa, 475 5th Ave.; Emily T. Burr, Ph.D., 421 E. 88th St.; Rev. Henry Sloane Coffin, D.D., Union Theological Seminary; Rev. Harry Emerson Fosdick, Riverside Church; Foster Kennedy, M.D., 410 E. 57th St.; Rev. Karl Reiland, D.D., St. George's Church; Charles T. Root, 32 Washington Sq.; Joseph C.

Roper, M.D., Neurological Institute; Rabbi Stephen S. Wise.

Rhode Island: Elizabeth M. Chace, 190 Hope St., Providence.

APPENDIX B

OFFICERS AND DIRECTORS
1940s
(From Gould Farm Brochure, op cit)

THE WILLIAM J. GOULD ASSOCIATES INCORPORATED 1929

Board of Directors

Resident Directors

Mrs. William J. Gould
Miss Caroline Goodyear
Mr. Sidney McKee
Miss Eleanor Goodyear
Miss F. M. Scovill
Mrs. H. F. Colt

Non Resident Directors

Mrs. Robert E. Speer
Dr. Richard C. Cabot (deceased)
Mr. Francis H. McLean
Rev. Sydney B. Snow
Dr. John B. Beebe
Rev. A. Phillips Guiles

APPENDIX C

OFFICERS AND DIRECTORS
1960s
(From Gould Farm Brochure, op cit)

REFERENCES

Rev. Kenneth D. Beckwith, Amherst, Mass.

John M. Billinsky, Ph.D., Professor of Psychology and Clinical Studies, Andover-Newton Theological School, Newton Centre, Mass.

Martha Brunner-Orne, M.D., Consultant, Harry C. Solomon Mental Health Center, Lowell, Mass.

Eleanor Clark, Director Social Service, Massachusetts General Hospital, Boston, Mass.

Eric Fromm, Ph.D., New York, NY

Gordon Granger, Executive Vice President, Great Barrington Savings Bank, Great Barrington, Mass.

Rev. Donald Szantho Harrington, D.D., The Community Church, New York, NY

Edgarton Howard, M.D. Berkshire Mental Health Center, Pittsfield, Mass.

Homer L. Jernigan, Ph.D., Associate Professor of Pastoral Counseling, Boston University School of Theology, Boston, Mass.

Rev. Howard Joslyn, Massachusetts Council of Churches, Boston, Mass.

Nathan S. Kline, M.D., F.A.C.P, New York, NY

John A.P. Millet, M.D., New York, NY

Rev. Frederick M. Morris, D.D., Rector, St. Thomas Episcopal Church, New

157

York, NY

Harold Pierce, Jr., Executive Vice-President, First Agricultural National Bank, Great Barrington, Mass.

V. Gerard Ryan, M.D., Medical Director, Elmcrest Manor, Portland, Conn.

Dorothy C. Sawyer, Consulting Rehabilitation Counselor, New York, NY

Douglas Steere, Haverford College, Haverford, PA

Samuel M. Tarnower, M.D., Pittsfield, MA

Rev. James M. Webb, Connecticut Council of Churches, Hartford, Conn.

Janet Wien, ACSW, Director Social Service Dept. of New England Medical Center Hospitals, Boston, Mass.

G. Montgomery Winship, M.D., Grove Hill Clinic, New Britain, Conn.

OFFICERS AND DIRECTORS

Chairman of the Board, Rev. Nehemiah Boynton, III, S. Dartmouth, Mass.

Vice-President of the Board, Dr. James Luther Adams, Andover-Newton Theological School, Newton Centre, Mass.

Treasurer, Edward Dunlop, Gould Farm, Great Barrington, Mass.

Clerk of the Board: Mrs. Albert V. Danielson, Wellesley Hills, Mass.

DIRECTORS

James Luther Adams, PhD., Andover-Newton Theological School

Mrs. James Luther Adams

James M. Bell, M.D., Clinical Director-Psychiatrist, Berkshire Farms for Boys, Canaan, NY

Col. Lawrence J. Bolvig, USAR, SICG, Dundee, NY

Rev. Nehemiah Boynton, III, United Church of Christ, S. Dartmouth, Mass.

David Colt, Attorney, Rackemann, Swayer & Brewster, Boston, Mass.

Mrs. Howard Colt, Gould Farm

Rev. Harold C. Criswell, Jr., Pittsfield Area Council of Churches, Pittsfield, Mass.

Albert V. Danielsen, L.H.D., D.D., Pres. Danielsen Fund, Wellesley Hills, Mass.

Mrs. Albert V. Danielsen, Treas., Danielsen Fund, Wellesley Hills, Mass.

Robert J. Donelan, Attorney, Great Barrington, Mass.

Rev. Leon Flanders, First Presbyterian Church, Greenlawn, N.Y.

Rev. Paul Kennedy, S.T.M., Trinity Lutheran Church, Worcester, Mass.

Mrs. Allan Larter, Treas. Wannalancit Textile Co., Lowell, Mass.

Richard V. McCann, Ph.D., Director of Educational Research, U.S. Office of Education, JFK Federal Bldg., Boston, Mass.

Rev. Sidney McKee, Gould Farm

Mrs. Sidney McKee, Gould Farm

Walter Pahnke, M.D., b.D., Ph.D., Chief of Research, Maryland Psychiatric Research Center, Baltimore, MD

H.B. Pearl, Chairman of the Board, Whitlock Corp., New York, NY

John Silard, Attorney, Rauh & Silard, Washington, D.C.

Mrs. Molly Simon, ACSW, New York, NY

Rt. Rev. Anson Phelps Stokes, Jr., Bishop, Protestant Episcopal Church, Diocese of Massachusetts, Boston, Mass.

Robert K. Wheeler, Wheeler & Taylor Real Estate, Great Barrington, Mass.

Mrs. Harold Winchester, Gould Farm

Arthur Wright, M.D., Albany, N.Y.

APPENDIX D

OFFICERS AND DIRECTORS
1980s
(From Gould Farm Brochure, op cit)

REFERENCES

George P. Adams, President, Great Barrington Savings Bank, Great Barrington, MA

John B. Billinsky, Ph.D., Professor of Psychology and Clinical Studies, Andover Newton Theological School, Newton Centre, MA

The Rt. Rev. John B. Coburn, D.D., Bishop of Massachusetts, One Joy Street, Boston, MA

Richard Culley, M.D., 30 E. Housatonic Street, Pittsfield, MA

John D. Gillespie, Ph.D., Psychologist, Westport, CT

The Rev. Donald Szantho Harrington, D.D., The Community Church, 40 East 35th St., New York, NY

The Rev. Seward Hiltner, D.D, Ph.D., Princeton Theological Seminary, Princeton, NJ

Edgerton McC. Howard, M.D., Consultant, Austin Riggs Center, Stockbridge, MA

Homer L. Jernigan, Ph.D., Danielsen Professor of Counseling, Boston University School of Theology, Boston, MA

William S. Morgan, Vice President, First Agricultural Bank, Great Barrington, MA

The Rev. Francis O'Hare, S.T.D., Rector, St. Ann's Church, Somerville, MA

Humphrey Osmond, MRCP, DPM, FWA, University of Alabama, Birmingham, AL

Robert D. Patterson, M.D., Lexington, MA

Dorothy C. Sawyer, Certified Rehabilitation Counselor, Pelican Cove, Sarasota, FL

Douglas Steere, Haverford College, Haverford, PA

Samuel M. Tarnower, M.D. Pittsfield, MA

The Rev. James M. Webb, Rhode Island Council of Churches, Providence, RI

G. Montgomery Winship, M.D., Assistant Chief of Psychiatry, New Britain General Hospital, New Britain, CT

OFFICERS OF THE BOARD
May 9, 1987

The Rev. Richard Lindgren, President, Boston, MA
Suzette Alsop, Vice-President, Tyringham, MA
Virgil Stucker, Treasurer, Monterey, MA
Sally Kelly, Clerk, Sheffield, MA

DIRECTORS

James L. Adams, Ph.D., TH.D., Harvard Divinity School, Cambridge, MA
James M. Bell, M.D., Clinical Director-Psychiatrist, Berkshire Farm Center & Services for Youth, Canaan, NY
Col. Lawrence J. Bolvig, USAR, SIGC, Dundee, N.Y.
Ellen Price Bowler, Simsbury, CT
The Rev. Virgil V. Brallier, Ph.D., Monterey, MA
David G. Colt, Attorney, Rackemann, Sawyer & Brewster, Boston, MA
Herbert Coyne, Goldman, Sachs & Co., New York, NY
Richard G. Culley, M.D., Psychiatrist, Pittsfield, MA
Jessie Danielsen, LT.D. Treasurer, Danielson Fund, Wellesley Hills, MA
Matthew Dempsey, Treasurer, Dempsey's Garage, Inc., Great Barrington, MA
The Rev. Canon Clinton Dugger, Rensselaer, N.Y.
Edward Dunlop, Monterey, MA
Tryntje Hawks, Concord, MA
Kingsley Kelly, Sheffield, MA
The Rev. Dr. Paul Kennedy, S.T.M., Worcester, MA
The Rev. Dale J. Lock, Pittsfield, MA
The Rev. Jon Luopa, Bloomfield, CT
Janet McKee, M.S.W., Bethesda, MD
John Montgomery, Houston, TX
Joan Nettleton, Spencertown, NY
Eva Pahnke, M.W.W., Shelburne, VT
H.B. Pearl, Chairman of the Board, Carlisle Capital Corporation, Fort Lee, N.J.
Lewis Scheffey, Monterey, MA

WORKS CONSULTED

The following are general references consulted, some of which are cited in the Reader. As such, it is not meant to be exhaustive of all works cited or referenced in text.

Anderson, Larry. *Benton MacKaye: Conservationist, Planner, and Creator of the Appalachian Trail*. Baltimore: The Johns Hopkins University Press, 2002.

Bordman, Gerald and Hischak, Thomas S. *The Oxford Companion to American Theater*. Oxford University Press. 2004.

Grob, Gerald N. *The Mad Among Us: A History of the Care of America's Mentally Ill*. New York: The Free Press, 1994.

Hopkins, June. *Harry Hopkins: Sudden Hero, Brash Reformer*. New York: Palgrave Macmillan, 1999.

Joselit, Jenna Weissman. "My Country, My Country." *The New Republic*. August 1, 2012. Accessed August 3, 2012. http://www.tnr.com/print/book/review/mary-antin-the-promised-land.

McKee, Rose L. *Brother Will and the Founding of Gould Farm*. Monterey: William J. Gould & Associates, [1963], 1975.

McKee, William J. *Gould Farm: A Life of Sharing*. Monterey: William J. Gould & Associate, 1994.

Rieff, Philip. *The Triumph of the Therapeutic: Uses of Faith after Freud*. New York: Harper & Row, Publishers, 1966.

Salz, Evelyn, Ed. *Selected Letters of Mary Antin*. Syracuse: Syracuse University Press, 2000.

Sheehan, Susan. *Is There No Place on Earth For Me?* New York: Vintage Books, 1983.

———. "The Last Days of Sylvia Frumkin." *The New Yorker*. Feb. 20 & 27, 1995.

Wyman, David S. *The Abandonment of the Jews: America and the Holocaust, 1941-1945*. Pantheon, 1985.

SELECTIONS

Adams, James Luther. "Notes on the Study of Gould Farm" (1955-56). From "Voluntary Associations: Socio-cultural Analyses and Theological Interpretation." Ed. J. Ronald Engel. Chicago: Exploration Press, 1986.

Anonymous letter to Gould Farm from a prospective resident. April 5, 1920.

Anonymous reflections by a former Gould Farm guest – 1980s.

Antin, Mary. Letter to Thomas A. Watson. October 2, 1924. (Satz, 99-100).

———. Letter to Caroline Goodyear. July 23, 1928 (Satz, 110-112).

Bowen, Clayton R. "The Work of Gould Farm." *Hospital Social Service*. Vol. VII 1923.

———. "What is Gould Farm?" *The Christian Register*. January 12, 1922.

———. A Sermon upon the death of William J. Gould.

Clarke, Jessica. "Field of Dreams: Group Crusades to Build Local Community for the Mentally Ill." *Daily News Record*. August 5, 2005.

Davis, Melodie M. "New Farm in the Valley for Persons with Mental Illenss." *Valley Living for the Whole Family*. Summer 2005.

Duhon, Anna Melinda. "Liminality in Paradise: A Dialogue with the Gould Farm Community." In partial fulfillment of the requirements for the degree with honors of Bachelor of Arts, Harvard University, 2004.

Elliston, Grace. *Gould Farm*. 1940.

"Farm of New Hope." *New York Times*. September 18, 1921. Rotogravure Section, page 7.

Farm Yarn. May 23, 1974.

Flach, M.D., Frederic. *Rickie*. New York: Fawcett Columbine, 1990.

Goodyear, Caroline. *The Story of Gould Farm*. 1936

Gould, Agnes C. Letter to Eleanor Roosevelt. November 24, 1952.

Gould Farm Charter. 1929. (Gould Farm Archives).

Gould Farm newsletter. "We Take Conscientious Objectors." Winter 1966. No author.

Gould Farm Pamphlet. 1960s.

Gould Farm Pamphlet. 1980s.

Gould Farm Pamphlet. 2011

Gould, William J. Excerpt from a letter to his family. October 18, 1896. From: *Brother Will and the Founding of Gould Farm*. 1963 (1975). Great Barrington: The William J. Gould Associations, Inc. 13-14.

———. "The More Abundant Life." *The Congregationalist and Christian World*. September 23, 1911. (Contribution to a prize contest on: "What makes the Christian religion worth while to any man?").

———. Sermon given November 24, 1924. (In McKee, R.)

Hiltner, Seward. "Faith and Health at Gould Farm." *Pastoral Psychology*. 1964. 27-30.

Hines, Kim. "Glimmers of Mutuality: Achieving Solidarity within the Social Relations of Philanthropy." Submitted to the faculty of the University Graduate School in partial fulfillment of the requirements for the degree of Master of Arts in the Department of Philanthropic Studies, Indiana University. April 2003.

Hopkins, Harry L. Letter to William J. Gould. March 3, 1915. (Gould Farm Archives).
——. Letter to William J. Gould. February 1, 1915.
Infield, Henrik F. *The American Intentional Communities: Study on the Sociology of Cooperation.* New Jersey: Glen Gardner Community Press, 1955.
Joseph, Charles H. "Random Thoughts." *Jewish Criterion.* Vol. 70, Issue 15. August 19, 1927.
MacKaye, Benton. Memo for Mrs. Gould Concerning the Gould Farm Woodland. May 29, 1945. (Gould Farm Archives).
——. Letter to Mrs. John Sherman Hoyt. March 10, 1932 (Gould Farm Archives).
McKee, Rose. "Introduction" from *Brother Will and the founding of Gould Farm.*
McMillan, Donald C. "The Story of Gould Farm." A Dissertation Submitted to the Graduate Faculty in Candidacy for the Degree of Bachelor of Divinity. The Meadville Theological School – Department of Practical Theology. 1935.
Martin, Earl. "From Earl's Files." Crossing Creeks newsletter. 2001.
Rockefeller, Abby A. Letter to Agnes Gould. May 20, 1925. (Gould Farm Archives).
Sacks, Oliver. "The Lost Virtues of the Asylum." *The New York Review of Books.* Vol. 56, No. 14. September 24, 2009.
Sheehan, Susan. *Is There No Place On Earth For Me?* New York: Vintage Books, 1983.
Smith, Kent D. Revised from a presentation at the International Association for Psycho-Social Rehabilitation Services, Washington, D.C., May 29, 1981.
Steere, Douglas V. *Work and Contemplation.* New York: Harper & Brothers, 1957.
Trelawny-Ross, Tamsin. "The Experience of Mental Illness and the Meaning of Work: 'If I'm just sitting, I don't feel I'm living.'" Thesis for Master of Science in Applied Social Studies. Oxford University. 1999.
Wald, Lillian D. Letter to Agnes Gould. May 24, 1920.
Wilder, Amos P. Letter to Agnes Gould. December 2, 1929
Wise, Rabbi Stephen S. Letter to Agnes Gould. June 9, 1933. (Gould Farm Archives).

INDEX